"THE SHOT HEARD 'ROUND THE WORLD"

The causes, course, and aftermath of the rebellion of the American colonies are analyzed in depth by a distinguished scholar and historian. Mr. Lacy goes beyond the obvious rationale of the revolution to scrutinize the social patterns and political practices that had evolved within the colonies during a century and a half of imperial mis-administration. He shows that the problems that precipitated crisis in the 1760's—regulation of trade, legislative representation, disposition of Western lands—remained at issue under the Articles of Confederation and were resolved finally in the drawing up of the Constitution. Mr. Lacy sees the American Revolution as both a conservative and a radical movement: the attempt of a sovereign people to preserve valued institutions, to initiate a new form of government that met the challenge of the times, and to ensure the future against tyranny and oppression with the greatest code of law ever written, the Constitution of the United States.

"The author sets out to show that the aims and ideals of the American Revolution were not merely a set of radical ideas which triumphed nearly 200 years ago and shocked the world of that era, but are 'as relevant and explosively revolutionary today' as in 1776. . . . Dan Lacy has produced a book based on sound scholarship and leading to logical conclusions. [illegible] a work of considerable originality."

—*Washington Star*

Other MENTOR Books on American History

DEMOCRACY IN AMERICA (abridged) *by Alexis de Tocqueville, edited by Richard D. Heffner*

The classic critique of freedom and democracy in 19th century America by a brilliant Frenchman. Mr. Heffner is a well-known historian, and commentator on current affairs. (#MT362—75¢)

A DOCUMENTARY HISTORY OF THE UNITED STATES (revised, expanded) *edited by Richard D. Heffner*

Important documents that have shaped America's history, with commentary. (#MT604—75¢)

THE FEDERALIST PAPERS *by Alexander Hamilton, James Madison and John Jay, edited by Clinton L. Rossiter*

Written to win ratification of the U.S. Constitution, these essays constitute a milestone in political theory. Introduction and notes by Clinton Rossiter. (#MQ556—95¢)

THE LIVING U.S. CONSTITUTION *edited by Saul K. Padover*

Complete text of one of the world's greatest documents and the history of its making. Portraits of signers. (#MP412—60¢)

The Meaning of the AMERICAN REVOLUTION

DAN LACY

A MENTOR BOOK

Published by The New American Library, New York and Toronto
The New English Library Limited, London

This book was originally published in a hard cover edition by The New American Library in 1964.

FIRST PRINTING, AUGUST, 1966

MENTOR BOOKS are published *in the United States* by
The New American Library, Inc.,
1301 Avenue of the Americas, New York, New York 10019,
in Canada by The New American Library of Canada Limited,
295 King Street East, Toronto 2, Ontario,
in the United Kingdom by The New English Library Limited,
Barnard's Inn, London, E.C. 1, England.

PRINTED IN THE UNITED STATES OF AMERICA

This book is for Hope with love

Preface

Two hundred years ago began a series of events that led through more than a decade of debate, years of war, and an era of creative political experiment to the birth of a new nation conceived in liberty and dedicated to the proposition that all men are created equal. It is clear that that proposition is as relevant, and as explosively revolutionary, today as it was in 1776. This book is an attempt to explore the meanings of those events as seen from the vantage point of our own era, when equality among men and among nations is again the crucial problem of our society. I have not hesitated to compress the detailed narrative of the Revolutionary generation in the effort to clarify and emphasize these meanings.

Among many debts, I should like to express my gratitude to Victor Weybright for his faith in an unlikely enterprise, to Beatrice Drucker and Elizabeth Eddy for their long labors with the manuscript, most of which was written on the tremulous commuter trains of the New York Central, and to the New York Public Library for the use of the facilities of the Frederick Lewis Allen Room. To the memories of Robert D. W. Connor and Albert Ray Newsome I owe love as well as professional obligation.

A very special debt is due the scholars listed in the bibliography, whose painstaking and creative research has brought a whole new illumination to our knowledge of the Revolution. The function of this book, indeed, is only to report, and in a measure interpret, their contributions, on which it depends.

Dan Lacy

Preface to the Mentor Edition

The appearance of this work in a Mentor edition has afforded an opportunity to bring the bibliography up to date and to make a few minor modifications in the text to take account of the most recent research. As a result of the work of such distinguished scholars as Richard Morris, Seymour Lipset, and Jackson Turner Main, for example, there has been a growing illumination of many aspects of the Revolutionary period, especially its diplomatic history and the sociological analysis of class structure in relation to politics. On the whole, however, such new knowledge has reinforced rather than altered the conclusions of the present work.

Dan Lacy

May 2, 1966

Contents

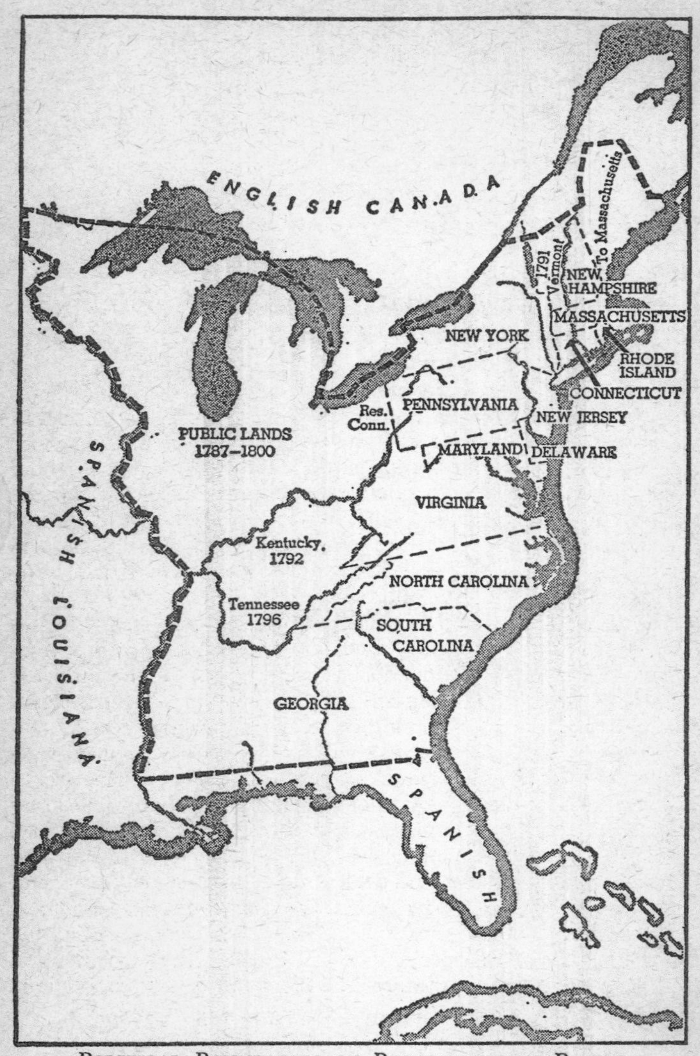

POLITICAL BOUNDARIES OF REVOLUTIONARY PERIOD

1★★★★★★★★★

The Eighteenth-Century World

The American Revolution happened less than two hundred years ago, a short time as human history goes. And yet those times now are further from us than the distant planets about which our earth-thrown satellites may orbit. In many ways the world of Washington and Jefferson lies closer to that of ancient Egypt than to ours. If we are to understand the Revolution, and why it happened, and what it meant, we shall have to think ourselves back into a very different age.

And we shall have to think not of the American colonies alone. Though it was here that the assemblies and congresses met, the resolutions and declarations were adopted, and the battles fought, the Revolution was not only an American event. It was a part of a reshaping of Western civilization itself. By the end of the Middle Ages there had been formed in Europe a body of ideas of enormous power. This body of ideas was to break the slow pace of change, almost imperceptible from generation to generation, that had governed all earlier history. Ceaseless growth, feeding on itself and moving faster and faster, was to become the central fact of the civilization built by the Europeans and by their descendants overseas. The new power of this civilization was to leap the oceans, peopling the Americas, subduing for a time the far older cultures of Asia and North Africa, and impressing the patterns of its technology and government upon the lives of all men everywhere.

This seething flow of power has continually required the shaping of new patterns of government and of society itself so that its forces can be contained and organized. Over the past four or five centuries Western civilization time and again has had to develop whole new bodies of political and economic thought and new ways of understanding itself. By peaceful change or by revolution it has had to reorganize its governments and its economy to keep up with the changes in science and technology and in the basic ideas that underlie its culture.

The American Revolution was one of the more important of those reorganizations carried out within Western civilization. The conditions that brought it about were in part peculiar to this country and its relations with Great Britain, but in part they were aspects of Western civilization generally. The ideas on which our forefathers based the Revolution were drawn from the general store of Western thought, and the new political and economic patterns that were created by the Revolution became in turn part of the organization of Western society as a whole. One may say that it was in the period of the American and French Revolutions at the end of the eighteenth century that modern Western civilization shaped its purposes and defined the ends toward which it was to move. In doing so, it crystallized ideas that had long been forming. When Jefferson drafted the Declaration of Independence, he echoed generations of earlier thinkers, just as in turn his ideas echo today in Asia and Africa.

What was the eighteenth-century Western civilization like? In what sort of matrix of institutions and ideas was the American Revolution formed?

In the first place, two hundred years ago there were fewer than one hundred and fifty million Europeans, even counting the two million of their descendants overseas. Most of them were still untouched by the currents of change already flowing in their society. Almost all of them still lived on farms and in rural villages. Paris, with a population of approximately a half million, and the much smaller but still highly urban London were beginning to take the shape of modern cities, but in most of Europe twenty-five thousand people would make a great city. Literacy had spread widely and was now the attainment not only of clerics and court scribes but also of a considerable educated class. Even so, probably not one adult in ten knew his letters, even in France or England; and in Eastern and Southern Europe illiteracy was still nearly universal outside the cities, monasteries, and courts. Superstitions and agricultural practices transmitted from centuries past, even from Neolithic times, still exercised an unchanging sway over the daily lives of most Europeans.

Life in the peasant villages at the beginning of the eighteenth century was more isolated than we can easily imagine today.

Roads were miserable, dangerous, and few. Travel was a tedious and painful experience and an expensive one. Most men walked where they must go. The well-to-do might ride and the rich be driven in coaches that bounced and slithered a torturous ten or twenty miles a day. Only toward the end of the century did stagecoach lines begin to afford a tolerably regular and dependable, though very expensive, means of going from place to place. It is probable that most men two hundred years ago died without ever having been more than twenty miles from the place of their birth.

Trade in the early 1700's was as restricted as travel. Except where ships or barges could go by sea or rivers, the transportation of heavy goods was almost impossible. Even where wagons could pass, a wagoner must charge half the daily pay of a laborer to haul a ton of goods a mile. Most overland merchandise was packed on the back of draft horses led along forest paths menaced by highwaymen. Even waterborne transportation was slow, hazardous, and costly. To bear cargoes of a couple of hundred tons or less, tiny vessels spent weeks and even months at sea exposed to the raids of pirates and to storms that overwhelmed their frail structures. The goods that moved in commerce were naturally the luxuries of the rich, with a value that could bear the high cost of transportation. Silks, spices, jewels, tobaccos, fine woolens, and delicate objects of exquisite workmanship were the merchant's goods. The peasant ate and wore and used what was grown and made in his neighborhood.

Intellectual isolation was even more complete than economic isolation. A few weekly newspapers in large cities reached some hundreds of subscribers. Each had four pages of print, only a part of which was devoted to the weeks-old news. Organized postal services connected only the largest cities. For the illiterate majority of Europeans neither newspapers nor letters nor books mattered. Only here and there did the brilliant flow of ideas in the seventeenth and early eighteenth centuries penetrate to the mass of men. A possible exception was the Protestant religious revolt that had swept through the parishes of all Northern Europe. Even after this revolt, however, the village communicant came to the same church and knelt before the same altar to worship, more often than not under the guidance of the same clergyman or of one so like him as to represent no abrupt change. The theological differences between the papacy and Luther, Calvin, and the other reformers were doubtless lost on the majority of their respective followers, who willingly enough practiced their religions under the forms dictated by their rulers or by the community generally.

Life was precarious. Illness, accidents, war, and lawless violence cut it short. The difficulties of transportation meant that a local crop failure could bring famine even though food was abundant a few score impassable miles away. Inefficient agricultural methods and the exactions of feudal dues and other forms of taxation required the constant hard work of everyone to make enough to live. When disorder came, through war or rioting or banditry, starvation followed.

Such a society, in which any disruption of the orderly patterns of life was likely to mean hunger and suffering, was naturally conservative. It was important that everybody have a defined place in society and an assigned job to do in a set way. In the rural village complicated formulas prescribed the allotment of fields and the rotation of crops. In the towns and cities, guilds controlled the trades; there existed a fixed technical procedure to be followed step by step in each craft, and there were detailed traditional regulations for buying and selling its product.

Every man had a status, which was usually his by birth. He was not merely a man, but a nobleman or a serf or a free peasant, a priest or a baker or a merchant. He held his land, if any, in a particular way, as a fief or by freehold or copyhold, and his tenure of it was probably hereditary. His status was a local one, attached to a particular place. He was not just a baron, but baron of a particular barony, held from the King on a particular basis that conferred rights and imposed duties that were different from those of other baronies. He was not just a serf, but a serf of a particular estate. A goldsmith who was a member of the goldsmiths' guild in one city could not transfer his trade and his membership to another city. Men were born to a particular status—or to the opportunity to acquire a particular status—which defined their roles in life, limiting their freedom but also giving them security. It was through such a status that a man enjoyed a relationship to society. A stranger who came to a town or village statusless could only with difficulty find any place to fit himself.

The patterns by which the lives of most Europeans were fixed were traditional and inherited, and it was their traditional character that gave them authority. A man farmed in a certain way not because it was the way that produced the highest yield, but because that was the way his fathers farmed and the way custom said men should farm. The duke enjoyed certain authority at law not because he had earned it or because it served the interest of the people to have him exercise that power, but because it was the power traditionally held by the reigning duke. In deciding whether any act was right or proper men did not look so much forward to its consequences as backward to its precedents.

The fact that tradition set the patterns of daily life simply reflected the basic ideas of philosophy, religion, and law. Standards of truth and legal rights were believed to have been fixed unchangeably in the past. Most of Europe remained Catholic, even after the Reformation, and of course continued to believe that the truths of religion had been finally revealed insofar as mortal men might know them and had been authoritatively interpreted by the Church. Though it was a different authority that the Protestants accepted, in their way they no less relied upon past revelation as the source of truth. Moreover, the area of belief controlled by religion was much larger than today. Reliance on a literal interpretation of unrelated passages of the Bible as the final authority on scientific matters seemed ridiculous in the 1920's when some American states legislated against teaching evolution or when the followers of some sects continued to insist the world is flat. But in the early modern centuries traditional religious texts—the Bible or writings of Church Fathers—were to most men the accepted source of authority in science, economics, government, and philosophy as well as in theology.

For centuries the works of Aristotle had supplied an authority on matters that the Bible and the Church Fathers did not treat. During the Middle Ages an elaborate system of philosophy had been developed from a synthesis of his writings with Biblical and Church teachings. This so-called "scholastic" philosophy was an impressive example of the application of great reasoning power, using traditional beliefs as an accepted base. It still commands great respect; and as late as the eighteenth century there were many who rejected the astronomy of Copernicus, Kepler, Galileo, and Newton because it seemed to conflict with Aristotle's views.

The tendency to refer all questions to the past for answer or justification was true in law and government as well. Political power in Europe was exercised mostly through a crazy quilt of local and provincial authorities and customs. These represented a survival of the Middle Ages, and were rooted in long history. As will be pointed out, national states were growing in power; but much of Europe was still a conglomeration of principalities, duchies, baronies, and independent cities. Even within such nation-states as France and Spain, individual provinces retained local laws, customs, and "estates," or parliaments, that were traditional in origin and that limited the power of the national government. Cities were likely to be governed by "corporations" of burghers that, like the guilds, cherished inherited and indefeasible rights.

The laws of the various provinces of France were known as the *coutumes,* or "customs," of Normandy or Brittany or the like, and as the name indicates, were tradition-based. Their justification was not that they were useful or necessary or rational or that they had been enacted by any present authority, but rather that they *were* the *coutumes.*

In all ages political philosophers have been concerned with the legitimacy of political power. What entitles a governing power to obedience? In the mid-eighteenth century Europeans still looked to the past for the sources of legitimacy. Legitimate power was that exercised by inherited authority in accordance with the customs of the particular locality. What had existed—in the words of Blackstone—"since the memory of man runneth not to the contrary" was right.

These traditional patterns of work, government, and thought had persisted as the controlling forces in the lives of most Europeans for two or three centuries past the time that we think of as the end of the Middle Ages. But for a long time new developments had been growing that were incompatible with these inherited institutions. Strains and conflicts were steadily increasing, and by the mid-eighteenth century the time had come when a radical reorganization of European civilization was inevitable. The American Revolution was one part of that reorganization.

Several currents of change were sweeping through Western civilization in the eighteenth century. One of these was economic. Since the end of the Middle Ages Europe had been undergoing a commercial revolution. The discovery of the Americas and the opening of sea routes to Asia were made possible by the beginning of this revolution. Once the flow of gold, silver, sugar, tobacco, tea, and spices began to pour in from overseas, economic life was further quickened throughout Europe. Prosperity grew, and with it the scale of economic activity.

Large corporations, like the Dutch and English East India companies, had been formed in the seventeenth century to assemble the capital for overseas exploration and trade. In the eighteenth century the joint-stock company came to be used for many other purposes—to build canals or turnpikes, to operate banks, to write insurance, and even to undertake manufactures. Stocks were traded freely in embryo stock markets in London, Amsterdam, and Paris. The corporation became a means of organizing economic enterprises vastly larger than any single merchant or merchant family of an earlier day could have dreamed of.

Other tools of commerce grew. In the seventeenth century were created the Bank of Amsterdam and, at the very end of the century, the Bank of England. Both operated very much like modern banks, providing a ready reservoir of capital, a convenient way of transferring funds, and a sound paper currency that circulated over much of Europe. Marine insurance came to be written systematically and relatively cheaply. Lloyd's Coffee House in London achieved its fame as the meeting place of underwriters whose policies covered a vast fleet of ships venturing into every corner of the globe from the China Sea to the Arctic.

The physical means of commerce expanded rapidly as well. Though ships themselves were little changed in the eighteenth century, they became somewhat faster and more seaworthy, and their number multiplied. The tons of shipping clearing English ports nearly tripled between 1700 and 1770. The invention of the sextant and a reliable chronometer and the improvement of geographical knowledge and navigational charts increased the safety and dependability of shipping, so that merchant vessels could voyage anywhere with assurance and postal packets could sail on schedule between Bristol and New York.

The flow of goods from abroad had to be distributed within Europe, and means had to be found to carry the increased internal trade created by the new prosperity. The miserable roads maintained by local parishes were replaced or supplemented in France by a system of nationally planned and maintained highways and in England by turnpikes built by private joint-stock companies and financed by tolls. The eighteenth was the great century of canal building. England and France and parts of Prussia were crisscrossed by canals and improved river channels, so that horse-drawn barges bearing heavy freight could traverse nearly all of those lands. It became practical, for example, to bring English coal to the sites of iron mines so that it could replace charcoal from the vanishing forests for use in smelters.

Manufacturing outgrew the handicraft tradition of the guilds. In villages and rural areas beyond their jurisdiction, tasks were "put out" to families working in their own cottages on materials supplied by early capitalists who were thus able to undercut guild prices. The beginnings of the factory system emerged in such establishments as the Gobelin tapestry works in France. Here, though work was still done by hand rather than by machine, large bodies of workers were brought together under one roof and under a single discipline, with a division of tasks among the various specialists. In England the factory system had reached a point at which simple power-driven machinery could be effectively used. A primitive form of the steam engine came into use at the beginning of the century and was greatly improved in the 1760's. The invention of the fly shuttle in 1738 sped up weaving and led to a search for means of spinning thread faster and cheaper to supply the busy looms. A number of inventions were produced to answer this need in the latter half of the century, and the foundations of the Industrial Revolution had been laid by its close.

The rise of cities and commerce, the quickening pulse of economic life, and the improvement in transportation opened new and wider markets for agricultural products. Fortune awaited the landowners who could increase production of crops and of sheep to satisfy the hungry cities and the woolen factories. Many new agricultural techniques were developed in France and especially in England, including deeper plowing, more intelligent crop rotation, use of fertilizers, and more careful stockbreeding. The use of these techniques, however, required the unified control of a large estate by a manager who could plan for years ahead. The patchwork of fields and land tenures inherited from the Middle Ages lay as a frustrating barrier in the path of agricultural progress. Goaded by the promise of great wealth from steadily rising prices, landlords and noblemen, especially in England, by agreement or by legislation wiped out traditional tenures, dispossessed peasant holders, and enclosed large acreages in single efficient estates, very much as the large mechanized commercial farm or plantation has tended to overwhelm the family farm of our day.

The most important product of this economic revolution was not the farms, factories, or commodities that flowed from them, but rather the world-bestriding capitalist himself. By the latter half of the eighteenth century there were businessmen who bought and sold the spices of Java and the beaver pelts of Canada, sent their ships to Canton and the Coromandel Coast, traded rum for slaves in Africa, built speculative empires on land grants in the American wilderness, traded stocks on the exchange, and saw the great, newly opening world of that century as one vast arena for their resistless enterprise. Wealth undreamed of in preceding centuries became the possession of a whole class of restless and powerful men who calculated every maxim of law and turn of public policy, not in terms of its sanction in tradition but in terms of its utility in serving their ends.

The new capitalist class was generally in close alliance with the newly powerful national governments that came to full growth in the eighteenth century. France and Spain strengthened their national identities. England, by solidifying its control over Ireland and uniting with Scotland, formed the United Kingdom. The Hapsburgs, losing possessions elsewhere in Europe, were able to unite their Central European territories into a more coherent Austro-Hungarian Empire as the Hohenzollerns were erecting a powerful kingdom of Prussia on the basis of their electorate of Brandenburg. Sweden and Russia entered the nation-system of Western Europe.

For the first time in history most Europeans were organized in a few great nations, each far outranging in size and power the feudal provinces of the Middle Ages and bound by no international order imposed by church or state. Before these new and greedy powers lay the prospect of immeasurable wealth to be gained by control of the Asian and American continents and the great sea routes. Ceaseless armed competition among them was inevitable. During half the years from 1689 to 1763 they were actively fighting in a series of dynastic and colonial wars: the wars of the League of Augsburg (1689–1697), the Spanish Succession (1702–1713), and the Austrian Succession (1740–1748), and the Seven Years' War (1756–1763). Even the interstices of peace were filled with diplomatic maneuvers, arming for new combat, half-legalized piracy of shipping lanes, and border brawls along the thousands of miles of colonial frontier.

To support the ceaseless combat, open or covert, of the great states, their rulers were forced to seize on every source of power. No temporary feudal levies bringing their own arms could suffice for this warfare. Navies of hundreds of great ships must be built and sustained. Professional armies paid in hard cash must be organized. Cannon by the scores of hundreds, muskets by the many tens of thousands, and uniform cloth in hundreds of thousands of yards must be manufactured and paid for. Money must be found for forts in the American wilderness, naval expeditions to the Niger, and armies in India. To meet these needs, new taxes of every variety must be levied; trade and business must be stimulated both to produce the needed arms, ships, and materials of war and to raise the level of economic activity that could be taxed to pay for them; large-scale bureaucracies must be created to bring unity and efficiency; transportation must be improved; the whole state must be pulled together into one vast instrument for achieving national strength. There can be little doubt that the most dynamic single force in the eighteenth century was the ceaseless drive of the national governments for power.

It was the conviction of seventeenth- and eighteenth-century statesmen that all the economic activities of a country should be directed toward increasing the power of the national government. This doctrine was known as mercantilism. It is remembered today principally for its emphasis on the importance of gold and silver and the lengths to which it would have a nation go to increase its stocks of those metals. This preoccupation with hard money arose directly from a ruler's need to maintain his armed forces and corps of administrators. The constant and urgent need of governments for gold and silver to coin, even more than the personal greed of the explorers, accounts for the almost frenzied search for precious metals by the expeditions opening the New World.

But few nations could mine their own money. For most, income in gold and silver had to be earned from foreign trade; hence governmental policy during the seventeenth and eighteenth centuries was largely devoted to creating a "favorable" balance of trade—that is, to bringing it about that exported goods were of greater total value than those imported. Tariffs and even outright prohibitions against certain goods held down imports. Exports were encouraged by subsidies. The shipping of gold and silver out of a country was usually explicitly forbidden.

But mercantilism went far beyond these export-import controls. Exports of manufactured goods were especially favored, not only because they were higher priced but also because, unlike many raw materials, they could not ordinarily be used by a competitor for his own further manufacture. To develop manufacturing industries a government might use general as well as export subsidies. It might give a monopoly of a product to a particular manufacturer to encourage his larger investment. Inspection and quality standards were established to assure the reputation and marketability of exports. In some countries, especially in France, standards might be reinforced by detailed regulations covering every step of manufacture.

Foreign trade was directly encouraged not only by subsidies but also by the incorporation of chartered companies charged with developing trade to given areas, like the British and Dutch East India companies, the Hudson's Bay Company, or the Royal African Company. These enterprises might receive capital from the government and many special privileges, including powers to govern the territories within the area of their concern and to maintain private armies and naval forces. Such companies did much of the work of exploring, conquering, settling, and administering the colonies and trading concessions acquired by the European powers.

Colonies, in fact, occupied a very special role in mercantilist thought. They might, as in the case of Mexico and Peru, be immediate sources of precious metals. In any event, they could provide raw materials for manufacture and exotic products such as sugar, tobacco, and dyewoods that would otherwise have to be imported from competing powers and paid for in specie. They might indeed provide essential materials for sale that competing powers must buy for cash. The labor of emigrants and natives in providing raw materials and specie could be paid for with manufactures from the home country. The colonial policies of all European powers were primarily devoted to assuring that their overseas possessions fulfilled the role assigned them by mercantile theory. The production of needed raw materials in the colonies was encouraged by bounties, and the export of those materials was usually confined by law to the mother country. Only the parent country could be the source of imports, and the development of local manufactures was restrained or forbidden. Indeed the European powers thought of their overseas possessions not as communities of men having a political relation with the mother country, but as economic enterprises—mining camps, plantations, or trading posts—whose relation to the mother country was almost wholly commercial. The blind pursuit of this policy, more than any other single factor, had all but ended European dominion in the Americas by the end of the first quarter of the nineteenth century.

But balances of payments and acquisitions of specie were not the sole objectives of mercantile policy. All measures that enlarged the power of the state were its concern. The supply of armaments demanded attention, and subsidies and other forms of encouragement were used to promote the production of weapons and naval stores. Above all, the maritime powers needed strong navies based on large and efficient merchant fleets. Hence a country's navigation acts confined trade to its own ships insofar as possible.

The removal of barriers to internal trade was also a necessary part of mercantilism. This involved not only the physical improvement of roads and canals but also the reduction or elimination of provincial and municipal tariffs and an attack on restrictive marketing regulations in individual cities. Even more important were the efforts of the economic planners to achieve a systematic and dependable internal revenue. The governments of the national states depended for their income on a patchwork of sources, including the rents and profits from the King's own estates, customs duties, fees, income from monopolies, and land taxes collected in a highly uneven way and often varying widely among provinces. In none of the European countries did these feudal sources of income provide an adequate revenue, and ministers of finance in every capital were pressing for new taxes more rationally laid and more effectively collected.

In this demand they came everywhere into conflict with provincial "estates," or local parliaments, of medieval origin, with municipal corporations, and with traditional courts like the *parlements* of France that asserted a power to grant or withhold all new taxes and were the defenders of the established pattern of provincial and municipal laws, tariffs, and trade regulations. In country after country ministers like Colbert and Turgot and rulers like Frederick the Great, Catherine of Russia, and Joseph II of Austria struggled with the bodies of aldermen, the provincial nobility, the monastic chapters, the estates, and the other corporate groups that embodied and defended the traditional local interests surviving from the Middle Ages. In this struggle the local groups, like states-rights advocates in the present-day United States, saw themselves as defenders of inherited freedom against the encroachments of a ruthless centralizing power; the monarchs and their ministers saw themselves, in contrast, as the reforming agents of modern and effective government.

But by the mid-eighteenth century mercantilist economic policies enforced by an administrative bureaucracy in the interest of the national state were losing acceptance. Initially the merchants for whom the policy was named, the emerging manufacturers, and the other members of the new capitalist class welcomed mercantilism and gladly associated themselves with the state. Protection from foreign competition, subsidies for exports and for new ventures, government-protected monopoly, and aid in breaking the local shackles on trade were all boons indeed. But in time mercantilistic regulations became as detailed and vexing as the guild ordinances they in part replaced. The chartered companies and monopolies that were the instruments of national policy, particularly in trade with Asia and Africa, smothered the enterprise of individual businessmen who sought a share of the opportunity. Many a chance for trading gain was barred by law or regulation because it might involve the export of coin or bullion. Agricultural interests were injured by policies that favored manufacture and trade.

During the course of the eighteenth century a new body of economic thought grew up that saw national wealth not in terms of stocks of gold and silver but as the sum of the wealth of individual citizens, and that believed that individual men best knew the way to augment their own wealth. This economic philosophy received its classic statement in Adam Smith's *Wealth of Nations,* published in the very year of the Declaration of Independence; but the ideas Smith so brilliantly brought together had been widely expressed for decades before. Their first systematic expression came in the writings of a French group headed by François Quesnay (1694–1774). They were called "physiocrats" and were perhaps the first real economists. "Physiocrat" means a believer in the rule of nature; and the core of the faith of Quesnay and his followers was that if the government let men do as they wished in their business affairs, the pursuit of their individual interests would lead them, by natural law, to serve the general interest. "Laissez-faire" was a term invented by the physiocrats. Similar beliefs were expressed by such precursors of Adam Smith in England as Sir Dudley North and Smith's friend David Hume. Even the seventeenth-century mercantilists of England had been less rigid than those of the Continent.

The significance of the new body of economic thought lay not only in its more sophisticated analysis and its greater conformity with the needs of emerging capitalism. It was significant because it substituted individual wealth for national power as the object of national policy. True, this shift of goals was justified or concealed by the argument that individual wealth was a means to national power, but the shift was nonetheless real.

This newer economic thought was one aspect of a major intellectual development in eighteenth-century Europe that is known as the Enlightenment. The Enlightenment was grounded in a brilliant series of scientific discoveries that had made the preceding century—the 1600's—perhaps the greatest epoch in the history of the human mind. In a dozen fields the scientists of the seventeenth and early eighteenth centuries laid the basis of modern knowledge. In astronomy, mechanics, optics, analytical geometry, calculus, anatomy and physiology, experimental chemistry, and biology, to mention only a few, science as we know it began with those generations. Their most important contribution, however, was in the way they conceived, and helped educated men generally to conceive, of the nature of the universe itself. To the medieval thinker every object had its own peculiar qualities that were part of its very essence and distinguished it from objects of every other kind, and indeed from other objects of its own kind. Infinite variety characterized the innumerable species of objects and beings with which the world was filled. Earth and silver and leather and air were not merely matter in different states, but utterly different things whose distinguishing qualities were unchangeable parts of their very being. All these varied things were related to one another in complex and essentially unpredictable ways that were imposed by the will of God and might be altered by him from time to time, almost capriciously, in the form of miracles. There appeared to be no way in which this bewildering profusion of being could be subdued to an abstract pattern of numbers.

Scientists from the days of Copernicus and Galileo had begun to find areas of order within this complexity, but it remained for Isaac Newton (1642–1727) to bring together a series of simple principles that seemed to his followers to reduce the whole universe to a pattern of law and reason. Though Newton made important discoveries in optics and mathematics, the achievements that shaped the thought of the next century were his formulation of the law of gravity and of the three basic laws of motion. Newton's principal work was published in 1687, but it remained for the next century to popularize it. Many dozens of simplified summaries of his work were published in England and on the Continent and were widely read. By the mid-eighteenth century Newton had become the sort of fad in fashionable intellectual circles that

Darwin, Freud, and Einstein were to become in later generations. Like the followers of those later geniuses, the followers of Newton erected upon the basis of his precise and modestly limited scientific conclusions a whole system of philosophy.

Among the principles of this Newtonian revolution was the uniformity of matter. Earth and silver and leather and air, it turned out, were not essentially distinct things, but merely matter in varying states. A body of a given mass would behave in a given way, whatever it was made of. All things could be reduced to one mathematical measure of mass and speed. Indeed mass, extension, and motion were the only real properties that matter possessed. The variety that adorns the world exists in the beholder's eye. The blue of the sky is merely the stimulation of the optic cells by light waves vibrating at a given speed, heat our sometimes painful perception of the rapid motion of molecules, sound the shaking of our eardrums by still other waves. The scientists of the eighteenth century did not know how all these effects were achieved, but they did sense that color, temperature, sound, and other qualities that the ancient and medieval thinkers endowed with separate and real existence were in fact but our ways of perceiving motions—motions that all obeyed a single set of laws.

The universe that consisted only of extended mass in patterns of motion was, moreover, a uniform universe. The stars swept across the sky in obedience to precisely the same laws that governed the fall of apples from trees or the roll of billiard balls across a table. Any one set of causes, no matter where or how often repeated, would produce the identical effect.

The laws of the uniform universe, moreover, were simple ones. To explain the motion of the stars one needed no elaborate hypothesis of spheres upon spheres moving in complex cycles and epicycles such as the Ptolemaic astronomers had been forced to construct. All that was needed was three easily stated laws of motion and a formula for gravitational attraction as simple as $G = \frac{M_1 M_2}{d^2}$.

It was in the nature of matter to obey these simple laws governing its motion. The universe stayed in exact and magnificent balance because every particle of matter everywhere moved as the inherent nature of matter dictated, and in so doing conformed to the grand pattern imposed by the mind of God. Any meddlesome effort to distort the naturally impelled motion of matter was certain to be fruitless and might be disastrous.

Finally, these simple principles that so clearly explained the workings of the universe were open to the mind of man. No miraculous revelation was needed. As a matter of fact, since Newton's discoveries happened to lie in fields in which, unlike biology and chemistry, no extended experimental work was required or, indeed, possible, it seemed to his followers that the mysteries of the universe could be unraveled—actually rather easily unraveled—merely by simple observation and thought.

Newton was himself a simple and devout man whose intellectual curiosity did not often run far beyond the scientific areas in which he worked. He was interested in neither the theological nor the political implications of his work. His own theology was "pre-Newtonian," owing little or nothing to his scientific thought. Not so with his followers. By a loose process of analogy they carried what seemed to be the spirit of his ideas into many other fields. The more popular Newton's thought became among non-scientists in the coffeehouses of London and the salons of Paris, the more remote the subjects his ideas were believed to illumine. If all matter was basically alike, differing only in such qualities as extension and motion, perhaps all people were alike, differing not in kind but only in the positions they happened to occupy at any given time. If the universe was governed by simple and uniform laws, rationally deduced, perhaps the political and economic world was also, and perhaps those political and economic laws were as readily discoverable by observation and thought. If it was the nature of matter to obey universal laws that brought the motion of all particles into harmonious relation with each other, perhaps it was wise in political and economic affairs to allow men freedom to pursue their natural bent, for they too in following their natural impulses might be led by a universal law into serving the general interest. And if the universe was governed by unchanging law, perfect and not to be tampered with, the role of God became that of an original Creator, remote from all subsequent contact with the workings of the perfect machine he had devised. All religious rituals designed to affect his actions or procure his intercession to change the course of events were vain superstition, and the organized religions that practiced them were, in Voltaire's words, "infamous" institutions that deluded the popular mind and expropriated resources that might have been used for public betterment.

The general body of thought we call Newtonian was most effectively applied to social issues by another Englishman, John Locke (1632–1704). Locke, as a secretary and agent for the Earl of Shaftesbury, was active in political affairs for most of his life. His writings reflect a common-sense application of the views of his time to important public issues. His most important political writings, his two *Treatises on Civil Government,* were written to provide a justification in political theory for the English Glorious Revolution of 1688; but however specific the occasion for which they were written, they dominated political thought for a century to come and provided the philosophical basis for the American Revolution. His theories of government will be discussed in detail in a later chapter; here it is necessary only to point out that Locke, like Thomas Hobbes and other English writers of his century, found the origin of legitimate political power not in mere past existence or tradition but in a voluntary act of those governed to attain their own ends, an act that could hence be revoked or amended as those ends changed or were poorly served.

Perhaps even more relevant was Locke's *An Essay Concerning Human Understanding* (1690), which explored a puzzle fascinating to thinkers of the period: how did human beings come to have knowledge? Most earlier thinkers believed in the existence of innate ideas, so that every individual was believed to have inherited much of his intellectual equipment. Locke asserted rather that the human mind was created naked of content—a *"tabula rasa,"* an erased blackboard, he termed it—and that all its subsequent collection of facts, beliefs, and ideas were acquired by experience. Among the many implications of this belief is a reinforcement of the idea that all men are inherently equal. Locke certainly did not mean to suggest that men's intellectual potentialities are equal; but after all, one *tabula rasa* must be very like another, and the differences we observe in men exist in large part because society has treated them differently rather than primarily because they inherited different characters. Moreover, if knowledge is gained only from observation and experience, the role of revelation is further reduced and the importance of observation and reason is increased.

The inferences from Locke's writing, like those from Newton's, lessened the importance of the past in fixing the patterns of the present and the future. Perhaps because the scientific discoveries that underlay seventeenth- and eighteenth-century thought were primarily in such relatively timeless areas as physics and mathematics, the thinkers of that epoch tended to see systems of ideas, government, or economics as existing essentially outside the flow of time, as devised by reason rather than inherited from former growth. Locke's rejection of innate ideas reinforced this conception. Society itself became a sort of *tabula rasa,* on which men could write out a new pattern of government created from their own rational contemplation of timeless natural law.

The intellectual movement expressing all these views reached its height in eighteenth-century France in the writings of such men as Voltaire, Condorcet, Diderot, Helvétius, and Holbach. They thought of themselves as indeed "enlightened" men, freed from a long burden of superstition that had smothered the human mind since the days of the Greeks and Romans. The past, they believed, could easily be done with, and the human mind could construct a new order, formed on the basis of reason rather than on inherited privilege. They were optimistic men, sanguine that the complexities of society and of government would fall neatly into patterns as simple as those discovered by Newton in the motions of the stars. They were perhaps shallow men, unaware of how much of the thinking of the medieval past they had imported into their own thought. Historian Carl Becker has pointed out that in their reliance upon reason rather than experiment, in their fascination with abstract formulations, and in their attention to ideal forms they were far more medieval than modern.

And yet it was they, the seventeenth- and eighteenth-century thinkers of England and France, that opened the door to our world. It was they who convinced enough of the politically active classes of their time that the inherited patterns of status, privilege, and tradition must be radically altered and replaced by a new order, looking to the future rather than the past, and shaped by reason to meet the newly opening opportunities and demands of Western civilization.

They were themselves humane men, concerned that all men should be freed of the burdens placed on them by ignorance and an irrational social order. For the first time men contemplated human misery not as something permanent to be alleviated in individual cases by acts of charity, but as a social evil created by an irrational social order, an evil that could be eliminated by a rational act of the will. For the reasons described above, they were disposed toward views of human equality and toward minimal governmental interference with what they believed was the natural tendency of individuals to behave in accord with natural law. But they were not democrats as we understand the term. The Continental thinkers wanted a government that could swiftly put into effect the policies they formulated, and they saw this as more likely under an enlightened despot than in the confusions of a popular government. Their predilection was strengthened because the guilds, the municipal governments, the provincial estates, the traditional courts, and the other "popular" bodies on the Continent, though they spoke of themselves as the protectors of liberty, actually sought to thwart progress in order to preserve inherited privilege. It was natural that Voltaire and his contemporaries turned to Louis XV in France, Frederick the Great in Prussia, Joseph II in Austria, and Catherine the Great in Russia. Even in England, where Locke and his followers insisted on the necessity of a popular participation in the government and on the supremacy of Parliament, they spoke for a tiny oligarchy of a relatively few thousand politically active Englishmen out of a population of millions.

By the late eighteenth century the tensions between the new world of science and industry and the medieval world of inherited status were so great that the work of radical reconstruction of society had to begin. That work of reconstruction—the creation of a modern social, political, and economic order—was to go on in Western civilization for a century and a half or more, and it is just beginning in the civilizations of Asia and Africa. The tools to make the future were at hand in the ideas of the seventeenth and eighteenth centuries, but the ends and the patterns were still ambiguous. A Marx or a Lenin or a Bismarck, as well as a Jefferson or a Madison, could strive to replace an old order with a new one, designed full-fashioned to express the new science and technology.

We shall now explore the causes that shaped the American Revolution as a particular response to this challenge.

2 ★★★★★★★★★

The British Empire in the Mid-Eighteenth Century

When George III came to the throne in 1760, Englishmen and envious philosophers from the Continent alike agreed that Great Britain had the best of constitutions. The freedom of the individual, they held, was guaranteed by laws to which the King himself was subject; the King's authority was powerful to act for good, yet was restrained from oppressing the people by the countervailing powers of Parliament. An independent judiciary was vigilant to protect the security of the subjects in their liberty and property. A loyal citizenry supported a just and loving King in a joint and harmonious dedication to the well-being of the realm.

Though there was a vast deal of fiction in this roseate account, it was not altogether without justification. Eighteenth-century Britain was politically blessed on several counts. One was that the medieval institutions that guarded traditional liberties were national rather than local, as they were on the Continent. The Tudor kings and queens hence had been able to establish a pattern of working with and through them rather than against them in the task of modernizing and nationalizing the government and economy of the country. The common law and the judges who rode circuit about the country enforcing it were powerful instruments for the uniform and effective exercise of national authority, not—like the *coutumes* and *parlements* of the French provinces—means of frustrating it. Parliament itself was an integral part of that embodiment of national sovereignty, the "King-in-Parliament," that was the center of national power, not—like the provincial estates of most Continental countries—a focus of separatist resistance to the central authority.

Because they were associated with rather than opposed to the growth of modern central authority in the state, the independent legislative and judicial institutions of Great Britain were strengthened as the state itself grew in power. This was in contrast to the situation throughout the Continent, where the comparable institutions that might have restrained the specific authority of the King set themselves also against the growing national authority, and were destroyed in the process.

This contrast had been demonstrated in the previous century, when twice the efforts of reigning Stuart kings to raise a revenue and otherwise govern without the participation of Parliament provoked successful armed rebellions by the people. The first led to a long war, the beheading of Charles I, and eleven years of a republican commonwealth and protectorate (1649–1660). The second, in 1688, was a bloodless affair that permanently displaced the Stuarts from the English throne. In neither of these cases, however, did the aggressive action of Parliament and other traditional institutions in the protection of vested rights involve resistance to the emerging commercialism and nationalism that elsewhere in Europe was in continual conflict with medieval survivals. On the contrary, it was the rebels who sought the stronger and more effective national government and represented the forces of modernity. In similar contests on the Continent over the taxing power or over the independence of the judiciary, the provincial estates and law courts everywhere lost their power to the new and unrestrained authority of the "enlightened despots." In England alone, the comparable institutions became part of the embodiment, rather than the victims, of the new political and economic order.

After the so-called Glorious Revolution of 1688 and the succession to the throne of William and Mary, all the politically effective elements in England joined in a settlement so universally accepted that internal disssension was greatly diminished for a century to come. It was not until new groups —agricultural laborers, factory workers, the urban poor—not included in the earlier settlement achieved political effectiveness and began to demand a voice in the commonwealth that serious tensions recurred.

The political system that emerged from this settlement was very different from the British government of today or even that of the nineteenth century. The King's ministers were still his own, individually responsible to him, not collectively responsible to Parliament. The maintenance of his independent authority, the royal "prerogative," was thought essential to the vigorous conduct of government. Parliament's powers were nevertheless real and beyond the King's reach. The King could raise no revenue but by Parliament's gift and make no law without its consent. Though there was no ministerial responsibility to Parliament as we understand the term today, any effort to govern contrary to Parliament's will could be paralyzed by its refusal to enact laws or to grant funds. It was hence part of the unwritten understanding embodied in the settlement that the King would not endeavor to pursue a major policy without the support of Parliament.

Parliament in turn was a very different institution from the one we know today. The House of Lords was no vestigial relic, but—save for money bills—an equal body to the House of Commons. Even the Commons in no sense represented the totality of the common people of Britain. Each shire elected two members, and all those who owned or leased land to the value of forty shillings a year could vote. This was only a tiny minority of the residents of the shires, and even these few electors voted openly under the eyes of their landlords and local squires. The fewer than one hundred shire members were democratically elected, however, in comparison with the more than four hundred members chosen by the boroughs. Throughout the medieval and early modern centuries the cities, towns, and even villages had been haphazardly added to the list of boroughs summonsed to send members to Parliament, with little regard to population or logic. Some had decayed to the point that only a handful of residents were left; newer cities as large as Birmingham and Manchester, on the other hand, might not be represented at all. In only a few boroughs, such as the City of London, was the election reasonably democratic even among the middle and upper classes to whom the suffrage was confined. The mode of election varied from borough to borough, and in most of them an oligarchy of one kind or another controlled the choice. In many so-called nomination boroughs a single landlord, usually a nobleman, could name the member or members personally. Some great magnates controlled several such seats; the King himself, through landholdings and patronage, could manage the choice of thirty to forty members. In all of England fewer than two hundred thousand out of perhaps five and a half million subjects participated in any way in the election of Commons; and a few dozen great families, if united in alliance with the Crown, could control the House against anything less than an overwhelming tide of public opinion.

What Parliament did represent, and represent effectively, was the great landed and mercantile interests of the country. Montesquieu thought he saw in the British Constitution a complete separation of legislative and executive powers; and partly because of his praise of that arrangement, such a separation was to become a fetish of Revolutionary political theory. But in fact it hardly existed. The Crown and Parliament, acting in fact as well as in theory as the King-in-Parliament, exercised both powers jointly. But there was a *balance* of powers in the sense that no major governmental program could go forward unless it balanced the interests and had the common support of the Crown, the nobility, the landed gentry, and the great merchants.

Meanwhile the disfranchised masses as well as the tiny political elite were protected in their basic liberties by the Bill of Rights of 1689, which guaranteed many of the rights later to be set forth in the first ten amendments to the Constitution of the United States. A booming economy throughout most of the century also helped to hold the loyalty of the populace. Not until near the end of the century were the poorer classes seriously oppressed by the displacement from enclosures and other rapid economic changes and by the sordid conditions of employment in the early factories. In consequence, the masses in England, both rural and urban, for the most part remained politically inert until after the beginning of the American Revolution.

The relative political harmony that prevailed in eighteenth-century Britain made it possible to leave local government in local hands without endangering national unity. Throughout the Continent, and especially in France, that century saw the steady displacement of the traditional local authorities by bureaucrats designated by and responsible to the central government. In France, for example, by the latter part of the century *intendants,* career servants of the Crown drawn from the middle classes and always serving in districts remote from their homes, governed the provinces with absolute authority. The provincial estates had ceased to meet or had become meaningless, and the provincial nobility had become a privileged and ornamental class divorced from all the actual business of government. Local administration looked to Paris for its authority and legitimacy, not to any grounding in local tradition, participation, or consent.

Not so in England. Though in each shire there was a Lord Lieutenant representing the King's authority, the office was very nearly hereditary and not subject to the King's free disposal; and in any event its power was nominal. The real power of local government was in the hands of the justices of the peace, both individually as the petty judges and ruling squires of their neighborhoods and collectively as the Court of Pleas and Quarter Sessions that both governed and administered justice throughout the shire. These worthies, though commissioned by the Crown, were in practice self-selected from the landowning "county families." Below the shires were the parishes, governed by vestries more democratically elected but still essentially representing the landed interest, the "squirearchy" of England.

In the growing towns and cities there was a bewildering diversity of forms of government. Many were ruled as "close corporations" in which an initially appointed board of aldermen was self-perpetuating, filling vacancies in its own membership. In a few, such as London, there was a free election of municipal officials, but even here the franchise was limited to propertied businessmen. Whatever the form of local government, the municipal authorities in practice represented the business and mercantile interests of the borough. Both in the shires and in the boroughs the same families and interests, even the same men, both administered local government and helped to make up that union of interests that was the King-in-Parliament and that ruled the nation.

For this reason no new corps of bureaucrats was necessary to subdue local interests to the national will. The national and the local governments alike were only different agents of the same dominant classes. No national police enforced the law. Only the smallest of standing armies was stationed in England in peacetime. Except in the seaports, where customs officials and naval officers were at hand, an Englishman might live out his life rarely seeing an officer from the national government at Whitehall. A union of interests rather than a hierarchy of authority held the realm together.

Nor was there in England the hostility between a traditional landed and military class and a modern commercial class that disturbed so many Continental countries. Daughters and younger sons of the nobility were commoners in England and entered all the trades and professions. Neither law nor tradition kept peers of the realm themselves from business, and the landed gentry avidly pursued the economic opportunities offered by the expanding commercial life of England. At the same time, men of trade aspired to the ownership of land as the surest evidence of social standing and hastened from the countinghouse to the country estate, uniting themselves in interest with the older gentry.

In the mid-eighteenth century the government of Britain, both national and local, singlemindedly represented not the traditions of England or its military glory, its feudal past, or its religious passion, but its property. Property, protected from arbitrary action by a system of law above the King himself, controlling the government through its representation in Parliament and its management of local authority, growing with rapidly accelerating speed, dominated the policies of the kingdom and empire. Like all governments of property, the ruling class of England sought order and economy, the steady and foreseeable courses of the law. They thought little of expensive glory and regarded the army as a costly nuisance to be held to a minimum and the navy as the escort and protector of trade. Challenging ideas and novel concepts they found troublesome. Though it was a brilliant age in English philosophy, there was no Milton or Hobbes or Locke, as in the preceding century, to bring bold speculation into the arena of government. The imagination and the world vision of a Pitt could be tolerated only in moments of desperate crisis. The empire itself was not a vast world-spanning realm, an England writ large across the known universe, but rather a species of property to be run as a mine might be run or a fishery or a wholesaler's warehouse, with due regard for the owner's profit.

When a greatness of view and a bold and creative imagination might have held intact a union of English-speaking freemen engirdling the world, eyes and minds were hardly lifted from the ledgers of trade and taxes.

By 1750 Britain was already mistress of a great empire, shortly to be made much greater through its conquests in the Seven Years' War. The North American coast from Newfoundland to Georgia and such Caribbean islands as Barbados, Jamaica, and the Leewards had already been acquired, as well as suzerainty over much of India. The acquisition of this empire had been almost solely the work of private enterprise. During the sixteenth and seventeenth centuries, when the European powers were asserting their claims to India and the Americas, England was a small, poor, maritime nation on the margins of Europe. With one fifth the population of France, one half that of Spain, and a fraction of the wealth of either, the English government could by no means support such imperial efforts as did those powers. During most of the seventeenth century, moreover, the English government was distracted by two revolutions and by bitter tension over its control that continued until the last decade of the century.

The enterprise of fishermen, half-piratical seamen, companies of merchants, and daring noblemen with capitalistic ambitions had made good the inactivity of the royal government. By the early seventeenth century they had begun to establish footholds at scattered points along the Atlantic coast. A great migration of Englishmen followed throughout most of that century as the civil wars, the sense of political and religious oppression, and the economic distress of those troubled years drove them from Britain. After 1690 this emigration decreased, but by then the Atlantic and Caribbean colonies were well established and continued to grow rapidly as a result of a high birthrate; migration from Scotland, Ireland, and Germany; and the importation of African slaves.

Because the empire grew in this unplanned, almost haphazard way as the product of private efforts, and because its early history fell in a period of such continuous disturbance in Great Britain, nearly a century elapsed before a systematic pattern for its government emerged. The Navigation Act of 1696, the commissioning of the Board of Trade and Plantations in that year, and the general revision of instructions to the royal governors that then occurred mark the initial completion of that pattern.

It reflected, as one might expect, the dominant concepts of the settlement of England's own governmental problems that had occurred just previously. Though Parliament never abandoned—and from time to time asserted—its ultimate authority over the colonies as over the home realm, its administration was recognized as an executive function within the royal prerogative. Hence, except for the general regulation of trade, Parliament until after 1763 rarely concerned itself especially with the colonies. The King, acting through the Privy Council, was the source of British authority in America. The role of the prerogative was clearly and forcefully conceived, as it was in England itself under William III.

At the same time, the prerogative was no more absolute in the colonies than the authors of the Glorious Revolution would have permitted it to be at home. The various experiments in ruling colonies without a local assembly attempted by the Stuarts, as in New York after its conquest from the Dutch or in the short-lived Dominion of New England, were abandoned. Thenceforward no one would think of ruling a colony of Englishmen without the participation of a local assembly. Nor was there ever any renewal of the effort made in Virginia and Jamaica in the 1670's to limit the power of the assemblies to the ratification of royally initiated legislation.

The British view of the colonies was shaped by the mercantilistic conception of government then prevailing. Their purpose was conceived to be to promote the trade and commercial well-being of Britain by providing needed raw materials, absorbing manufactured products, and giving employment to the merchant marine that underlay Britain's naval strength. It is more than symbolic that not until the eve of the Revolution was there any colonial office or equivalent agency that could have considered colonial problems as such. Colonial matters were dealt with primarily in the Board of Trade and Plantations. This was a small committee, of eight members, whose meetings might from time to time be attended by privy councillors or other high officials. It was created by William III to inquire into and make recommendations concerning the trade and commerce of the realm. The drafting of instructions to royal governors and the handling of correspondence with them, the preparation of legislation affecting the colonies, and the drafting of reports on colonial matters were all in the hands of the Board of Trade as an advisory body to the Privy Council and the executive departments. Yet it dealt with all these matters as a part of, and in the context of, its primary commercial mission. All colonial questions hence tended to be seen simply as matters of trade and to be acted upon in that light.

The absence of an executive office devoted to colonial affairs was significant not only as evidence of a mercantile rather than an imperial conception of the colonies. It meant also that they escaped effective control from Great Britain. During most of its existence the Board of Trade was a reasonably efficient body, but its concern for the colonies was limited in scope and its powers were purely advisory. Any authority to act with respect to the colonies was dispersed among many offices. The Secretary of State for the Southern Department among his many duties had a general responsibility for the overseas possessions. The Treasury had fiscal responsibilities. The War Office maintained the handful of troops in the New World.

The Admiralty maintained naval squadrons and undertook to suppress smuggling. The King and the Privy Council had an ultimate executive responsibility but exercised it only desultorily prior to the reign of George III. These offices were scattered over London, lacked competent staff, were little used to working together, and during the half century before the Seven Years' War were directed by no effective or driving overall authority. This divided and indifferent administration was no match for a single-minded colony that knew what it wanted. In large part, the administrative inadequacy of British rule accounts for the successful maintenance of colonial autonomy against British efforts to limit it, and ultimately for the failure of British authority when it was finally and directly challenged.

Though the administration of the colonies was weak and confused, the objectives of British colonial policy and the British conception of colonial status were reasonably clear. A series of acts defined the economic role that Parliament conceived for the colonies. Oldest among these were the Navigation Acts, to use the term narrowly. In 1651, when Cromwell began to bring order out of the chaos into which economic life had fallen during the English Civil War, the principle was laid down that all commerce to and from the colonies and among them could be carried only in vessels of British or colonial build and ownership, the captain and most of the crew being British or colonial subjects. These provisions were reenacted and strengthened upon the return of royal authority in 1660 and again upon the general reorganization of colonial administration in 1696. By clauses included in the instructions to royal governors from 1717 onward, the colonial legislatures were forbidden without the prior consent of the Crown to tamper with this system by the passage of acts affecting the trade or shipping of Great Britain. Though a part of the purpose of the Navigation Acts was to impede the smuggling of European products into the colonies, their primary objective was to assure the construction and employment of an extensive merchant marine. In the eighteenth century the distinction between a vessel of war and a potentially armed merchantman was slight, and the training of seamen and the encouragement of shipyards served both naval and commercial purposes. In her strength upon the sea Britain saw, and saw rightly, her single basis of security in a world of competitive and often hostile powers with far greater population and wealth.

Moreover, it seemed natural in that era that every power should reserve to its own merchant marine the carriage of goods within its own dominions and to its own colonies. Even today coastwise commerce in the United States, including trade between the mainland and the overseas states and possessions, is reserved to American ships. Though the colonies were discriminated against in that they could not receive into their ports, as could the homeland British, the ships of Spain, Portugal, France, Scandinavia, and other countries bearing the goods of their respective nations, the colonial ships, masters, and seamen were benefited by being allowed to enter the reserved trade on the same basis as the British themselves.

A second group of statutes was intended to reserve for Great Britain all the products of the colonies that it might otherwise have to buy outside the empire. The Navigation Act of 1660 "enumerated" sugar, tobacco, cotton, indigo, ginger, and fustian and other dyewoods as goods that could be shipped from the colonies only to England. In 1663 all direct commerce between the colonies and the European continent—with a very few exceptions—was forbidden, though the export of nonenumerated articles to French, Spanish, and Dutch colonies in the West Indies and elsewhere remained permissible under British law. The list of enumerated articles was from time to time extended. Rice, for example, was added in 1706, and copper and beaver and other furs in 1722. Because the whole purpose of the enumeration was to reserve the supply of products for British use and to obtain for British merchants the profit on the reexport of any surplus, enumeration of a commodity was usually accompanied by measures to forbid the importation of that commodity into Great Britain from any other source. Thus, though the colonies were denied potential markets outside the British empire, they were usually assured a monopoly of the market within the empire. In the case of tobacco, Parliament went so far as to forbid its cultivation within England.

Certain exceptions to the principles of the enumeration were permitted when the colonies produced a greater quantity of any commodity than Britain could absorb, and when its transshipment and reexport from Great Britain to the continent of Europe would so raise the cost as to make its resale impossible. Fish, for example, rice after 1730, and sugar after 1739 could be shipped directly from the colonies to Southern Europe. The shipment from the British colonies to those of Spain, France, and the Netherlands of such goods as lumber, foodstuffs, and horses—of which Britain produced enough for her own needs—was actively encouraged as a means of drawing off hard money from those empires.

A special and annoying aspect of the policy of monopolizing colonial products for British use was embodied in acts reserving white pine trees above specified sizes for the exclusive use of the British navy for masts, yards, and bowsprits.

To free Britain further from dependence on imports from outside the empire, Parliament offered bounties for the colonial production of some specially desired items. Beginning in 1705, for example, a series of efforts was made, through bounties, regulations, inspections, and other measures, to increase the quantity and improve the quality of the colonial production of "naval stores"—the general term for tar, pitch, turpentine, rosin, hemp, timbers for masts and yards, and other supplies needed for the growing navy and merchant marine. In 1739 a similar set of bounties was provided for the production of indigo. Each of these programs appears to have been reasonably successful, both in stimulating production, especially in the Carolinas, and in relieving Britain from dependence on foreign sources of supply, especially Baltic naval stores.

A third element in British policy was intended to assure that the colonies served British manufacturing by purchasing its products and avoiding any competitive efforts. The Act of 1663 that forbade all exports directly to Europe also forbade all direct imports from that continent, with such necessary exceptions, not competitive with British products, as Madeira wine and salt for drying fish. This assured English manufacturers a monopoly for their products and English merchants the profit on the importation and resale of the commodities England could not provide directly. The provisions of this act, making England the staple through which almost all European imports must be drawn, remained in effect for most of the colonial period.

Not content with protecting the English manufacturer from European competition, Parliament sought to protect him from his American competitor as well. Though in fairness to the Americans it rejected or ignored many of the more apprehensive pleas from English producers for protection, it did not hesitate to act when any prospective development of manufacturing even slightly threatened the British market. This was true not only when American products were feared in the British market itself—in which they rarely appeared in the colonial period—but even when by supplying colonial needs they threatened to diminish British exports to the colonies. In 1699 the export of raw wool and woolens from any colony was forbidden. In 1732 the production of hats for other than local use was banned. When an iron industry began to develop in certain of the colonies in the mid-eighteenth century, the British authorities were presented with a more complex problem, in which the interests of the British makers of raw iron were in conflict with those of steelmakers and fabricators of ironware, who were dependent on Sweden for much of their material. The upshot was the enactment of the Iron Act of 1750, which encouraged the colonial production of bar iron by admitting it duty-free to London (though to London only), but which also forbade the establishment in the colonies of any rolling or slitting mill, plating forge, or steel furnace. The act thus proposed to leave the Americans with no use for the bar iron they were encouraged to produce, save to ship it thousands of miles across the sea for whatever price it might bring, to be returned to them made up into goods that bore in their prices the cost of British manufacture and two sea voyages and the profits of several sales. Undoubtedly a similar legislative fate would have awaited any other competitive industry that might have developed in the colonies.

Any efforts the colonies themselves might make to encourage manufacturers were checked by instructions to the royal governors issued between 1724 and 1732 and remaining in effect throughout the remainder of the colonial period. These forbade the governors' approval of any act laying down duties on goods imported from Britain, whether the produce of Britain or not, and any act discriminating against British subjects in favor of colonials.

British trade policy not only subjected the interests of the colonies to those of the home island but also subjected the interests of the less favored colonies to those of the more favored. The most striking example of this practice was in the regulation of the molasses trade. A cheap supply of molasses was essential to the New England distillers of rum, a principal export of the region and an indispensable element in the slave trade. During the early eighteenth century molasses and sugar from the French West Indies came markedly to undersell the products of the British West Indies. Parliament, rather than raising the price of sugar to Englishmen by excluding French sugar entirely from Britain, chose to raise the price of molasses to Americans by levying a prohibitive duty on the sugarcane products of foreign colonies imported into the British American colonies. Had this Molasses Act of 1733 been effectively enforced, it would have been seriously damaging to the North American economy.

Beyond these specific regulatory acts, two aspects of British commercial policy need to be mentioned. One is the fact that the colonies were not considered to be within the bounds of the British customs barriers. Hence their exports to Britain paid the regular import duties at British ports; many of their imports bore in their prices the burden of a British export duty. These duties had only a slight regulatory effect, and their impact was lessened by the rebate of duties on commodities reexported from Great Britain and by the inclusion of a number of items on the free list to encourage their colonial production. Nevertheless, colonial trade was levied upon for a significant contribution to the British treasury, in considerable part at the expense of colonial residents; and the mere fact that the colonies were beyond the realm for customs purposes was in itself symbolic.

A final element in the British commercial program lay in the area of monetary supply. British mercantile policy was intended to promote a flow of precious metals from the New World to Britain, and in this it succeeded. The export of tobacco, indigo, and similar products from the North American colonies to Great Britain was never sufficient to balance the unending demand for imports from that country. Balances due could be met only by bills of exchange on London acquired from British West Indian planters for lumber, horses, and foodstuffs, and with silver from the Spanish and French Indies paid for the same sort of product. Most of the Spanish dollars, or "pieces of eight," followed the bills of exchange to London, and all of the colonies, lacking precious ores themselves, were chronically short of coinage, both to pay London merchants and to carry on their own business. British mercantile policy in effect forced the colonists into a reliance on paper money, often secured by land, as the medium of exchange. Yet this same policy viewed such issuances fearfully, as threatening the repayment of British debts with cheap money. During most of the colonial period instructions to the royal governors forbade them to approve bills for the emission of paper currency without a clause suspending their operation until they received the royal approval in London. After 1751 an act of Parliament forbade the passage of any such act in any colony without a suspending clause.

On the face of it this extensive pattern of legislation would appear severely damaging to the interests of the colonists, limiting the sources of their supplies, narrowing markets for their products, suppressing their manufactures, and depleting their money supply. In fact, however, the impact was probably relatively slight. For the most part the Navigation Acts and related statutes simply legislated what would have happened in any case. Had there been no such laws, the bulk of the commerce between Britain and America would have moved in British and American ships, most American products would have been sold to British merchants, and most American imports would have come from or through British sources. This indeed continued to be the case long after the Revolution had ended the entire system of restraints. Similarly, so long as abundant land attracted workmen from the mill or forge, holding labor high, there was little likelihood that manufacturing would flourish in the colonies.

When the Navigation Acts or related laws did try to shape the flow of commerce into unnatural patterns, they were largely ignored. Great Britain was simply not powerful enough to enforce an unpopular law across thousands of miles of ocean, among the innumerable harbors and inlets of the Atlantic coasts, and in all the inland hamlets of America. The Molasses Act, for example, which attempted to lay a prohibitive duty on the importation of sugar products from the French and Spanish West Indies, proved entirely impossible to enforce. In Newport and Boston especially, but in other New England ports as well, the smuggling of foreign molasses and sugar was an established and respectable business. So with some aspects of the Iron Act: the industry would have developed only scantily in any case; but where a forge or slitting mill was needed and served a definite economic purpose, it was likely to be built—law or no.

The fact that many of the laws were easy to evade whenever they attempted to force a seriously inconvenient course of action may explain the rarity of colonial complaints against them prior to 1763. It has even been suggested that on balance the colonists may actually have benefited from the British commercial system. The bounties for indigo and naval stores were a boon, especially to the Carolinas. The enumerated articles excluded from the European market were generally given a compensating monopoly of the British market. New England shipbuilding and the colonial merchant marine generally profited from the exclusion of foreign ships from the colonial trade. It is probable that of all the British acts for the regulation of trade, only the prohibition of exports of tobacco to the European continent seriously injured the colonies.

It should be remembered, however, that all of these apparent concessions to the colonies were enacted primarily for British, not colonial, benefit. Both the bounty system and the monopoly of the British market granted certain colonial products had as their purpose not the enrichment of the colonies but the conservation of the empire's currency resources through forbidding imports from foreign sources. A cheap supply of ships for England's growing commerce, not the prosperity of New England shipbuilders, was the aim of the relevant provisions of the Navigation Acts. Indeed if the demand for ships had slacked off to the point of producing truly damaging competition between British and New England shipbuilders, legal restrictions on the latter would almost certainly have followed.

It was the clear intent of British commercial policy to consider the colonies not as overseas portions of a single realm whose economic well-being was cherished equally with that of the home island, but as inferior communities whose economy was to be at all times subservient to the interests of Great Britain. An equal loyalty was demanded in exchange for an unequal protection. Though the legislative acts through which Britain sought to enforce this system did not in practice prior to 1763 weigh heavily on the colonies—or were evaded when they might have—a deep conflict of interests existed, probably unbridgeable by any solution an eighteenth-century British government could have devised. If British strength rose to the level of effective enforcement of the system against a rapidly maturing American economy, and if the system itself remained unchanged, an explosion was inevitable.

The political pattern of the empire took longer to shape and was more variegated than the commercial pattern. Most of the American colonies were founded as business ventures, and their administration as political communities came as a distinct afterthought. For nearly a century after the early settlements, England was too distracted by its own internal governmental problems to give consistent thought to the political relation of these overseas enterprises to the home government. By the end of that time a tradition of substantial self-government only lightly and intermittently controlled from London had been so firmly established that it was never to be overcome. Following the consolidation of the Glorious Revolution of

1688, however, William III moved to regularize colonial administration as well as the commercial organization of the empire. The Board of Trade was set up as a coordinating authority, and uniform instructions were drawn up for the royal governors.

Any plan for uniform administration, however, was frustrated by the prior haphazard granting of charter rights that had set up some colonies as almost entirely self-governing and had conveyed to "proprietors" royal rights over others. James II had in fact sought to end this diverse independence by voiding the charters of the New England colonies and uniting them with newly acquired New York in a Dominion of New England, which should be ruled absolutely by royal authority without even the limitation of a colonial assembly. This action was an egregious example of the contempt for vested legal right that led to his dethronement, and Parliament under William and Mary moved promptly to restore at least most of the earlier charter rights. But it became a consistent policy of the Crown and the Board of Trade, as rapidly as was legally practicable, to bring all of the colonies directly under royal authority in a uniform pattern.

Efforts to do this all at once by act of Parliament failed, for Parliament disliked both to tamper with a charter once granted and to increase royal authority. But the long-pursued policy in time had a considerable success. By the outbreak of the Seven Years' War all the American colonies were directly under Crown rule except Rhode Island and Connecticut, which retained their early charters and elected their own governors, and Pennsylvania, Delaware, and Maryland, in which governmental authority was still exercised by hereditary proprietors (the Penn family in the case of Pennsylvania and Delaware, the Calverts in Maryland).

In every colony some formal document defined its government and the relation of the colony to the royal authority. In the corporate and proprietary colonies this document was the charter. Once issued, a charter bound the Crown as well as the recipients, and could not be rescinded or modified by the King except by court action based on a violation of its terms. In the other colonies the basic document was the governor's commission, issued under the Great Seal and having the force of law. The commission, unlike the charters, terminated with the death of the King or the end of the governor's service, and could be modified by the King at any time. In practice, however, the governors' commissions were relatively unchanging and similar from colony to colony and provided a stable and largely uniform pattern of government.

Whether the colonies were corporations, proprietorships, or royal possessions, it was clear to British legal theorists that they were not political communities enjoying even partially the attributes of sovereignty. In their view the corporate colonies were simply chartered companies, precisely on a footing with the chartered guilds or trading companies or at most the incorporated boroughs of England. The proprietary colonies were considered feudal possessions in which, as in the bishopric of Durham, the proprietor had been granted some subsidiary powers of government as an incident to his property ownership. And the royal colonies were possessions of the Crown, in which any popular assembly authorized by the governor's commission existed only by the King's grace and to perform only such functions as he thought proper within such limitations as he might from time to time impose. As late as the eve of the Revolution Chief Justice Mansfield equated the colonial governments with the business corporations of London, having the power only to make limited bylaws for their internal management.

Though it was held that an act of Parliament did not extend to the colonies settled prior to its passage unless it expressly mentioned them, there was no question in British minds as to the complete freedom of Parliament to legislate for the colonies. And it often did so, not only in such general statutes affecting the whole empire as the Navigation Acts, but also in laws relating to specifically colonial matters such as regulating the colonial manufacture of iron, hats, and woolens, the issuance of currency, and the naturalization of immigrants. Parliament's actions were, however, almost entirely confined to those colonial problems that involved relations with Great Britain. All the foregoing acts, for example, though operating internally within the colonies, had as their object either protecting British manufacturers and creditors or obtaining a uniformity of legislation throughout the empire. Parliament made no effort to legislate on matters that concerned only the colonies.

The tension between Crown and Parliament over the scope of the royal prerogative, though it was not very active during most of this period, was sufficient in fact to strengthen the relative independence of the colonies. The Crown had no wish to see Parliament, by a specific concern with colonial matters, invade an area in which the prerogative still had wide scope.

Parliament, on the other hand, though not wishing to encourage the pretensions of the colonial assemblies to an independent share in the legislative authority, yet did not want to intervene to strengthen the power of the Crown in its contests with them. In consequence the Crown, unaided by Parliament, dealt with colonial assemblies that were the sole legislative authority for a million and a half Americans inhabiting an area larger than Britain and having the vast and novel political problems of a new world to solve.

In this situation it is natural that the colonists had quite a different view of the status of their assemblies. From the earliest days they saw them as colonial versions of the House of Commons, exercising within the respective colonies all the legislative authority and enjoying all the privileges of that venerable body. And indeed to century-and-a-half-old communities with whole new constellations of problems peculiarly their own, located across thousands of miles of sea and wilderness from Westminster, the legal theory of Lord Mansfield and his colleagues seemed meaningless. The great London corporations, to whose governing councils Mansfield likened the colonial assemblies, were voluntary associations of men seeking particular ends. These particular ends could define their legislative scope: the governors of the Bank of England need deal only with financial matters, the council of one of the guilds only with the regulation of its trade. The members of each of those corporations lived, as individuals, within the encompassing matrix of the ordinary British political institutions, which could provide for their general security and well-being. Not so with the colonists. For better or worse, they were linked together for all the purposes of society. Whatever the theory, each of the colonies was in fact a total political community providing for its residents all the services that political communities of the eighteenth century offered. In default of other sources of law, the lawgiving power in each of these communities necessarily exercised many of the legislative aspects of sovereignty.

These conflicting conceptions of the status of the colonial assemblies were expressed in intermittent controversy over nearly a century before the outbreak of the Revolution. The Crown sought to define a very limited role for them as early as 1678, when the governors of Jamaica and Virginia were instructed to confine the assemblies of those colonies to the ratification of legislation presented by the governor. Both assemblies rejected this status. By a stubborn refusal to legislate or vote funds, the Jamaica assembly won its point, and the proposal was subsequently dropped in Virginia as well. This was in the pattern of many similar controversies over the following decades. Many of these concerned the formal status of the assemblies—whether the governor under royal instruction or the assembly itself could determine its meeting-place, the constituencies to send delegates and the number each could send, the privileges of members of the House, the right to choose a speaker, the right to originate money bills, and the like. Others were concerned with the substance of the assemblies' acts, as when the Crown instructed the governor to veto legislation or to suspend it until it could be submitted to the Crown for approval. Many such instructions were issued, seeking to remove or severely limit the power of the colonial assemblies to make laws that lessened the royal revenue, provided for paper currency, affected the King's prerogative or the trade or shipping of Great Britain, laid duties on imports from the home country, affected the valuation of foreign coins, provided for the naturalization of aliens, or granted divorces—among many other things. Other instructions sought to prevent evasions of the royal disallowance of legislation by forbidding the reenactment of laws previously disallowed or the passage of temporary revenue and other acts that would escape royal scrutiny by lapsing before they were examined in London, thus permitting their unreviewed reenactment year after year.

When the will of the colonial assembly was resolute, the colonists were usually able to win in these controversies. Few of the services of the central government of each colony were essential in the daily lives of the individual settlers. Their common needs were largely met by the town governments or the county courts, and they were quite willing to endure a paralysis at the colonial capital. The colonial governor, in contrast, lacking any other source of revenue, was entirely dependent on the assembly for funds with which to administer the colony, maintain the forts and armed services, and pay the salaries of employees, including his own. During the wars that filled so much of the late seventeenth and eighteenth centuries, the Crown was peculiarly dependent on the assemblies for troops, supplies, and funds for carrying on military operations in North America. Each new governor, especially in wartime, was likely to come bearing instructions to solicit from the assemblies a variety of actions to support the imperial program.

For the needed funds and aid, the assemblies exacted a price. Part of this price was a recognition of their own status and privileges. This had been almost universally won by 1763. Whatever the theories still held in the lawcourts of England, in practice the assemblies enjoyed a status and exercised a kind of power substantially identical with those of the House of Commons. They normally fixed the dates and places of their meetings, determined the constituencies from which representatives were elected and the number to be chosen from each, set the qualifications of voters and of representatives, controlled their own procedures, and successfully asserted a complete control not only over the voting of taxes but also over the expenditure of funds from the colonial treasuries. Though there were no "ministers" in the British sense to be made responsible to the assembly, most of the colonial legislatures had won the freedom to name a treasurer who would receive and disburse funds authorized by the legislature and an agent in London who reported directly to the assembly, not to the governor.

The victories of the assemblies by no means, however, related only to their own constitution and powers. They used these powers in turn to win victory after victory on substantive issues, particularly in wartime, when their control over the purse had added and crucial importance. Royal governors in instance after instance were compelled to assent to legislation on such matters as paper currency or the creation of new courts, which the letter or spirit of their instructions should have required them to veto. In the day-to-day conduct of his office as well as in his legislative functions, the governor was compelled to follow courses approved by the assembly unless he was prepared to accept the risk of governmental paralysis that would follow on legislative noncooperation.

By the mid-eighteenth century the colorful assemblies had indeed become, in the language of the day, epitomes of the House of Commons. Their histories had paralleled that of the older body; the power over the purse had been used in the same way to gain the same kind of victory over the royal authority. But with a difference. The Crown and the Commons in their long rivalry had been but different manifestations of the sovereignty of England and later of Great Britain. As power moved gradually from one to the other, that sovereignty gradually altered the form of its expression while remaining itself unchanged. But in the present case the assemblies represented not only the commons as a class but also the American colonies as a whole; the governors represented not merely the royal prerogative, but Britain. A shift of power between them altered not only the expression but the residence of sovereignty. By the victories of the assemblies all British authority was diminished, and not merely that of the Crown.

As in the administration of the shires of Britain, the imperial authority was present in the colonies in the common law and the concept of loyalty to the Crown rather than in the form of troops or bureaucrats. In all the colonies—royal, corporate, and proprietary—there was a handful of royal customs officials in the ports, but not nearly enough for the effective enforcement of the law. Most of the actual customs employees, moreover, were colonial residents with a primary loyalty to their home communities. In the royal and proprietary colonies a governor with a very small entourage of assistants was almost the sole personal representative of the authority of Britain. Other officials—an attorney general, a secretary, sheriffs—might be appointed by the King or the governor, but they were almost always colonists with a primarily colonial loyalty. Judges were appointed by the Crown, but in most colonies for life, and as in Britain they were vigilant to protect the rights of the individual against the Crown. Only the Vice-Admiralty Courts established primarily to deal with customs and maritime matters really represented the prerogative.

In 1750 there were in all North America only a handful of ill-equipped, half-forgotten British troops at New York and Charleston supplemented by the very occasional visit of a British naval vessel. For all the million and a half Americans, scattered over more than a thousand miles of frontier, menaced to the north and west by the French, to the south by the Spanish, and everywhere by the Indians, the British simply maintained no present force, either to defend them or to control them.

The local government within each colony, far closer to the daily lives of the settlers than the provincial officials, was almost wholly under local control. The town governments of New England were inclusive democracies with popularly elected officials; the few city governments, though often oligarchical, represented a local oligarchy; the justices of the peace who made up the governing county courts in the South, whatever the formalities of their designation, in fact made up a self-perpetuating local group. The authority even of governor and assembly ran but feebly to the interior towns and counties, that of King and Parliament hardly at all. Many a colonist might live his life out without seeing a soldier or sailor or civilian officer of the imperial government.

The exercise of the national sovereignty by locally chosen officers worked well within Britain itself, where the same squires and merchants chose the burgesses and knights of the House of Commons and the aldermen and justices of the local governments. There the various levels of government all reflected a common national purpose derived from the relative unity of the group to which they jointly owed their authority. No such harmony of purpose united the local and provincial powers in America with the imperial authorities. The special interests of the Americans were unrepresented in Parliament, not only technically but actually. The British authorities themselves deliberately chose to distinguish the interests of Britain from those of the colonies and to require that when they conflicted the latter be subordinated to the former. The royal authority as represented by the governor and the local power expressed through the assembly were in almost continual tension and potential conflict throughout the colonial period. That this tension did not earlier lead to an open break was due partly to the fact that on most internal matters of greatest concern to the colonists, the imperial authorities were indifferent and glad enough to leave both policy determination and administration in local hands. Partly it was due to the lack of any effective enforcement machinery, which made it easy to evade many imperial regulations by smuggling or carrying on other unlawful enterprises. But when controversy could not be avoided, it was almost always the royal authority that yielded.

It could hardly be otherwise. Every instrument of power—military force, control of funds, the machinery of local administration—was in colonial hands. The loose administration, leaving the real sources of power in autonomous local hands, that was adapted to the harmony of interest within Britain could not master the conflicts of interests with the colonies.

By the mid-eighteenth century such authority as Britain held over the colonies existed not in military or naval power or in bureaucratic machinery, but only in the minds and loyal attitudes of the colonists. It was tolerated very largely because it was little exercised; it could end with a change of minds and attitudes. And such a change was ready to come at the first evidence of a serious effort to make that authority real and vigorous.

3 ★★★★★★★★★

The American Colonies in the Mid-Eighteenth Century

By the eve of the Seven Years' War—or French and Indian Wars—the little settlements along the American coast had grown into important commonwealths. Their population was more than a fourth that of Great Britain itself, and larger than that of many of the independent nations and principalities of Europe. But their people were still widely scattered. Philadelphia, Boston, and New York had twenty thousand to forty thousand residents each and were beginning to compare with the larger provincial towns of England and France; but beyond these three, only Newport and Charleston, with five thousand to ten thousand, had any urban pretensions. Nine Americans out of ten still lived in completely rural surroundings.

Settlement had moved west across the piedmont and southwestward from Pennsylvania until it lapped against the mountains from New Hampshire to South Carolina, and groups of pioneers were moving into the coves and valleys of the Shenandoah and even beyond. Fur trappers and Indian traders fanned out far beyond the settlers to the Great Lakes and the Ohio Valley. Already the land speculators dreamed of empires on Western waters and were beginning their plotting for the grant of princely domains beyond the hills.

Yet the seaboard and piedmont areas were far from filled. Labor was dear and land was cheap at first; agricultural techniques were ignorant and careless; and the crops of the New World, like Indian corn and tobacco, quickly exhausted its soils. As a result, farmers restlessly moved from place to place, and planters constantly sought purchases of new domains, each wanting virgin tracts of rich soil that could be hastily exploited for a few years with limited labor. Already the older

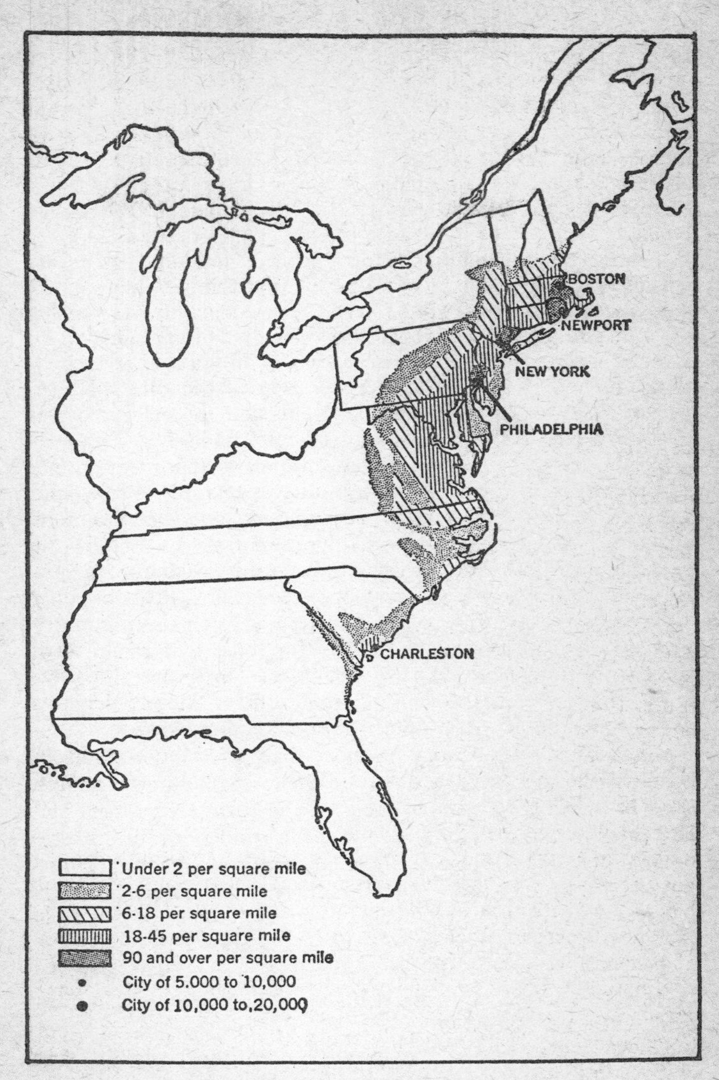

Distribution of Population, 1750

tobacco areas along the Chesapeake and the great rivers of Virginia were beginning to decay from soil exhaustion. Moreover, the miserable condition of the roads made it important for any large farmer or planter to live near navigable water so that he could bring his crops to market. Settlement threaded out along the streams as it moved inland, and the wealthier farmers were likely to control the better lands along their banks.

The expansive methods of farming and the scarcity of transportation scattered the growing population thinly over an enormous area. Travelers of the day were conscious of moving through endless miles of forest, broken only at long intervals by isolated farms. Beyond the seaport cities only a tiny and occasional village of a few dozen houses varied the rural pattern.

The isolation of most Americans outside the larger coastal cities was one of the central facts of colonial life. The few villages and towns were small; over large areas there were none; and even the farms were remote and far apart. Only a few main roads could bear wagon traffic, and men and goods had to move on horseback or on foot along wilderness trails in most of the back country. In the countryside beyond the towns human contact was limited to a degree now hard to imagine. Probably only a minority of Americans were literate, and in the back country the minority was a small one. Even for those who could read, there were in 1750 fewer than two dozen newspapers, appearing weekly or less frequently and distributing "news" that was usually many weeks old before its publication; their subscription lists were tiny, usually no more than a few hundred each. Public gatherings were rare outside the towns, and even church services were infrequent in most of the rural settlements and generally attended by only a few of the residents. Cultural life among the colonists as a whole probably reached its lowest point in the first half of the century. The cultural capital brought from Europe had eroded in the wilderness, and local institutions had not yet attained the size or strength to restore it.

The isolation and cultural poverty of most rural life in the colonies led to a narrow particularism. This was to help frustrate intercolonial cooperation in the French and Indian Wars, goad the British into efforts to enforce an imperial unity, and make impossible the development of a broad vision that could bridge the differences between Great Britain and her colonies. It was to persist as a severe limitation on the ability of the Continental Congress to organize or sustain an effective army during the Revolution or to create thereafter a united government that could deal with broad national problems.

It was also to mean that a very large part of the colonists, perhaps half or more, were to have no part in the coming Revolution or the long and embittering series of events that were to lead up to it. The passivity of the majority of the settlers, in large measure ignorant of the war and the issues preceding it, left the colonies' dispute with Great Britain in the hands of the more informed and politically more active minority along the coast, in the towns, and on the more prosperous farms.

The colonial population was not only growing rapidly and spreading west to the Appalachian barrier; it was markedly changing character. The heavy migration that had flowed from England to the New World throughout the seventeenth century had dwindled to a relative trickle. The immigrants that now landed, for the most part at Philadelphia and New York, were likely to come from Scotland and Ireland and increasingly from Germany. French Huguenots had come to form an important element in several colonies. With the acquisition of New York had come its substantial Dutch population. Largest of all was the influx of African Negroes, which rose swiftly throughout the eighteenth century. In 1700 it was proper to speak of the American colonies as English. The majority of their residents had been born in England, and few indeed were more than one generation away from the English land and loyalties. By the 1750's this was no longer true. Only about two thirds were of English descent, and of these the majority were American-born, and many had generations of American life behind them. To the German settlers who already occupied much of Pennsylvania and were flowing southward east of the Blue Ridge and down the Shenandoah Valley as far as North Carolina, England was a remote and strange land to which no loyalty bound them. Even the Scotch and Irish, for all their English speech, had little love for England. Though an American identity was yet to become distinct among the colonists, their English identity was already fading. It would not much longer in itself provide a bond of empire.

The society created by these colonists along the outer margin of the eighteenth-century world formed into three principal patterns: in the plantation colonies of the South; in the Middle colonies from Delaware to New York; and in New England. In all the colonies the principal economic activity was subsistence farming and household industry—growing the food and hewing the lumber, spinning and weaving the fiber, by which everyday life was sustained. Every colony, however, had an endless need for English and European goods—manufactures, wines, and luxuries and conveniences of every sort. The earliest settlers depended on imports to live; and as the ability to supply daily necessities from local production grew, so too grew the cities and manor houses and the ever more complex life of the colonies demanding more and more from across the sea.

The colonies paid for these imports in various ways, and the means they devised for this purpose did as much as anything else to shape their differing societies. It was easy for the Southerners. Their soils and climate gave forth exotic crops that could not be grown in Europe—rice, indigo, and above all, tobacco—for which the new-rich English and their Continental customers had an almost unfillable demand. The pine forests of the Carolinas yielded as well the tar and pitch on which the Royal Navy and merchant marine were dependent. Many of the provisions of British trade policy described in the preceding chapter favored these colonies, giving their products a monopoly of the British market, allowing their rice to be shipped directly to Southern Europe, and offering a bounty for their indigo and naval stores.

The sort of commercial agriculture that could produce these crops for export, however, demanded large-scale farming, with access to navigable water, capital for equipment and for financing operations pending the sale of the annual crop, large resources of land to bring fresh soils into cultivation as older lands were exhausted by one-crop use, and extensive business and marketing contacts. A labor force large enough to man such establishments could not be brought together voluntarily, as wages meant little to men who could strike out for themselves along the still-free margins of the colonies. This was equally, or even more, true of the island colonies of France, Spain, and Britain in the Caribbean that were growing sugar for the European market. The labor need was met by capturing and enslaving African Negroes and bringing them to the Caribbean and Southern colonies to be kept in perpetual and hereditary forced labor.

For all its successes the plantation system, with its heavy reliance on one-crop exports to Britain, had its own major problems. Among these was dependence on British merchants and factors for the marketing of crops and the purchasing of imported goods. Their too ready willingness to advance credit to the planters as a means of ensuring the handling of their future crops, coupled with the planters' often extravagant desires and their perennial optimism as to the proceeds of each year's crop, brought it about that by the middle to the late eighteenth century most tobacco planters were enmeshed in a growing web of debt from which they saw little chance of escape. Overproduction was the consequence of the desperate effort of planters to enlarge their crops and hence the income available to meet their obligations. With overproduction came glutted markets, collapsing prices, and a further worsening of the planters' situation.

Soil exhaustion too played a role in the growing distress of the tobacco producers. Tens of thousands of acres of once fertile land in the Virginia and Maryland tidewater had been abandoned, and those that remained in cultivation had to meet the competition of the freshly cleared lands of the piedmont and later of the Shenandoah Valley. It is not surprising that in the middle years of the century many planters, like the master of Mount Vernon, shifted their interest from tobacco culture to wheat. Many more looked with increasing urgency to fresh western lands as the answer to their problem, while nearly all sought some break in the trading pattern that seemed to assure an annual worsening of their situation.

Because the ownership of capital played so essential a role in plantation production, class lines were more sharply defined in the Southern than in other colonies. The endless succession of acres that must be mined and exhausted in the production of tobacco, the costly slaves that must be imported to work them, were beyond the means of all but a few colonists. Those who could afford and effectively use these resources grew in wealth and in political power, which they used in turn to open opportunities for wider landholding. Those who could not afford them tended to be pressed back to less fertile and more remote lands, and unable to compete with slave labor in the production of export crops, to be restricted to a narrow subsistence farming.

The plantation society that developed in its classic form in Virginia and in some degree in the other Southern colonies had not yet, however, hardened into a rigid caste system. Even the oldest of the colonial families could hardly count three generations of opulence, and most of their wealth had been wrung from a stubborn environment by its immediate holders. The storied plantation mansions to which so much tradition attaches were then but freshly erected in the ostentation of new riches. The slaves that worked their acres were not the faithful retainers of a later legend, but African tribesmen not often more than a generation from their savage freedom. The acres themselves were likely to be raw red clay newly hacked from the wilderness. Beyond the nearby Blue Ridge the marauding Indians were still a real and bloody threat. No security of long-settled rents sustained the planters as it did the landed gentry of England. Bankruptcy awaited any owner who relaxed his ceaseless energy or failed in his power to manage men and events. The planter elite were imperious and able men who possessed great power, but not inherited privilege.

The pattern of government that developed in the plantation colonies was very like that in eighteenth-century England. In all of the colonies an assembly or house of burgesses had absorbed most of the powers of government. In each it represented the property owners of the colony, being made up principally of larger landowners—including in South Carolina great merchants—elected by the freeholders of the colonies. The class that dominated the colony as burgesses or assemblymen also, as in England, managed its local affairs as members of essentially self-perpetuating county courts and parish vestries. As in England, the power of the larger landholders to maintain this control depended on their ability to keep up a personal contact and community of interest with the enfranchised freeholders generally, that is, with the landholding small farmers. This contact was, however, far more important than in England because there was no system of rotten or disproportionately represented boroughs to overwhelm the county representation and because the definition of "freeholder," though not greatly different from that in England, embraced a much larger proportion of the white population because of the wider distribution of land ownership.

In all the Southern colonies representation in the assembly had marked inequalities. In the Carolinas the older counties, or parishes, had five delegates each, whereas the newer areas had two. There was a reluctance to create new counties as settlement poured into the west, with the result that very large areas along the frontier might be filled with settlers and yet gain no separate representation. The consequence of these devices was that political control in all the Southern colonies remained rather firmly in tidewater hands.

This unequal representation was one basis of a sectional hostility between the older and newer settlements throughout the South. Other bases were social and economic. The western settlers in each colony were likely to be in large part Scotch-Irish or German, the easterners almost entirely English. The westerners were likely to be Presbyterian, Baptist, German Reformed, Lutheran, or Moravian and to take their religion seriously; the easterners were likely to relax in an unzealous Anglicanism. There were few slaves as yet in the piedmont or beyond the Blue Ridge, and the yeomen doing their own labor resented the competition with the slaves of the tidewater. Colonial assemblies were reluctant to establish courts or other governmental services along the frontier, so western settlers might be weary days away from the nearest essential courthouse. Nor were the assemblies willing to levy taxes to build roads or provide protection from Indian raids or meet other needs that the frontiersmen felt keenly. The taxes they did levy drained the western areas of their little silver and gold, or so the settlers thought. At the same time, eastern merchants were ruthless, from the westerners' point of view, in collecting debts and foreclosing mortgages.

These sectional differences were to cut across the later Revolutionary controversy in curious ways. The eastern planters, because they dominated the assemblies throughout the period, led in all the fights that asserted the powers of the colonial legislature against the royal prerogative vested in the governor. When the Revolutionary break later came, it was the same elite that led it in every Southern colony. As the embodiment of the colonial government, they had the largest stake in resisting British efforts to curtail its freedom and ultimately in asserting its complete independence. Yet in the sectional controversies the royal governor and the tidewater group were almost always allied. The Crown distrusted the turbulent west, desired to restrain its troublemaking penetration into Indian country, and was firm for law, order, and hard money. Many westerners, and especially the Scotch-Irish, were later to be fervent Revolutionists, attacking the royal forces not only as agents of foreign control but also as instruments of domestic privilege. But more of the uplanders, and especially the Germans, distrusting both, were indifferent when Crown and planter fought. And in North Carolina, where the sectional controversy broke out into actual fighting in the War of the Regulators in 1771, there was active disaffection to the American cause among many former Regulators when their planter enemies became Revolutionary leaders.

Save for its towering white pines, the climate of New England permitted it to produce little that England needed. No sugar grew there, or exotic spices, or soothing tobacco, no indigo dyes—none of all the strange and sought-for riches of the South. Hard labor on its farms could grow the basic necessities for home consumption, but there were no opportunities for commercial agriculture. Farms stayed small, within the labor of one family, and were largely self-supporting units, as contrasted with the capitalistic enterprises of the plantation area.

The need for British manufactures was great, nevertheless; and with growing wealth, great too became the appetite for imported luxuries and wines. These were paid for in a variety of ways. Shipbuilding became a major New England industry, supplying many British as well as colonial needs. Some hundreds of vessels a year were built in New England shipyards, and perhaps the majority were sailed to England and sold there. Those that remained in colonial hands carried a significant part of the imperial trade, earning shipping charges for their owners. In the same tiny vessels several thousand New England fishermen sailed over the North Atlantic in pursuit of the cod and other fish, and over all the seas in search of whales. Though England supplied her own fish, there was a ready market for the New England catch in Spain and Portugal; the poorer grades were sold as food for the slaves of the sugar islands of the Caribbean.

The ships that trafficked in such numbers with those sugar islands carried not only fish but also lumber, flour and other foodstuffs, whale oil, candles, soap, and other products of New England handicraft. In the aggregate, exports to the Caribbean islands from all the colonies totaled about seven hundred and fifty thousand pounds by 1769, of which five hundred and fifty thousand pounds came from New England and the Middle colonies. Payment from the British Caribbean colonies was largely in bills of exchange on London, with some hard coin. From the French and Spanish islands came silver and molasses.

It is difficult today to comprehend the importance of molasses to the colonial New England economy. It was consumed itself as a cheap form of sweetening, but its principal value was as the raw material for rum. Many dozens of New England distilleries were engaged in this transformation. Rum eased the northern climate and the frigid watches of the fishing fleet. More important, it was a staple of the Indian trade by which furs were obtained for sale to England; and more important yet, it was the basic item of exchange for Negro slaves on the coast of Africa. A considerable part of New England commerce consisted in shipping rum to Africa for slaves and slaves to the West Indies for molasses and money. The molasses went back to New England for more rum, the money to Britain to pay for manufactured imports.

The significant thing about the New England trade, in contrast to that of the South, was that almost all of it was in violation of the precepts of mercantilist doctrine. Except for masts, New England did not supply British needs for raw materials. Their incipient manufactures threatened to compete with those of Britain in the other American colonies. Already their fish and foodstuffs and candles competed with British products in the Caribbean so successfully as to dominate that market. New England shipyards underbid those of the home country and were booming, whereas their British competitors were sometimes idle. Moreover, much—perhaps most—of its trade was with England's commercial enemies: France, Spain, and their colonies. Sending New England fish, like Southern rice, to the mainland rivals for cash was not objected to; but the trade to the Spanish and French West Indies was a constant sore point to the British West Indies. Yet it was indispensable to New England's prosperity. The British West Indies simply were not large enough to absorb the exports from New England and the other mainland colonies or the slaves brought from Africa in New England ships. Production costs of sugar and molasses were higher in the British than in the French and Spanish islands because of a scarcity of fertile and unexhausted land. Prices were hence prohibitively high to New Englanders, whose rum must compete with that distilled in the Caribbean area itself. Nor were the British island colonies large enough to supply the mainland needs for sugar and molasses, even were the price competitive.

There arose, therefore, a sharp conflict between the two groups of colonists themselves. The British West Indian planters would have liked to deny cheap slaves and inexpensive products to their French and Spanish competitors and to retain a monopoly of the supply of sugar and molasses to the mainland. Opposing them were the New England colonies, to whom the trade with the foreign islands had become, quite literally, a matter of economic life or death. The influence of the West Indian planters was the greater in Parliament, in part because a number of them sat as members from English boroughs and in part because it was not easy for many in Britain to understand why the irritating New Englanders should have access to a lucrative trade denied to the English merchants themselves. This influence had led to the passage of the Molasses Act of 1733 already referred to. If its prohibitive duties had been enforced, it would have throttled the traffic completely.

The act was not, however, enforced in practice; and indeed the administrative authorities gave the foreign West Indies trade their tacit approval. They recognized that it drew gold and silver from their commercial rivals and made it possible for the northern colonists to buy an ever-increasing quantity of British manufactured goods. In the minds of the British officials the role of the colonies as a market for the output of the factories of the home country was coming to assume an importance as great as their more traditional role as a supplier of raw materials. The flouting of the Molasses Act was so open and so universal as hardly to constitute smuggling. Nevertheless, the whole New England economy rested on the thin edge of official toleration. More than any other section, it was vulnerable to any determined effort to enforce the whole British trade policy as embodied in the Navigation Acts and related statutes. And as the most dependent on trade, it was also peculiarly vulnerable to new taxes or regulations that would disturb the delicate balance of commerce by which it lived.

In the patterns of society and government, as in the patterns of its economy, New England differed sharply from the South. The absence of forced labor and hence of large plantations meant that land ownership was very widespread among the rural population and was relatively equal. The family farm was the economic type of the region.

This independence and equality were reflected in politics as well. In the New England colonies the requirements for voting in provincial elections were substantially those for voting in elections for members of Parliament from the English shires, which were based primarily on the "forty-shilling freehold." But though this requirement disfranchised the great majority of Englishmen, it is probable that the wider distribution of property gave the vote to the overwhelming majority of heads of families in New England. Young unmarried men, drifters, and laborers without property were unable to vote in provincial elections, but even these could usually vote in town meetings, where the public business most intimately affecting the individual citizens was transacted. The New England town meeting, though indifference often limited attendance, afforded those who chose to participate the freest democracy the world had known. This was in sharp contrast to the Southern colonies or England, and even to the cities of New York and Philadelphia, in which popular participation was sharply restricted.

Religion and education as well reinforced the democratic egalitarianism of New England. The Congregational Church, to which the majority of New Englanders belonged, had no hierarchy and was governed by its lay membership in relatively democratic fashion. Indeed, in an age when theological issues were more important than they are today, participation in the government of the church may have been a more thorough grounding in democracy than sitting in town meeting. Most of the political theories expressed in the writings of early New England related to control of the church rather than the state. The church itself had become more democratic during the eighteenth century, as church membership had been greatly broadened and the oligarchic intensity of the early church had mellowed toward a growing tolerance and secularism.

Education was more widespread in New England than in any other area of the world, and illiteracy was diminishing. Graduates of Harvard and Yale were to be found in almost every town, and entrance to these institutions was opening to promising boys of even quite limited means.

The egalitarianism and the sense of independent political unity of these colonies were further strengthened by their peculiar constitutions. As the discussion of corporate colonies in the preceding chapter pointed out, Rhode Island and Connecticut were substantially self-governing states, bound to the empire only by the oath of allegiance to the Crown taken by their officials, by the deference to the English common law in their courts, and by the British customs and naval officers in their ports. Massachusetts could look back on a history of similar independence, so firmly asserted that its charter had been amended in 1691 to bring it at least partially under royal control. Even after the amendment, the council was still chosen by the assembly rather than appointed by the governor.

Because executive authority was wholly in Connecticut and Rhode Island and partially in Massachusetts responsible to the people rather than the Crown, because the people were homogeneous in nationality and religion, because few who cared about politics were disfranchised from practicing it, and because inequalities were fewer than elsewhere, the New England colonies were less plagued than others by the class and sectional rivalries that marked the period. Even here, however, there were gulfs between the lordly merchant princes of Boston and the mob of Boston laborers, between the settled farmer along the coast and the pioneer on the frontier, that were to affect the Revolution and the years that followed.

The New England colonies were also distinguished by their having a distinct sense of corporate identity. The original settlements at Plymouth, Boston, New Haven, and the many other towns that formed the several colonies were community efforts. In each case the body politic was formed before the settlement and imposed itself upon the land. This was in contrast with most of the South, where government and a sense of community had to grow up later in areas that had first been settled by independent pioneers pursuing their individual purposes. The compactness and religious and racial homogeneity of New England towns helped to reinforce the sense—even a rather fierce sense—of being united as a community. Though the singleminded religious motivation of many of the original settlers had long since been diffused, so that Congregationalism was now a comfortable part of the general pattern of life rather than its demanding whole, there remained an intense sense of high purpose. John Adams was as convinced as John Winthrop had been that the settlers of New England had been called out of a corrupt world to establish a better political order in the new land and that nothing must divert them from that goal.

For these many reasons the New Englanders were ripened for independence. Their political connection with Great Britain was but tenuous. Their economy was more gravely imperiled than that of other areas by the prospect of a vigorous enforcement of British mercantile policy. They had more to gain from any development that would free them to enlarge their area of trade. They were schooled in a religion of dissent, and a long experience of substantial democracy in all the aspects of their lives had made them sensitive to the first steps toward its abridgment. The relative absence of class and sectional conflicts and the sense of common purpose maintained through the generations armed them to move promptly and effectively when any such abridgment threatened.

In contrast to the homogeneity of the New England colonies, the Middle colonies—New York, New Jersey, Pennsylvania, and Delaware—were heterogeneous assemblies of nationalities and religions. The original Dutch settlers of New

York retained vast estates and great power, and families like Van Rensselaer, Van Cortlandt, and Philipse still exercised a ducal power over much of the colony. Almost equally prominent were some Huguenot families like De Lancey and Jay. New York City, though little more than a good-sized town, already showed signs of its later role as the American melting pot, and men from all over Europe mingled on its streets. The upper settlements along the Hudson had been little changed by English control since 1664, and as late as 1750 Dutch was still a common language on the streets of Albany. The Dutch Reformed Church shared with the Anglican the role as the "established" church of the colony; and New York City, in addition to its variety of Protestants, had a healthy sprinkling of Catholics and Jews.

In Pennsylvania the admixture was still more complete. By mid-century half the population was German and one fifth Scotch-Irish, with only one fifth still Quakers. Along with a few Anglicans among the official classes and merchants, there were also Baptists and a variety of other minority sects. As in New York, these various national and religious groups were concentrated in various parts of the colony. Quakers still dominated Philadelphia and the counties immediately adjacent. The Germans had settled next to the west, in the rich agricultural counties that still make up the Pennsylvania Dutch country. The Scotch-Irish Presbyterians lay along the western edge of settlement, breaking the forests and confronting the risks of the still savage Indians along the border.

The checkered history of the two proprietary colonies that had been united to form New Jersey had produced a bunching of religious groups in that colony as well. Quakers predominated along the Delaware, and Scotch-Irish Presbyterians in the northern and northeastern counties. The counties along the western bank of the Delaware that were emerging as the colony of that name retained traces of their original Swedish settlement to add to the variety of the region.

Nor did the distribution of land fall into the homogeneous patterns of New England. The desire of the Penn family, indeed, as proprietors of Pennsylvania, to get the largest possible revenue from the disposal of their lands led to rapid sales on favorable terms to individual farmers. But in New York the Dutch pattern of vast and vaguely bounded patroonships was continued, often corruptly, by many of the British governors, who often issued enormous grants, running even to hundreds of thousands of acres. Intermarriage of the great families and the general practice of primogeniture held the vast domains intact, and the majority of the land of the whole colony was in the hands of little more than a dozen families. The soil and climate did not lend themselves to the plantation agriculture found in the South; and the actual working units were, as in New England, small one-family farms devoted primarily to subsistence agriculture. The difference was that almost all the farmers of New York were tenants, often of uncertain tenure, with little hope of acquiring title to their homesteads, and subject to the political and economic domination of their landlords. Land titles were not only monopolized, but were confused by border disputes with New Hampshire and by failure to define precisely the boundaries of a number of the princely grants.

Confusion and bitterness affected New Jersey land tenure as well. The two groups of proprietors of East Jersey and West Jersey had retained their ownership of the land of the colony when they surrendered its government to the Crown in 1702. Subsequent grants from their heirs and assigns were often confused and irregularly made, and involved lands already settled by squatters. The rights of the proprietors, now divorced from any governmental power or responsibility, were held in little regard. For several years before and after 1750 continual riots frustrated the efforts of the proprietors to assert them. A bit later in New York the embittered claims of the tenants were to lead to violence that approached open warfare.

Though Pennsylvania largely escaped controversy over land tenure, there were severe sectional disputes between the aggressive Scotch-Irish along the frontier, who bore the dangers of Indian attack, and the pacifist Quakers in the safe and settled eastern counties, who from principle as well as thrift were unwilling to support border warfare against the Indians.

Oligarchies ruled both New York and Pennsylvania. In New York the ruling class was made up of the great landlords and merchants, who were split, largely on personal grounds, into two factions. The suffrage itself was reasonably widely distributed, being available not only to all freeholders but also to all tenants with lifetime leases. But elections were almost entirely managed by the landlords, under whose eyes the public voting took place. Almost the only consideration of the needs of the artisan and small farmer came from the rivalry of the aristocratic factions who from time to time needed to court the favor of the poorer voters.

In Pennsylvania the descendants of the original Quaker

settlers maintained control of the colony until the French and Indian Wars, even though their proportion of the population had fallen to less than one fourth. In part this control was the result of their greater wealth, education, and organization; but primarily it was due to the heavy overrepresentation in the legislature of the Eastern Quaker counties, the underrepresentation of the Scotch-Irish frontier settlements, and the political apathy of the majority of Germans. When the Quakers were compelled to abdicate their power over the colony so that it could be governed by men whose principles would allow a more vigorous prosecution of the war against the French and Indians along the frontier, it was to the small group of Anglicans rather than to the Germans or the Scotch-Irish that their power passed.

Indeed, in none of the Middle colonies was there the corporate sense of a unified self-governing body that so stamped New England and that so shaped the convictions of the ruling classes in the South. The internal divisions in these colonies tended to make the various factions look for royal aid in their contentions with each other rather than to unite in opposition to British power. When it is considered also that the Middle colonies were less affected than others by British commercial regulations and were more dependent on British protection from French and Indian attack, it is not surprising that in the coming struggle the loyalists were to be stronger here than in any other region.

But if diversity enfeebled the actions, it freed the minds of the Middle colonists. No one religious or national group could assert its dominance, and the intellectual life of Philadelphia and New York was the most varied and brilliant in the colonies. A Benjamin Franklin and an Alexander Hamilton were to bring to the political thought of the new republic bodies of ideas far more powerful and original (if for that very reason perhaps less influential) than the more patterned thought of the New England and Southern leaders.

For all their diverse economic and social patterns, the American colonies shared alike in one vast blessing. Most of the cumulation of inherited privilege that burdened the labors and chained the progress of Europeans had not survived the Atlantic crossing. On the Continent hundreds of thousands of lives and suffering so bitter its traces still remain were to be spent in the following century to win freedom from constraints the colonists had simply left behind them.

Even in Britain itself, partly liberated by its own seventeenth-century revolutions, there lay ahead decades of political struggle, still manifested as late as the Labor Party victory of 1945, to be rid of privileges that had never been established in the colonies. The American Revolution was very different from the French Revolution, the European revolutions of 1848, and the Russian Revolution because its targets could be very different.

Royalty and nobility were unknown in the colonies. Even in the royal commonwealths, in both power and expense, the governor was but a pale reflection of his master at home. His powers were negative and restricted and were diminishing throughout the eighteenth century. He was supported in most of the colonies in a relatively niggardly fashion. No regiments of guards protected him; little of the panoply of royalty surrounded him. The governorship was a modest burden indeed on the public purse. Nor were there gubernatorial estates like the vast royal domains in Britain or on the Continent on which the labor of peasants was made to produce a surplus for royal enrichment.

Scattered efforts were made to introduce orders of nobility into the colonies. The Carolinas were to have their landgraves and caciques, according to the visionary Fundamental Constitutions drawn by John Locke. Manors whose lords were to have feudal powers had a brief and flickering existence in Maryland. The nearest to a real order of nobility were the patroonships inherited from the Dutch in New York. Most of the population of Europe submitted to the local government of a hereditary nobility and paid over to them in dues and rents a large and painfully won share of all the product of their labor. This greatest single incubus inherited from the Middle Ages was simply left behind by the voyaging colonists.

Also absent from the New World was the clerical hierarchy of the Old. In all the British colonies there was no bishop of a widely organized church. Most of the New Englanders and many of the colonists elsewhere belonged to denominations, like the Congregational, Quaker, Baptist, or Reformed, that were democratically governed by lay members. Even such relatively hierarchical churches as the Anglican passed essentially under lay control, as the rectors came to be ruled by the resident vestry rather than the far-distant Bishop of London. Though most of the colonies levied taxes for the support of an established church or churches, the burden was light

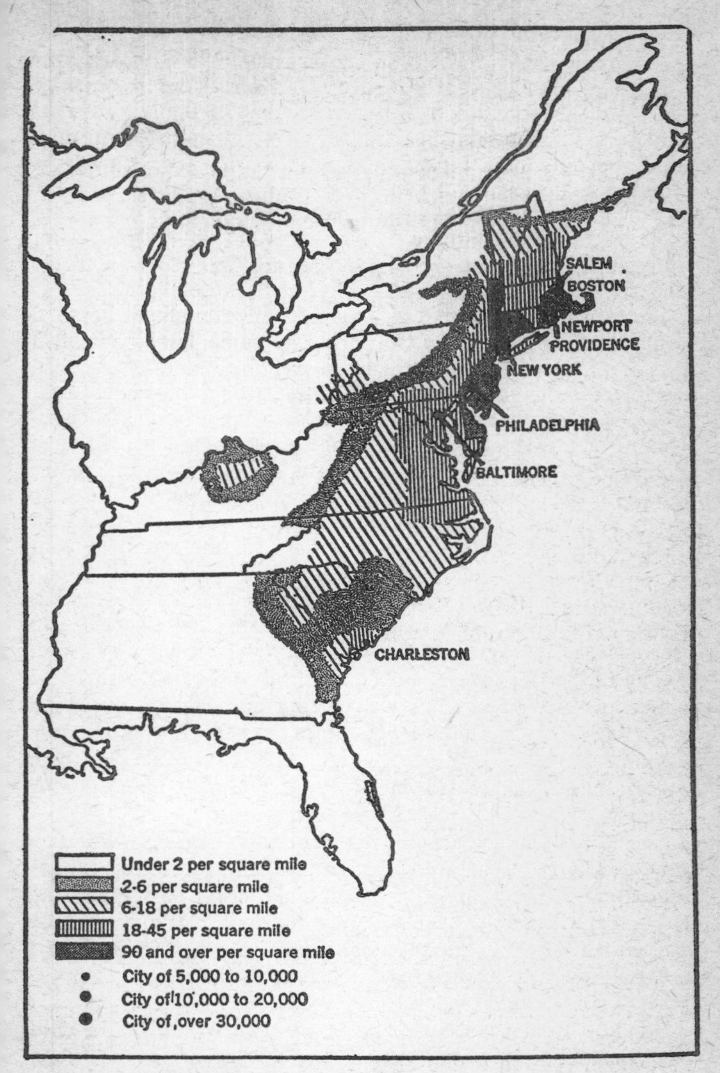

DISTRIBUTION OF POPULATION, 1790

and the expense of the sparse ecclesiastical establishment was tiny. In a number of the colonies dissenters could arrange that their church taxes went to the support of their own faiths rather than the established church. No monasteries or nunneries occupied the lands or consumed the produce of the colonies; no peasant-worked estates lay in mortmain for the support of the church. The anticlerical and hence often antireligious bitterness of the French Revolution and the later revolutions in Europe and Latin America was almost entirely absent from the American Revolution because the church in America had not become an important instrument of political control or economic exploitation. The same laity controlled the church that controlled the town meeting, the county court, and the colonial economy; it had no need to rebel against itself.

Nor was there a standing army or navy to support, constituting a burden on the colonial economy and providing a privileged officer caste, as in Britain and to an even greater degree on the Continent. The British navy policed the Atlantic waters. In times of war or Indian foray the colonies relied on a local militia officered by men drawn for the moment from civil life.

In other professions as well, there was little or nothing in the way of a fixed caste. There were few doctors and perhaps even fewer lawyers, and entry into either profession was easily had at the expense of a brief and often haphazard apprenticeship. Most of the doctoring and lawing was done by out-and-out amateurs—plantation owners with *The Poor Planter's Physician* in their hands giving physic to their slaves, farmers schooled in *A Perfect Guide for Studious Young Lawyers* sitting as justices of the peace.

Nor was there any rigidity in economic organization. The only chartered companies of any significance were those formed near the end of the colonial period to exploit the Trans-Appalachian lands, and few of their plans ever came to fruition. Guilds failed to make the Atlantic crossing, and one man was as free as another to set up as barber, silversmith, baker, or candlestick maker.

Wealthy men there were aplenty—Southern planters with their thousands of acres and dozens or hundreds of slaves, Quaker merchants in their Philadelphia countinghouses, Boston capitalists whose ships traversed the remotest seas. And their power extended far beyond their wealth, to hold sway in legislatures, influence courts, affect land policy, and name

EASTERN NORTH AMERICA

rectors. But they did not make up a closed circle of burdensome and impenetrable privilege against which the excluded could only rebel in rage. They made up a new-rich and constantly changing class. There was room in it for the sons of farmers, like John Adams, and sons of relatively small planters, like Washington and Jefferson, and even for the sons of the poor, like Franklin and Hamilton. For white men the American colonies of the mid-eighteenth century were as open a society as was then known.

In one area, and among one class of men, however, the colonies erected their own monstrous structure of privilege. That was by the enslaving of African Negroes. In a sense slavery was a response to the freedom of the colonies. In the days before the tractor and other forms of farm machinery, large-scale commercial agriculture was profitable only if the labor was wrung from workers who got little more than the food to keep them alive. This was true of the slaves on the Roman latifundia, the serfs of the medieval baronies, and the landless peasants of eighteenth-century Europe. Lacking the power to compel labor from men with no choice but to work for their masters or starve, the New World planters devised a legal bondage in place of the bondage of economic pressure. The slave market was a counterpoise to the free land on the frontier.

By 1750 there were more than two hundred and twenty-five thousand slaves, existing in every colony but concentrated overwhelmingly in the South. Only here and there, among Quakers and others with an odd view of life, was the equity of this institution questioned. Even in the Revolutionary age to come, when into the very ears of the Founding Fathers slavery screamed its denial of the truths they saw as self-evident, there were few who noticed.

The situation of the colonies was at no time static. Throughout the whole colonial period population was rapidly growing, settlement was pushing west, new industries were being founded. New social, economic, and political forms were being created every year to meet the unprecedented requirements of the kind of society growing up on the wilderness frontier. Every aspect of colonial life we have described should be thought of not as a fixed institution, but as an evolving pattern in a process of constant change.

In the last three decades of the colonial period this steady growth rose to a surge. The population of the colonies more than doubled between 1750 and 1775, more than matching in one short quarter century the growth of the preceding century and a half. The lapping of settlers against the mountain barriers and their infiltration through the passes brought them into direct and open conflict with the Indian and French occupants of the Trans-Appalachian region. Economic activity grew at an even swifter pace. Exports to England alone rose from £815,000 to £1,920,000, and as much again went to Europe and the West Indies. The colonies were beginning to be reckoned a power in the world markets.

The colonies were not only growing but also maturing. Such institutions as Harvard were no longer little wilderness academies, but major seats of learning. New colleges were founded between 1745 and 1775 in New Hampshire (Dartmouth), New York (now Columbia), New Jersey (now Princeton and Rutgers), and Rhode Island (now Brown). Such institutions as the American Philosophical Society in Philadelphia were being formed. Scientists were beginning to explore the plants and animals of the New World and to study astronomy. Franklin's contributions to physics were winning international attention.

The urban life of the largest cities was assuming a modern shape. Wealth expressed itself in large and well-capitalized businesses, elegant mansions, and sophisticated and luxurious patterns of living.

It has often been pointed out that the colonies were outgrowing their dependent relation to Great Britain. In a sense this is true. But it is more revealing to consider rather that they were outgrowing the isolation from Britain, the rest of the world, and each other in which they had independently developed over the course of the colonial period. In 1750 there was little that truly bound them to the British empire: the diminishing authority of a lone governor—and not even that in all colonies—more often flouted than respected; acts of navigation and trade that were freely violated whenever they seriously damaged the colonies' interests; a fading memory of a homeland and a dimming loyalty to a distant Crown. Even less bound them in those years to the rest of Europe: common intellectual interest on the part of a very few scholars and advanced thinkers, an illegal trade with the Caribbean, the sale of fish and rice to the Mediterranean powers. Even with each other the bonds were then almost nonexistent: a trickle of trade, infrequent mails, a small flow of migration and marriage back and forth. Sheltered between the sea and the wilderness, guarded by forests and mountains to the west and the British navy to the east, each separate colony had worked out its childhood in large degree disengaged from the rest of society.

That period was ending. The American colonies were growing into an economic power whose commerce was enmeshed with the whole Western economy. Overflowing their frontiers by ocean trade to the east and by fur traffic and settlement to the west, they came into military and commercial conflict with France and Spain and with the Western Indians. In order to sustain themselves economically, to maintain military and naval power adequate for their protection, and to achieve a political organization of such scope and power as to marshal that economic, military, and naval strength, the colonists had now reached a point at which they must outgrow their provincial isolation and enter integrally into a larger grouping. It was rather that they had become too big to remain aloof from the emerging British imperial organization than that they had become too big to remain within it.

The British realized that a new order must be devised, but their leaders lacked the wisdom and the political genius to create an imperial organization of equal commonwealths. The few Americans who were reaching toward such a vision spoke to closed minds on both sides of the Atlantic. The British efforts to enforce a closer but an unequal organization were resisted with arms, and successfully; but in resisting, the colonists themselves found the necessity of creating a larger organization. Eventually, after some years, they devised a means of uniting equal commonwealths in a common government, and the problem of imperial organization that had so long vexed the little settlements along the edge of the great and remote continent was at last solved. In resisting the British solution and in creating their own, the colonists gave shape to a body of ideas that in the long run proved to be more important than the events that gave them being.

In its simplest terms, this is the story of the Revolution that was to come. The long march of events that led through 1776 to 1789 and the establishment of government under the Constitution began with an event that was itself a great and earth-spanning cataclysm—the French and Indian Wars or Seven Years' War, which was really the first world war. Let us turn now to that vast and half-forgotten conflict and see how it created an insoluble situation that led, one unforeseen but inevitable step after another, to the Declaration of Independence, to Yorktown, and to the Constitution of the United States of America.

4 ★★★★★★★★★

The End of Isolation

The isolated independence of the American colonists became unworkable when the first streams of trappers and pioneers began to pour through the Appalachian passes into the unbroken forests of the West. The Indians beyond the mountains, threatened by the invasion of their hunting lands, and even more by the disturbance of their control over the fur trade with the tribes farther west, raised musket and tomahawk against the frontier settlers. They were spurred to attack and were aided with weapons and men by their trading allies the French. Though the charters drawn long ago in England by men who never knew the empty vastness of America spoke easily of colonial boundaries following parallels of latitude "from sea to sea," the words were meaningless. The hundreds of unending miles of forest lying beyond the blue mystery of the Alleghenies and stretching unbroken over an area greater than all Britain were too wild and vast for the Boston town meeting or the drawing rooms of Williamsburg. The Indians defrauded by the trader of one colony might seek their bloody revenge on the settlers of another. The French saw not Virginians or Pennsylvanians but only the English pressuring against their trading areas. The savage forces of the wilderness were fluid, touching bloodily now here and now there along the unmarked frontier. They could be dealt with only by a coordinated effort beyond the power of any single colony.

For different reasons a like situation existed across the world in India, where the death throes of the Mogul empire churned tens of thousands of armed men back and forth across India, tearing apart all the tidy trading patterns of the East India Company and laying open a vast continent that must be mastered. All across the world an empire was demanding to be born, an empire unplanned for and unwanted in the countinghouses of London, Calcutta, and Philadelphia alike.

As the tide of traders and settlers flowed west from Pennsylvania and northwest from Virginia, the French moved to protect their fur trade by a chain of fortified posts stretching from Lake Erie toward the strategic forks of the Ohio. The Virginians, ambitious claimants of an empire of forest by reason of their original charter's vague reference to lands lying west and northwest to the far sea, and even more by reason of the relentless land hunger of their planters, first took up the imperial challenge. In 1753 Governor Dinwiddie sent a young surveyor, woodsman, and militia officer named George Washington to warn off the encroaching French and lay hold upon the wilderness for Virginia. Words were not enough, and Washington had to be back the following year with a small company to drive the French from the future site of Pittsburgh, which they had meanwhile occupied. He failed, was defeated, and surrendered his little army; and Virginia's inability to deal alone with the imperial problem of the West was made clear.

Meanwhile the Iroquois, middlemen for the English in the Ohio Valley fur trade and their allies against the French and the Hurons, were frightened by the French cordon cutting them off from their fur sources and angered by the English movement west to bypass them and deal directly with the tribes of the Ohio country. They threatened to turn against the English and ally themselves with the French. If this had happened, the whole frontier down to the Carolinas would have been open to invasion.

The crisis demanded an imperial organization, and the British authorities besought the colonies to make a first step by conferring on a common treaty with the Iroquois. In June, 1754, delegates from New Hampshire, Massachusetts, Rhode Island, Connecticut, New York, Pennsylvania, and Maryland met in Albany for the purpose. They were led by Benjamin Franklin, whose vision of the British empire was to be matched only by Pitt's and who as long as three years before had sketched out a plan of organization for the colonies. Under his guidance the delegates went far beyond their instructions and drew up a plan of union for the colonies to meet the new problems now confronting them that so far transcended their individual capacities. This was the first of a series of efforts extending over thirty-five years to achieve an organization of the American commonwealths capable of meeting their common needs, efforts that found success only in 1789.

Franklin's plan provided for a President General, appointed and supported by the Crown, to be the chief executive officer and military commander of the North American colonies. A Grand Council, whose members were to be elected by the lower houses of the colonial legislatures in proportion to the tax revenues derived from each colony, would serve as a continental legislative body. It would have authority over Indian affairs and defense, could raise and sustain military and naval forces, and for these purposes would have an unrestricted power to levy taxes. Control over the Western lands would be given to the new government, with the assumption that there would be turned over to it not only lands outside any colony's boundaries but also the unsettled wilderness vaguely claimed by the older colonies that were of "inconvenient" size.

Had this plan been approved, the whole subsequent course of American history would have been different. A colonial organization competent to deal with the imperial problems of the West would have been created. The military forces of the New World could have been financed without the parliamentary exaction of taxes from the unrepresented colonies, and the series of issues that forced secession might have been avoided. It is probable that as time passed other intercolonial matters, in addition to Western lands, Indian affairs, and defense, would have passed into the hands of the Grand Council. At the same time, the Grand Council would surely have used its control of the purse against the President General in the way that the House of Commons had used it against the King and the colonial assemblies against the royal governors. The office of the President General would no doubt have dwindled in time to a formality, a sort of governor-generalship, and the British authority expressed through the office would have atrophied. In time the Grand Council would almost certainly have emerged as the sovereign parliament of an independent nation within a loose aggregation like the present British Commonwealth.

But it was not to be. The colonial assemblies, jealous of their separate near-sovereignties, were flatly unwilling to cede their authority to any distant government. The power to tax, even by a council in which they were represented, was feared in Philadelphia as it was in Westminister; and it was not to be granted to any central government—not the Parliament or the Continental Congress or the Congress of the Confederation—until the ratification of the Constitution. And even then it was to be granted in much more restricted terms. Moreover, the vital interests of many wealthy and enterprising colonists were tied up in the claims of their respective colonies to Western lands. Many a beautifully contrived speculative scheme would be disrupted if control passed to a less easily managed central government. None of the colonial assemblies ever ratified the proposals of the Albany Congress.

The British government in turn had contemplated no such ambitious proposals when it suggested the Albany Congress; indeed it feared any self-created colonial union, which might challenge British power in the New World as readily as French. Moreover, the more Whiggish members of Commons might well see in the Albany proposals a scheme that would give the Crown an income independent of Parliament, enable it to maintain a standing army and navy without parliamentary controls, and indeed rule the whole western empire without consulting Parliament. In terms of the British Constitution as it was emerging in the long century of Whig rule, the Albany Plan of Union would have been wholly unconstitutional.

The British government therefore joined the colonial assemblies in rejecting the plan, but urged an overall military commander and an overall civilian official to deal with Indian affairs, thus undertaking to unite colonial efforts in meeting the most immediate and critical problems of the West without placing those imperial officers under colonial control.

Such a commander was appointed in the person of General Edward Braddock, and with him came a substantial body of British regular troops. The forces of the entire empire were being drawn, willy-nilly, into meeting the situation along the frontier. Braddock's fatal defeat by a French and Indian ambush in the summer of 1755 has become one of the schoolboy legends of American history. With it came war and a series of stunning defeats for the British, relieved only by victories won that summer by the colonials themselves at Lake George and along the Bay of Fundy. The French were successful all along the frontiers, holding Louisburg and Fort Duquesne at the opposite ends of the crescent-shaped area of conflict and driving the British back along Lake Ontario and in the Lake Champlain-Lake George region.

Meanwhile in India the increasing chaos as the Mogul empire stumbled toward collapse compelled both the British and French trading companies to grasp for political power, directly or indirectly, and drew them into open conflict. A few hundreds of Europeans, audaciously maneuvering the hordes of troops of Indian princes, played a desperate game with each other for the mastery of the subcontinent. Ultimately the handful of British led by the genius of Clive were to win, but in the early years of the war the future of empire hung as uncertainly in India as in America.

On the Continent of Europe the contest for dominance that began on the outer margins of European power was now joined at its center. Britain's old continental ally Austria joined forces with France; and Frederick the Great, formidable ruler of little Prussia, became the ally of the England he had so often fought. With the completion of this diplomatic revolution, war broke out on the Continent itself in 1756, two years after the first skirmishes along the Ohio. We are concerned with this Continental Seven Years' War only as it affected the imperial struggle. It was the greatest war in sheer size of forces that had ever been fought. Prussia was almost alone on the Continent, and Frederick was able to sustain himself only with massive British subsidies. The vast sums paid out by Britain helped lead to its post-war financial crisis, but they enabled the ministry to limit narrowly its military commitment on the Continent and to concentrate its troops and ships in the wider imperial struggle. Frederick meanwhile was able to force France to maintain her principal armies on the Continent. On such battlefields as Minden, as well as at Quebec and Plassey, was the British empire won.

On every front the war went badly for the British until William Pitt was called to the cabinet as Secretary of State at the end of 1756. Pitt was a man of truly imperial vision, a Winston Churchill of the eighteenth century, scornful of the narrow calculation and commercial morality of his predecessors. He was determined that Great Britain, which had defeated Spain in the sixteenth century and Holland in the seventeenth, should now in the eighteenth finally triumph over France and end the long series of imperial wars with that power. At whatever cost, Pitt fixed as his goal a British empire stretching from the Mississippi to the eastern coast of India.

His energy and his unconstrained use of Britain's resources made themselves felt. The subsidies to Frederick were greatly enlarged and backed up with troops when they were indispensable. The navy was invigorated, the army was enlarged, and thousands of British regulars were dispatched to America. The participation of the colonies was encouraged by promises to refund their expenditures in the war effort. Brilliant and aggressive young commanders were brought to the fore. The turn of the tide was dramatic. Frederick the Great, in astounding victories at Rossbach and Leuthen, beat back the overwhelmingly larger forces of France and Austria and gained a year of respite. When those two enemies recovered and again seemed about to overwhelm his much smaller forces, British aid and the skill of the Duke of Brunswick again threw back the French. Pitt's support enabled Prussia alone to occupy the armies of all the hostile European powers until Russia's shift from the Austrian to the Prussian side in 1762, following the accession of Czar Peter III, ended Austria's hope of victory.

During those same years there was an almost incredibly brilliant series of victories in India, culminating in the capture of Pondicherry in 1761. This conquest owed more to the genius of Robert Clive than to any direct aid from home, but it left Britain the dominant political as well as commercial force in the whole of the east of India.

Pitt's own genius was shown most clearly in the war at sea, which ended in total British victory, and in the fighting in North America. In America he arranged for attacks all along the frontier. In 1758 the British took Louisburg in the east and Fort Duquesne in the west, and began to press down Lake Champlain and up the St. Lawrence. In 1759 Ticonderoga and Quebec were captured, opening up both passages to the center of French power at Montreal, which easily fell in 1760.

These victories were made possible by James Wolfe's brilliant generalship, by tens of thousands of British regulars shipped to the New World, and by British naval victories that cut the supply lines between France and her forces in Canada. When the French, desperate after their defeats in 1759, called their Spanish allies to their assistance, the only consequence was that Britain added Havana and the Philippines to its list of conquests.

Colonial contributions to the victory, in both men and money, were not inconsiderable; but they were given grudgingly and undependably and hedged with conditions. Colonial troops were often forbidden to serve outside their own colonies, or for other than specified purposes, or under officers not of their own province. They stood upon the day and hour of their terms of enlistment, regardless of the state of the campaign in which they might be engaged. Colonial financial contributions were reluctantly made, and the price of obtaining them was often a major concession by the royal governor to the assembly's claim of power. In almost every colony Britain's desperate need was used as a means of driving hard political bargains and exacting further recognition of the rights and privileges of the colonists.

Even more enraging to the British was the active continuation by the colonists of their trade with the French and Spanish West Indies. Though forbidden as trade with the enemy, this commerce was carried on by a variety of subterfuges and on a massive scale. To have foregone it would have crippled the economy of the Northern colonies, but its continuation was a boon to the French and Spanish West Indies, which were cut off from their homelands by the British navy.

In spite of the effective participation of colonial troops in many campaigns and the indispensable, if niggardly, provision of supplies, to many Britons the conduct of the colonists seemed not merely selfish but little short of treasonable. A bitter determination to discipline them and set in order the slack colonial administration was one of the consequences.

When the war was concluded in 1763, the British found themselves masters of such an empire as had never before existed in the history of the world. Even after returning Martinique and Guadeloupe to the French and the Philippines to the Spanish, and swapping Cuba for Florida, they possessed all Canada, what is now the United States east of the Mississippi, many islands of the Caribbean, British Honduras, strategic trading posts along the coast of Africa, and political as well as commercial control of eastern India. Not since Rome had a nation so dominated the world; it would have demanded all the Romans' imperial skill to organize such a realm. The political institutions of Britain were fiercely insular; developed intensively to meet the specific needs of that moated realm, they were not well adapted to the organization of a diverse and complex empire. A unitary sovereignty of freemen was all their political tradition comprehended. Either all the rest of the empire would be subordinate to that unitary sovereignty or else the concept would spawn other unitary and independent sovereignties. A concept of distributed and mutually limiting sovereignties, linked in a system in which absolute power had no focus, was beyond the capacity of British political thought of the eighteenth century.

Nevertheless, Britons realized they confronted a whole new range of problems. A government must be provided for the empty reaches of Canada and for its seventy thousand French-speaking, Catholic inhabitants lacking the English tradition of self-government. The Floridas must also be organized. The Trans-Appalachian West, over which the whole war had started, had been safely won from the French, but none of its other problems had been solved. Some orderly control of settlement, the fur trade, and Indian relations must be worked out. The last of these was particularly urgent. British victory had alarmed rather than quieted the Indians, who foresaw correctly that it meant the final opening of their lands to the white horde; and even as the war with France ended, they were preparing a last desperate effort to drive the English back beyond the mountains.

Though most Englishmen still thought of India as a commercial problem of the East India Company, the new political problems there too were demanding, and the incapacity of a trading company to deal with them was to lead to the East India Company's early collapse. That crisis in turn was to set up the series of events that led directly to the outbreak of the Revolution.

Then there were the older colonies to deal with. After every previous colonial war, with its similar experience of laggard American cooperation, there had been a British resolution to assert a more effective control over the transatlantic commonwealths. In the subsequent eras of peace all these efforts had dwindled to nothing in the face of colonial resistance and fading British interest. But now the British meant it. They were compelled to mean it.

Pitt had spent lavishly for his victories, and England was left at war's end with a debt of nearly one hundred and forty million pounds. Interest charges alone on this sum were nearly five million pounds. Other annual expenditures were running at about eight million pounds. On the other hand, revenues were running at only about seven million pounds a year. The British tax system was inefficient and inelastic. New excise taxes were bitterly resisted, and almost the only convenient source of additional revenue was increases in the land tax. This had already been raised from two shillings in the pound to four. The valuation of land for tax purposes was artificially low so that such a rate did not really mean an annual tax of twenty percent of the actual value of all real estate. Even so, the tax had already been pushed to the uttermost limit that the country landowners, who dominated Parliament, would tolerate even in wartime.

The vast gap between income and expenditures was being met by a variety of unsound and temporary expedients, including the sale of annuities to wealthy men who would pay for them in immediate cash. But these could not be long continued. Major economies and major increases in revenue were imperatively necessary.

Yet these demands ran head on into the demands for imperial planning. The enlarged empire could ultimately bring great riches, but immediately it could only bring expense. And the more effectively administered the new possessions, the more costly they would be. All the ambitious plans for the protection and orderly development of the American West, for example, called for thousands of British troops. An end to the unregulated independence of the colonies would require not only troops but also a corps of administrators and civil servants receiving their salaries directly from Britain. If the Crown were ever to take over from the East India Company its new political responsibilities in India, another heavy burden would be added to the royal treasury. Major increases in revenue from sources other than the British taxpayer were hence an essential component in all planning for the future of the empire.

Yet the experience of more than a century had shown that every increase in revenue from the colonies had been won only at the price of further concessions to colonial autonomy. The consequence of attempting simultaneously to curb colonial independence and to exact a colonial revenue was quite predictable. But the inexorable pressure of the new imperial problems would no longer admit the procrastination and lethargy toward the colonies of such earlier prime ministers as Walpole, Pelham, and Newcastle, whose inertia had so long preserved the empire by obscuring its major internal conflicts.

The imagination and imperial vision of a younger and healthier Pitt might have seen a way out of this dilemma. Unhappily, the awesome problems of the new empire had to be faced by a shifting series of governments, none firmly grounded in popular support and all limited by a narrow and insular view. In 1760, at the height of Pitt's triumphs but before final victory, George II had died. He was succeeded by his grandson, the twenty-two-year-old George III. The personality of the new King was to have a fateful effect on British history during his sixty-year reign. His relations with his father, who had died before acceding to the throne, and with his aged grandfather were bitter. He had been viewed with hostility and rejected from public affairs by George II, jealous of every attention to his heir that might suggest his own death. He was neurotically dependent on his mother and on Lord Bute, the Scottish nobleman who was his tutor and allegedly his mother's lover. He was determined to oppose at every point the pattern of Hanoverian rule established by the two earlier Georges—their personal immorality, their indifference to British politics, and their preoccupation with Hanover, their ancestral domain in Germany. It was his intention not merely to reign but to rule—to rule under the Constitution, according to law, and with the concurrence of Parliament, but to rule.

Pitt's imperious grasp on affairs did not long survive the change of monarchs. George III wanted an early peace to increase his popularity and leave his hands free to work out reforms at home. As if to prove that he had reversed the German orientation of his forebears, he was indifferent to the outcome of the war on the Continent and to the fate of his ally Frederick. Pitt was determined to fight on to a victory so complete that France would never again be able to challenge Britain's imperial dominance. Beyond this clash of purpose, George III resented Pitt and his co-minister Newcastle as remnants of his grandfather's system of government, and he was vexed in his juvenile pride by Pitt's lofty and dominant manner. George wanted his own men in power; he insisted on Lord Bute's admission first to the cabinet and then, in 1762, to the Prime Ministry. Pitt was excluded from the solution of the imperial problems presented by victory in 1763 as Churchill was from the solution of imperial problems left in 1945.

Bute negotiated the Peace of 1763, which, while generally welcomed, offended Pitt and the imperialists by leaving France footholds in the Caribbean and in the northern fisheries. His clumsy attempts to increase the revenue by an excise tax on cider offended countrymen all across England. His Scottish origin, his reputed connection with the Queen Mother, and his role as a symbol of private friendship elevated to public power all tended to make him increasingly odious to Englishmen. He himself disliked the responsibility of publicly holding power. He devoted himself therefore to attempting to organize for the King a ministry more dependent on the Crown than on any faction in the Parliament, which would endeavor to carry out the King's wishes and in which Bute himself could have influence without office.

Such a ministry was not difficult to assemble. There were no parties in the modern sense of the word. The Whigs, who comprised the great majority of the House of Commons, had been held together since 1688 as a loose confederation of factions united rather for the distribution of patronage than for the exercise of power. When the control of patronage was removed from the hands of the Duke of Newcastle and taken over by the King, the cement that held the party together was dissolved, and the party itself disintegrated into a group of personal factions, most of which were eager for a share of power on the King's terms.

George Grenville emerged as the King's choice. A brother-in-law of Pitt, he was in many ways his opposite—earnest, humorless, thorough, pedantic, devoted to the Constitution, thrifty to the point of parsimony, lacking in flair and imagination. His systematic efforts to reduce the empire to a solvent and tidy unity were to begin its destruction.

Grenville's imperial plan for North America embraced eight points, many of which had been developed in Bute's administration:

1. A line would be drawn, approximately along the crest of the Alleghenies, beyond which settlement and unlicensed trade would be forbidden for the time being.
2. Royal Commissioners of Indian Affairs would control relations with the Indians west of the line. They would regulate the commerce carried on by traders licensed by the colonial governors, make treaties with the Indians, and prevent unauthorized settlement.
3. Purchases of land from the Indians would be made only by the Crown for subsequent granting or resale to individuals after a plan for orderly settlement had been worked out.
4. A large force of British regulars would be stationed in North America.
5. New colonies would be organized in Nova Scotia and the Floridas, which would follow in time the existing pattern of the older colonies.
6. Canada would retain for the time being its autocratic government, but with recognition of the right of the French colonists to retain their language, religion, and local laws and customs.
7. With naval assistance, enforcement of the trade and navigation laws and collection of the customs duties would be greatly tightened.
8. A revenue would be raised in the Americas to defray the cost of these services and especially of the troops in the New World.

Many British officials with experience in colonial administration had also urged that the political relations between Britain and the colonies be reorganized at the same time in order to assure a firmer British control. Their suggestions, of which the most systematically presented were those of Governor Bernard of Massachusetts, included such proposals as bringing all the colonies under a uniform pattern, rescinding charters and providing for royally appointed governors and upper houses in every colony, and setting up a civil list of colonial officials whose salaries would be free of control by the local assemblies. Grenville wisely avoided these proposals. They would have brought an appearance of order and system but they in fact would have added little to the actuality of British power, which was not really any greater in a purely royal colony like Virginia than in a charter colony like Connecticut. Councils and civil lists could not down a mob or enforce a law the colonists had decided to nullify. But these proposals would have added greatly to the intensity of colonial opposition. That opposition, confronted with such clear evidence of a systematic plan to curtail colonial autonomy, might have passed, ten years earlier than it did, from resistance against particular acts into outright secession.

The Grenville program was put promptly into effect. In March, 1763, even before Grenville came to office, the Bute ministry in the annual Mutiny Act for the authorization and support of the British standing army had provided for ten thousand troops in North America. In October, 1763, a royal proclamation established provisions for the government of Canada, the Floridas, and the newly acquired territories in the Caribbean. Moreover, it retained for the Crown all lands west of the Allegheny watershed and closed them to settlement and to unlicensed trade. Another act of 1763 extended to all the colonies the parliamentary ban on the issue of paper currency hitherto applicable only to New England. In the same months, absent colonial customs officers, who had administered their offices from England as sinecures, were ordered to their posts and stringently reminded of the requirements of their commissions and bonds. The navy was ordered to aid in enforcing customs law.

So much could be accomplished without legislation, but the program was to go much further. In March, 1764, Grenville laid before Parliament an extensive series of recommendations for measures to alter customs duties—both to regulate trade and to increase revenues—and to tighten the enforcement of the Acts of Trade and Navigation. Though a substantial financial return was expected from these proposals, Grenville also pointed out that more revenue would be needed and that a colonial stamp tax would probably be proposed in the following year. The recommended measures were enacted in the Sugar Act of 1764. Since it was this act and the executive measures already taken that laid the tinder that the Stamp Act of the following year was to explode, it is worth considering their content and their impact on the colonies in further detail.

The tripling of British forces in the New World was thought of by British leaders as an unselfish act for the defense of colonists, who should welcome the opportunity to pay for this protection. The colonists did not see it so. There had been no British arms for their defense when the Indians had been not a rumored menace along a distant frontier but a present and deadly threat to every cabin in the newly settled wilderness. No redcoats helped in the life-and-death struggle of King Philip's War or the Tuscarora War; none had been in the Shenandoah or beyond the Blue Ridge in Pennsylvania when the raiders left smoking ruins of cabins and scalped bodies over miles of frontier. When French forces hovered along all the northern and western borders, for years only a handful of British, and they in the safe and distant coastal towns, opposed them. Now that the French threat was ended and the Indians, though still dangerous, were well behind the mountains, the colonists felt little need for troops they might have welcomed a generation before. They were in America at Britain's decision, not the colonists' request.

As Bernhard Knollenberg has pointed out, the troops were not selected or trained or stationed in ways that would provide an effective defense against Indian attack. The ranger battalions, trained for forest warfare, were disbanded, and the regular regiments that were retained were stationed in the new colonies or in coastal cities or else in remote posts like Detroit, where they could watch the French *habitants* and control the fur trade but where they were of little value in protecting the frontier settlements to the east. The colonists suspected that insofar as the British troops were intended for defense, it was the defense of Canada, Florida, and the Western lands that had been taken from the colonies' hopeful control by the Crown rather than the defense of the existing colonies themselves. They suspected that so far as those colonies were concerned, the troops were intended to control rather than to protect. For neither of these purposes were the colonies willing to give their taxes.

Though British troops were in fact to be used almost immediately in campaigns against the Cherokees in the South and the tribes in the Midwest that joined in Pontiac's Rebellion, the ineptness of General Amherst, the British commander, in dealing with the Indians and his ineffectiveness in the campaigns themselves did little to increase colonial estimation of their value.

The colonists were suspicious also of imperial restraints on Western settlement. Though some temporary restriction was certainly important to any program for the peaceful and orderly occupation of the Trans-Appalachian region, the colonists saw other motives as well. Many of them realized or suspected that important figures in the British government thought it wise to hold the colonists to the narrow belt of settled land along the coast. Here they would be within the reach of British authority and of British trade, and would not be as likely either to manufacture or to govern on their own as they would be in the wilderness beyond the mountains. Confined to their present bounds, the insubordinate old colonies would remain weak in the face of growing British power, and the vast new areas could in time be organized from the beginning in patterns that did not brook the authority of Whitehall. The limitations on Western settlement cut across one of the most persistent drives in American society—the relentless movement westward to the free lands. Planter, speculator, and landless farm laborer alike felt cut off from their hopes, just when the end of war and the defeat of the French and Indians opened the West before them like a great treasure chest. The ruling elite in colonies like Virginia that had large Western claims were particularly angered at the frustration of their well-worked-out schemes for the grant to their land companies of near-imperial domains along the Western rivers.

The banning of paper currency issues in the colonies south of New England was a serious economic hardship. Though such currency had at times been issued in an irresponsible and inflationary way, it was a genuine necessity in colonies that simply did not have enough gold and silver to serve as a medium of exchange. The need seemed especially acute in the post-war years when new British trade regulations were limiting the opportunity to earn coin from Europe and the French and Spanish West Indies, when British merchants were pressing for payment of their war-inflated accounts, and when a post-war depression was settling over the colonies.

Most severe of all in its impact upon the colonies was the

Sugar Act of 1764. This statute took its name because it continued the earlier tariffs on sugar imported into the colonies, but that was among the least of its provisions. Duties were also levied or continued on certain textiles and on a number of products originating elsewhere and exported to the colonies through Great Britain. A heavy duty on Madeira wine sharply curtailed colonial trade with the Canary Islands, which had been a principal market for colonial lumber and other products as well as the source of the colonists' favorite vintage. The heart of the bill, however, was contained in a reduction of the duty on molasses imported from the foreign West Indies from a prohibitive but universally ignored sixpence a gallon to a burdensome threepence a gallon that the Crown was determined to collect.

This determination to enforce the British trade laws was made evident in many ways. Not only were the customs officers returned to their often neglected posts with stinging rebukes for past laxity. The navy was enlisted to assist them, and literal-minded naval captains were given an opportunity to share in the bounty of condemned cargoes that might have been ignored by more understanding customs officers who had to live day-to-day with the merchants in the port cities. A rigid new set of controls required the owner of every vessel, even little river craft, to get clearance on his cargo from the nearest customs officer for every intercolonial voyage. This might mean a trip of thirty miles to do the paperwork for ferrying a load of lumber or produce across the Delaware from New Jersey to Pennsylvania, or across the Hudson to New York, or across the Potomac from Maryland to Virginia. It also meant smuggling was made far more difficult.

Too often the British had seen notorious smugglers caught only to be tried and acquitted by juries of their neighbors. Indeed much of the laxity of customs officers in bringing smugglers to book could be laid to their knowledge that in most jurisdictions conviction was hopeless. The Sugar Act gave Parliament's sanction to the contention that customs cases could, at the Crown's option, be brought before the Admiralty Courts. These were so-called "prerogative" courts in which trial was held without jury and under procedures that gave the defendant a far more limited protection than he enjoyed in the common-law courts. Lest even these prerogative courts be affected by a local complaisance bred of cozy association with the merchants of the port, a new Admiralty Court was set up in

Nova Scotia, far from the mobs, the lawyers, the witnesses, or the influence of the smugglers, and customs officers were allowed to take their prizes there for condemnation if they chose.

This combination of measures pressed hard on the colonists. Barred from the West, denied the use of paper currency, narrowed in their trade, occupied by forces not of their inviting, and laden with new taxes, the colonists—who already lived under a system of trade regulations designed to subordinate their interests to those of Great Britain—were confined and burdened in ways that left them embittered.

The pressure upon them was the greater because it came at a time of severe post-war depression. The cessation of British military expenditures and the contraction of the colonies' own outlay helped to start a downward economic spiral that the new trade restrictions aggravated. The years 1764 and 1765 were a period of almost unrelieved gloom in the colonies. Trade stagnation everywhere, debts uncollectable from hard-pressed tradesmen and farmers, debts unpayable to insistent British merchants and factors—these were a depressing sequel to the exciting victories of the years before that had seemed to promise the colonists an open avenue to the riches of a continent.

The measures of 1764 did more than bring economic hardship on the colonists. They evinced a new British determination to show, once and for all, who was master and who subordinate. A navy off shore, an army in colonial posts, a revivified customs service, and courts free of local juries would see that the law was enforced. As the colonists saw it, even more strictly than before they were required to grow nothing, make nothing, buy nothing, and sell nothing except as their labors contributed to British commercial enrichment. The British government, not the colonial governments, would determine the issues of Indian affairs, defense, and Western settlement on which the future of the colonies depended. The colonists, not the British, would pay for these measures, and in amounts and in ways that the British Parliament determined.

For it was the Sugar Act rather than the immediately following Stamp Act in which British authority to levy taxes upon the colonists was first asserted. From the beginning the colonists had admitted in theory, even if they often evaded in practice, Britain's rightful power to regulate the trade of the empire and to set up tariffs as a means of doing so. They ignored the earlier Molasses Act, aimed at shutting off their imports of foreign sugar and molasses; but they did not question Parliament's right to enact it. But the Sugar Act was something else. The lowering of the molasses duty and its rigid collection meant that Parliament intended not to prevent the molasses trade, but through it to levy a tax upon the colonists without their consent. A grave constitutional challenge was presented. The colonists now faced not only a condition but also what was more important, a theory.

Before the colonies could respond effectively to this aggregation of grievances, the theory of Parliament's power to tax was put even more nakedly into practice. The maximum return from the Sugar Act and the more effective customs enforcement could not go more than halfway toward meeting Grenville's goal of putting the cost of North American colonial administration upon the older colonies. In his budget message of 1764 he had announced his intention to ask also for a colonial stamp tax similar to that for some time levied in Great Britain, but deferred action for a year in order to work out details and to give the colonies a chance—or so he said—to raise the money in alternative ways.

The colonies, or some of them, indicated a desire to raise needed funds by the traditional method of grant in response to royal requisition, but Grenville never formally communicated with them and in conferences with their agents in the intervening year refused to specify either the sums or the modes of raising them that he would consider satisfactory. Grenville and his ministry wanted money to meet the empire's immediate needs, but they wanted more than that. The refusal to consider any alternative that might be proposed by the colonies made it clear that Grenville was determined to place the imperial revenues in America firmly and permanently in the hands of Parliament. Royal governors, he hoped, would never again have to bargain with assemblies and exchange concessions of colonial liberties for grants of funds the empire had to have. Nor could the Crown draw on funds raised by the colonial assemblies as a possible source of support for royal programs unsanctioned by Parliament.

The Stamp Act therefore raised fundamental constitutional questions quite beyond the obvious one of taxation without representation. It would give a new constitutional frame to the empire. It raised these questions at a time when the colonists were already feeling oppressed by confinements of their trade and their westward expansion and were suffering from an acute economic recession. Nevertheless, the Stamp Act was passed in March, 1765, with little debate and almost no opposition. The die was cast.

5 ★★★★★★★★★

The Colonial Response

It almost seemed that Grenville had drawn the Stamp Act to assure the greatest and the most effective colonial opposition. Nearly every class and profession among the colonies in a position to organize and lead opposition was singled out for special taxation. The act provided that a tax stamp must appear on every issue of every newspaper, on every legal document, on every paper relating to customs and ship clearances, as well as on a large variety of other documents such as tavern licenses and college diplomas. The lawyers who provided most of the political leadership of the colonies, the newspapermen who controlled the most effective organs of public opinion, the tavern keepers who spread the political gossip, and the merchants, businessmen, and large planters who used the ports and made up most of the rest of the colonial elite were all directly hit. The isolation and political inertia of most of the middle- and lower-class rural population left the governmental and intellectual control of the colonies largely in the hands of a small group in the port towns; and it was precisely this articulate group whom the stamp tax most immediately and painfully affected. In the larger northern ports the artisans and workingmen had also become a loosely organized but self-conscious and politically effective group. These too—especially the printers, the mariners, and those working in ships' supplies—were hit by the tax because of its depressing impact on the trades in which they worked.

Every condition therefore existed for a violent colonial reaction against the Stamp Act. But it was difficult to organize. There was not a body, either formal or informal, that could act or speak for the colonies as a whole or concert their opposition. Leaders of one colony were in but limited touch with those of another. Organized political parties that could have mustered and presented opinion were not yet born. All the limitations of communication that were described earlier lay in the way of a concerted colonial response.

Indeed when the Stamp Act was first passed, no one expected more than grumbling from the colonies. The Grenville ministry knew that the act would be resented, but never questioned that it would be obeyed. Upon the passage of the act, so vigorous a representative of colonial interests in London as Benjamin Franklin resigned himself to its burdens and indeed thriftily sought some minor return by recommending his friend John Hughes as stamp distributor for Pennsylvania. But what happened turned out to be not merely resentment or resistance, but in a very real sense rebellion.

The act was passed on March 22, 1765, to go into effect on November 1 of that year. Even after the slowly carried news reached the colonies, they had six months in which to respond. Their response went through three stages—an assertion of the unconstitutionality of the act, coupled with declarations of the rights of the colonies; violent action to prevent the distribution of the stamps; and pressures to force the customs houses, courts, and newspapers to continue their business without stamps.

The first colony to respond was Virginia. The planter aristocracy that dominated the legislature was apparently little disposed to add anything to a fruitless and unread petition of the previous year. But in the dying days of the spring session of the assembly, when two thirds of the members had already departed to their homes, a young backwoods representative named Patrick Henry rose to his feet and delivered an inflammatory address that the Speaker thought came close to treason. He proposed a number of resolutions; just how many is buried in the dust of records long lost or destroyed. Five of them apparently passed, and one was rescinded next day. The four that remained on the record were moderate enough. They said what the colonies had said all along in their petitions and through their agents: that by charter and by inheritance the colonists possessed, and had never yielded, the rights of Englishmen and that these included the right to be taxed only by representatives of their own choosing. They asserted a right but did not propose an action.

What Henry had had in mind, what the newspapers in other colonies reported as passed, and what may have been in the rescinded resolution went further. The resolutions reported in newspapers elsewhere and undoubtedly sent them by Henry and his friends said that any attempt by anyone other than the assembly to tax Virginians had a manifest tendency to destroy American freedom, that Virginians were under no obligation to obey laws not passed by the assembly that purported to levy such taxes, and that anyone who upheld such unconstitutional laws was an enemy of the colony.

It was this more inflammatory resolution, bearing the mistaken prestige of adoption by the largest of the colonies, that set the pace elsewhere. Rhode Island followed suit almost immediately, with resolutions identical in tone and often in words, denying the right of Parliament to tax the colonies and encouraging resistance to the Stamp Act. During the summer and autumn most of the other colonies—Massachusetts, Connecticut, New York, New Jersey, Pennsylvania, Maryland, and South Carolina—joined in with their individual declarations.

But the colonists could not deal with the British in isolation from each other any more than they had been able to deal separately with the French and the Indians on the frontier or with the organization of the West. At the initiative of Massachusetts, which had earler sought intercolonial cooperation in remonstrating against the Sugar Act, a congress was called to meet in New York shortly before the Stamp Act was to go into effect. As the Massachusetts legislators phrased it, the congress was "to consider of a general and united, dutiful, loyal and humble Representation of their Condition to His Majesty and the Parliament; and to implore Relief." Nine colonies sent delegates chosen in one way or another, and Virginia, North Carolina, and Georgia would doubtless have joined them if their governors had permitted the assemblies to meet to choose delegates.

The actions of the Stamp Act Congress are of the greatest importance. It was the first intercolonial assembly whose acts were ratified by most of the colonies; and the resolutions of the congress were thus the first official declarations, on behalf of the colonists generally, of their rights in relation to Great Britain. After protesting their loyalty to the Crown and their "due Subordination to that August Body the Parliament of Great Britain," they asserted their rights both as Englishmen and as freemen. They held that it was unconstitutional to tax the colonies in any way save through their own representatives in their own legislatures or to deny the right of trial by jury.

Taxation without representation was indeed held to contravene not only the specific rights of Englishmen as guaranteed by the British constitution but also the essential rights of free peoples generally. Moreover, it was contended that the specific taxes levied under the Stamp Act were grievously burdensome and incapable of collection because of poverty and lack of hard currency and that they were inexpedient for Great Britain itself because they would limit the colonists' ability to import British manufactures. The specific resolutions of greatest interest are:

"III. That it is inseparably essential to the Freedom of a People, and the undoubted Right of *Englishmen,* that no taxes be imposed on them, but with their own Consent, given personally, or by their Representatives.

"IV. That the People of these Colonies are not, and from their local Circumstances cannot be, Represented in the House of Commons in *Great Britain.*

"V. That the only Representatives of the People of these Colonies are Persons chosen therein by themselves, and that no Taxes ever have been or can be Constitutionally imposed on them but by their respective Legislatures.

"VIII. That the late act of Parliament, entitled *An Act for Granting and Applying Certain Stamp Duties, and Other Duties, in the British Colonies and Plantations in America. &c.,* by imposing Taxes on the Inhabitants of these Colonies; and the said Act, and several other Acts, by extending the Jurisdiction of the Courts of Admiralty beyond its ancient Limits, have a manifest Tendency to subvert the Rights and Liberties of the Colonists."

In their first joint declaration of their rights, the colonists defined the position to which essentially they were to adhere throughout the years until the Declaration of Independence. They asserted constitutional limitations on the powers of Parliament to contravene the rights of Englishmen in the colonies, and specifically to levy taxes. Though they were prepared to concede a vague and deliberately undefined authority in Parliament, their earlier use of the power of the purse made it certain that if their sole authority to tax themselves were confirmed, the colonies would remain in an essentially independent position, and from decade to decade would strengthen that independence. The degree and character of their subordination to general imperial purposes would in fact, if not in law, be determined by the colonies themselves. If they could make good the assertions of the Stamp Act Congress, no such imperial plan as that devised by the Grenville ministry could be put into effect without their consent; and the empire, if it were to be preserved, must be a decentralized commonwealth.

The congress itself voted to send its resolutions to King, Lords, and Commons, but since it met only weeks before the Stamp Act was to go into effect, it was obvious that its appeals could not be acted on, even if Parliament were willing, in time to avert a constitutional crisis. It made no recommendation as to how that crisis was to be met.

Weeks before the congress convened the colonists began to provide their own answer to that question. The "unconstitutional" act would not be obeyed. If disobedience meant violence, then there would be violence. The first step was to assure that no stamps would be available. Mob action was the instrument for this. In the colonial cities, as in those of Great Britain, there was no police system in the modern sense, and rioting was a commonplace of political life of the period. Boston especially was a frequent scene of this activity, with flying fists and brickbats and blazing torches an almost expected accompaniment of such celebrations as Guy Fawkes Day. This turbulence could easily be harnessed to the colonial cause, since the workingmen who made up the rioters had little love for pomp or circumstance or for England and England's law.

It began hence in Boston on August 14, 1765, when Andrew Oliver, who had been named stamp distributor, was hanged and burned in effigy, saw an office building of his destroyed and his home wrecked, and escaped physical harm and possibly even death only by fleeing to the royal fort in Boston Harbor. Less than two weeks later a similar mob in Newport forced Augustus Johnston, the Rhode Island distributor, to take refuge in a British man-of-war and forswear his not yet received commission. No mob was necessary in New York and New Jersey, where the collectors resigned as soon as they heard of the Massachusetts action. In some other colonies the distributors were more stubborn. In Maryland Zachariah Hood, after his house was pulled down, escaped to New York rather than resign, but by late November the New York mob finished the work and forced him also to abandon his commission. In Connecticut Jared Ingersoll and in Pennsylvania and Delaware John Hughes held out until September 15 and October 7, respectively, but ultimately surrendered as well. William Houston in North Carolina received his commission belatedly, after the act went into effect, but prudently refused to accept it. Distributors in the other colonies that were later to secede were in England or at sea when they were commissioned. Threatened with mobs ashore, they all resigned before or promptly after landing. Only in the infant colony of Georgia, where the distributor did not arrive until January, were any stamps ever actually sold. And within a few days the distributor for that colony had also fled. When the law went into effect on November 1, nowhere was there an officer ready to enforce it.

This was only half a victory, however. The British officials could still hope that when debts had been long enough uncollected because the courts were closed for lack of stamps, when newspapers had gone long enough unpublished, and when ships had rotted long enough at the wharves awaiting stamped papers for their lading and clearance, the leading men of the colonies would themselves come pleading for stamps. But the colonists not only did not propose to pay the tax; they did not propose even implicitly to admit the validity of the Stamp Act by permitting publishers, judges, or port officials to suspend their functions in the absence of stamps.

Immediately after November 1, committees of Sons of Liberty and similar groups, with the unspoken or half-spoken threat of the mob at their command, as well as with all the manifold economic and legal pressures available to the leading citizens, made their views clear to all those called on to use stamps. Newspapers responded almost immediately, perhaps aware that they could be prosecuted only in courts that could themselves sit only in violation of the same act. Few issues of most newspapers were missed.

The port officials were a greater problem. Their consciences looked to their oaths, their prudence to their bonds as well as to the mob's threats. They gained a few days' or weeks' respite from the fact that most colonial vessels had cleared to sea in the last days of October. But the pressures mounted soon after. In Georgia, where there were at first no stamps, no distributor, and indeed no official notification of the act, business simply went on as usual. In Virginia the ports were closed for hardly a day. In a flurry of legal opinions and evasions, other collectors followed in issuing unstamped dockets and clearances in Rhode Island, Pennsylvania, New York, Connecticut, Massachusetts, and New Hampshire before the end of the year and in the remainder of the colonies by mid-February, 1766.

Fewer courts opened, in part because of the greater legal scruples of the judges, in part because the colonists needed them less—and indeed feared them as a forum for the prosecution of offenders against the Stamp Act itself. Those in Rhode Island, however, sat throughout the life of the act, and courts in a number of other colonies—New Hampshire, Maryland, and Delaware, as well as lower local courts in Massachusetts and elsewhere—had begun to hear cases before it was repealed. The victory of the colonies was total.

Indeed, most of the imperial issues involved in the later Revolution were actually decided in 1765 and 1766. In practice, whatever the constitutional theory, Britain had always governed the colonies by consent rather than by force. In 1765 Grenville chose to lay taxes without that consent and without providing adequate force as an alternative. The slender and already weakening bond of colonial respect for Britain's and Parliament's authority snapped. The colonists simply invalidated an act of Parliament. In view of the complete demonstration of the inability of Britain to tax the colonies, further argument as to its right to do so was empty. And what was true of taxation could be true of any other exercise of governmental authority. Hereafter, clearly, it would be the colonies, not the Parliament and courts of Britain, that determined the boundaries of the authority of the Crown and Parliament in the colonies. There would be an empire of decentralized authority and voluntary association or, so far as the colonies were concerned, there would be none.

Had George Grenville remained Prime Minister, the issue would doubtless have been tested in 1766. British troops would have been used to protect new stamp distributors, the customs officials would have been backed up by the navy in requiring the use of stamps, the newspaper publishers who forwent their use might have been hauled before Admiralty Courts for trial without jury. The Revolutionary test might have been forced a decade earlier upon colonies not yet prepared by years of consultation and propaganda and without the added strength that was to come from the very rapid growth of the ensuing ten years.

But Grenville had resigned as the King's first minister in June, 1765, before the Stamp Act had gone into effect and before the first riots. Personal differences with the young King rather than his American policy explained his departure. His ministry was succeeded by one under the Earl of Rockingham, who recalled to office the "Old Whigs" who had formerly been followers of the Duke of Newcastle and who represented a long tradition of lenient and hands-off policies toward the colonies. Rockingham was also seeking, though unsuccessfully, to strengthen his cabinet by the return to office of William Pitt.

That statesman firmly believed that the levying of an internal tax like the stamp tax by a Parliament in which the colonists were unrepresented was unconstitutional and was to express his pride in American resistance. Hence, when Rockingham encountered the colonists' violent refusal to obey the Stamp Act, his thoughts turned to retreat rather than to armed enforcement.

The temper of Parliament and of the King would not, however, permit an unqualified repeal of the act. Rockingham fell back on two devices. Residents of Boston and a few other ports had made pledges not to import British goods while the Stamp Act was in effect. Though the actual effect of this nonimportation agreement was probably slight—an estimated decline of about twenty percent in exports to America probably was due principally to the general economic depression—British merchants were frightened by the prospect of a distinct drop in trade, and they feared lest the colonists' little supply of gold and silver would go all to the British Treasury, leaving little or none for the settlement of their by now very large accounts. Encouraged by the ministry, merchants in London and most of the port towns submitted petitions urging repeal as a measure for their benefit and for the relief of Britain's trade. These petitions could be honorably heeded when colonial riots could not. Their faces further saved by the passage of a Declaratory Act that asserted Parliament's complete authority over the colonies, the honorable members finally felt free to repeal the Stamp Act as a deed of grace to the injured British merchants. This was done on March 18, 1766, to be effective May 1.

Britain had picked doubtless the worst possible path out of the dilemma. The revenue, which she desperately needed, was abandoned; yet by the Declaratory Act she made sure that she would get no benefit from the abandonment. By continuing to assert an authority that, as had just been demonstrated, Britain had neither the power nor the will to exercise, she forfeited any claim upon the affections of the colonies for a generous or understanding action. The constitutional *fact* had been decided: Britain could not successfully levy a tax upon the colonies; a useless constitutional *theory* was left to rankle into rebellion.

The immediate reaction of the colonists was to celebrate; but the more thoughtful ones, after the initial elation had passed, realized that they were dealing with a government in London that had explicitly, formally, and well-nigh unanimously set forth as its permanent position that the colonists had no rights save by England's grace and that a distant Parliament in which they had no representation was empowered to govern them on any point it chose and to tax them in any way and to any degree its wisdom or whim decreed. The colonists might choose to ignore the assertion of such an authority, but they would remain hereafter vigilant against its exercise. Dozens of earlier parliamentary enactments over a century and more had on one point or another regulated their affairs or in one incidental way or another taxed them, and these had been acquiesced to because the colonists had not often seen them as parts of a pattern of arbitrary control. But hereafter, even the slightest effort to legislate for and especially to tax the colonies, no matter how mild and reasonable in itself, was certain to be linked with the policy of the Declaratory Act and resisted not for its actual effect but because it was a manifestation of a theory that could not be tolerated.

Britain had hoped that the simultaneous repeal of the Stamp Act and passage of the Declaratory Act would impress the colonists with both the firmness of Britain's will and the generosity of her intentions toward the colonists. Instead it made the colonists understand that Britain's intentions were hostile, but that she could be intimidated from putting them into effect.

Meanwhile Britain's financial problems remained unsolved. They had been mitigated by the return of peace, a reviving prosperity, and the rewards of Grenville's persistent economies. But ends were still not meeting, and in particular only a negligible American revenue was forthcoming to meet administrative and military costs in the New World, now estimated at close to four hundred thousand pounds a year. Rockingham's response was to propose abandonment of the Western effort. He would make permanent the Line of 1763, which had been designed to hold settlement to the east of the Appalachians pending the orderly extinction of Indian rights; remove the British troops from the frontier forts to the more cheaply supplied seaport towns and reduce their number; and abandon the imperial West to nature and the Indians. The policy was feckless—as well might Britain try to hold back the tides themselves as the westward flow of settlers—but Rockingham's ministry fell before it could be put into effect. It was never a powerful or united cabinet, and, made unpopular by its necesssary stand on the Stamp Act repeal, it was unable to survive differences over West Indian legislation. Rockingham resigned in August, 1766.

The King now turned to William Pitt, who was made Earl of Chatham. Pitt had shown a willingness to serve the King's purposes and to create what the King desired—a government not dependent on any party or faction. He still thought in imperial terms. He would revive a vigorous Western policy in America, guarding and extending Western settlement. He would recognize fully the freedom of the colonies from internal taxation by Parliament and would support their claims to autonomous development. While they were strengthened, however, they would be ever more closely bound into the British imperial economy. Pitt declared himself ready to bombard American cities to the ground if ever they began to manufacture in harmful competition with British industry.

He turned his imperial eye equally to India. As almost no one else in Britain yet did, he saw that in that vast land his country had acquired not only a commerce but an empire that could not continue to rest in the corrupt and mercenary hands of the East India Company. Pitt would assert the sovereign rights of the Crown in the political control of the newly mastered domain while leaving the company to its trading. The tribute of Indian princes and the territorial revenues would flow into the royal rather than the company treasury and would provide the revenue required to strengthen and extend the Crown's domain in America.

Pitt—or Chatham as he is now properly called—ruled singly and made no effort to weld his ministers into a unit or to establish a common cabinet policy. By no means all of the ministry, whether from scruples against the amendment of charters or from personal involvement in the vast and richly corrupt net of the company's finances, were willing to follow Chatham's lead as to India; and his efforts to enact his proposals in that area failed. Though no general reorganization of the company was possible, its dividends were limited to ten percent, and an agreement was reached in June, 1767, under which it was to contribute four hundred thousand pounds annually to the Treasury.

This contribution promised to reduce, but it by no means eliminated, the need for an American revenue. Meanwhile relations with the colonies, which it had been hoped would improve with the Stamp Act repeal, were exacerbated by the Mutiny Act. This was the annually enacted statute that provided for the government and support of the British standing army. Its provisions required communities in which troops were stationed to provide for their quartering in the absence of barracks and to provide certain incidental supplies such as beer, vinegar, salt, soap, and candles. In 1764, at General Gage's request, the act was extended to the colonies; and thereafter, with modifications from year to year, it was continued.

Its practical impact began to be felt in 1765 and 1766, especially in New York, the British Army headquarters for North America. The statute required the assemblies to vote specified quarters and supplies on demand and without debate. In 1766 the New York and Massachusetts assemblies simply refused to do so. The New York assembly's action was particularly contumacious. It was the view of the colonies that an act of Parliament requiring a colonial assembly to appropriate funds in amounts determined by a British official was taxation by Parliament as direct as if Parliament had itself made the particular levies. That the colonies should refuse to grant the quite modest sums required for providing minor needs of British troops while the people of Great Britain were raising the forces from their own number and taxing themselves to pay, arm, clothe, feed, and transport them—and all, so the Britishers told themselves, for the aid and defense of the colonists—was to members of Parliament intolerable if not treasonable. The sore and grumbling resistance to the repeal of the Stamp Act was inflamed into open anger against the colonies and a new determination to bring them to heel.

This reaction would at best have made it difficult to achieve Chatham's goal of a complete and amicable solution of the American problem. Its achievement was made completely impossible by Chatham's illness. Following the frustration of his efforts to form a ministry that could rise above all "faction" and to reorganize the East India Company, he withdrew to his home, affected with gout and with a depression so deep it approached madness. For nearly a year he abandoned responsibility to the Duke of Grafton, an earnest young man who was nominal head of the cabinet as First Lord of the Treasury. Grafton's only policy was to carry out Chatham's will, and he could not learn that will from the darkened room at Bath to which the great man had retreated.

At a time when it was urgently necessary that the British government redefine its imperial program following the Stamp Act defeat, the cabinet drifted aimlessly. A deal took the place of a policy in India. Chatham's visions of a magnanimous

American program remained visions. The Earl of Shelburne, whose departmental responsibility it was, worked slowly and systematically on a revised plan of empire. This would have reversed Rockingham's abandonment of the West and would have returned to the policy of its planned and orderly development. Indeed, Shelburne would have encouraged a swift westward movement, convinced that though British authority might be more feebly exercised in the interior, the ready availability of an abundant supply of free and fertile land would indefinitely entice the colonists from manufacturing in competition with Britain's factories and would preserve the colonies as purveyors of raw materials and profitable markets for British products. Shelburne would have protected the westward movement with British troops and forts and would have paid for them with an anticipated flood of income from land-grant fees and quitrents for the newly settled lands. Though nothing in the experience of royal or proprietary officials with quitrents in the seaboard areas suggests that similar rents on the Western lands would have been a practical or, indeed, a collectible source of revenue, Shelburne's plans were at least a constructive effort to create a policy.

They were never to be put into effect. In Chatham's absence no one in the cabinet had the power to adopt them as administration policy and put them through Parliament. Grafton was too weak; General Conway, the leader of the House of Commons, was flirting with the possibility of resigning and joining the opposition; and the most brilliant member of the cabinet, Charles Townshend, was pursuing his own erratic and irresponsible fancies. All that preserved the headless administration in office was the fact that the opposition was equally headless and even more divided, with each of its factions tempted by the possibility of joining the government at a high price in patronage.

On one point, however, the enemies of the administration could unite. That was in opposition to the wartime level of land taxes. In the spring of 1767 a measure was pressed through that reduced this tax from four shillings in the pound to three, depriving the Crown of an annual revenue of five hundred thousand pounds. Immediately the financial crisis was upon the ministry again. With Chatham's hopes of a major Indian revenue frustrated, Shelburne's plans for a revenue from Western lands still but half formulated, and the domestic revenue slashed, the Treasury thought it could only turn again to the project of American taxation.

In the minds of most English and some American leaders there was at the time a confusion about a difference between "internal" and "external" taxes. Almost all Americans agreed that Parliament was without authority to levy a land or excise tax on them; and the English, whether or not they accepted this position, understood it and knew that internal taxes could be collected from the Americans only by the use of more force than they were prepared to employ. Most Americans, however, agreed that Parliament could regulate the trade of the empire and that as a means of doing so it could levy duties. Some duties that Parliament had levied—most recently in the Sugar Act—had been intended in considerable part to raise revenue as well; and these, though often evaded, had nevertheless been accepted by the colonies. From this, many British leaders concluded that it was only to *internal* taxes that the colonies objected and that so long as they were levied as customs duties and collected at seaports, Parliament might lay such taxes as it chose, even though for revenue only, without successful colonial objection. Relying on this fatuous distinction, Townshend, the Chancellor of the Exchequer, had hinted as early as January, 1767, that he knew a way to extract an American revenue without colonial objection. It was in part in reliance on this statement that Parliament cut the land tax. That action forced Townshend to make good his hints.

What he delivered was trivial as a revenue measure. It consisted of a proposal for modest duties on the importation into the American colonies of paper, paints, lead, glass, and tea. The total revenue hoped for from the measure was forty thousand a year, less than a tenth the income lost by the reduction of the land tax and but a small fraction of the cost of administering the colonies. But though the Townshend duties could offer little to the British Treasury, their cost in colonial opposition was enormous. Other provisions of the bill enacting the duties made clear a redoubled British determination to eliminate smuggling. A resident American Board of Customs Commissioners was created, independently responsible for the collection of duties and enforcement of trade laws in American ports. New Vice-Admiralty Courts were established at key ports with authority to try those accused under the new act and to do so without a jury and without the defenses of the common law. General search warrants, hated in England and in the colonies, were authorized as an aid to customs enforcement. Coupled in the minds of Americans with the Townshend duties were the provisions of a companion act suspending the New York assembly until it should comply with the Mutiny Act.

Perhaps most alarming of all was the provision of the Townshend Act that the revenues derived from the new duties should be used as necessary to pay the salaries of governors, judges, and other officials of the colonies, thus making them independent of the financial control of the assemblies.

In order to gain a trivial revenue, Parliament had undertaken to reassert its unilateral power to tax the colonists without their consent, to alter the common law to their detriment by shifting cases in which the British government was directly interested from common-law courts to "prerogative" courts sitting without juries, to authorize general search warrants that were unlawful at common law, to remove colonial officials from the financial control of the colonial assemblies, and to dispose of those assemblies themselves. Had the precedents created by these acts been allowed, colonial freedoms would indeed have existed by British grace. The threat to those freedoms, though perhaps less immediately palpable to the colonists than the threat presented by the Stamp Act, was actually a far more sweeping one. The wonder is not that the colonists again resisted, but rather that their resistance was so slowly and spottily organized.

No doubt this delay was due in part to the absence of so dramatic a departure from custom as that presented by the Stamp Act. The colonists were, after all, used to tariffs. Admiralty Courts they had known before, and the suspension of the New York legislature as yet touched only that colony. The colonists' own minds were by no means clear as to the location of the line that separated unconstitutional taxation from permissible trade regulation.

The acts had been approved on June 29, 1767, to take effect November 20. News of them reached the colonies in late summer, and there was a ripple of local nonimportation agreements among the merchants of Boston, New York, and smaller New England ports in the following months. General colonial resistance, however, was slow to mobilize until the appearance of John Dickinson's *Letters from a Farmer in Pennsylvania to the Inhabitants of the British Colonies*. These appeared originally as a series of contributions to the *Pennsylvania Chronicle*, a Philadelphia newspaper, beginning in November, 1767, and extending over two months. They were subsequently reprinted in more than a dozen editions in Great Britain and America and became one of the greatest "best sellers" of the colonial period.

Dickinson was an essentially conservative Pennsylvania lawyer whose primary concern was to rest the colonists' rights on a solid basis of constitutional law. His essays were quiet and even legalistic, but they were most effective in dignifying the colonial opposition to the Townshend Acts, raising the whole question from the area of a dispute over twopenny duties to a debate over the rights of men and Englishmen. Relying solidly upon John Locke, Dickinson again asserted the unconstitutionality of any effort to tax Americans by a Parliament in which they were unrepresented. Similar arguments at the time of the Stamp Act by Dulany and others, including Dickinson himself in his earlier *Considerations upon the Rights of the Colonists to the Privileges of British Subjects,* had not had to confront in detail the distinction between taxation and the regulation of trade, since the stamp tax itself was a tax and nothing else. Dickinson disposed of the illogical distinction between "internal" and "external" taxes, but found a clear-cut distinction between taxes and trade regulations on the basis of the primary intent of the legislation. The only consequences of the Townshend duties for trade would be to discourage British exports to the colonies and to encourage American manufactures, objects the Parliament could not be supposed to seek. Moreover, the Townshend Act explicitly stated their purpose to raise a revenue. Hence they were, in Dickinson's view, wholly unconstitutional even though as customs duties they were cast in the same form as many acts for the regulation of trade that had been accepted by the colonies as valid.

Following the publication of Dickinson's *Letters,* the colonial opposition to the new duties became general and explicit. It took three forms—the adoption of official resolutions condemning the Townshend Acts, pledges to cease the importation either of all British goods or at least of those bearing a duty, and mob violence against customs officers. The first official action was a resolution of the Massachusetts House of Representatives, adopted February 11, 1768. This denounced the Townshend duties in terms similar to Dickinson's and added a vehement attack on the idea of paying governors and judges from funds other than those voted by the colonial assemblies. Moreover, the resolutions were to be transmitted to the other colonies as a circular letter urging united action.

Royal authorities viewed this as close to treason, and Governor Bernard dissolved the assembly.

Townshend was now dead, his early demise coming too soon to permit him to see the consequences of his blithe irresponsibility. Chatham's illness had led him to resign in 1768, and Grafton had become the actual as well as the nominal Prime Minister. He and other members of the ministry who had originally joined under Chatham's leadership in the hope of a permanent and amicable settlement of relations with the colonies were disturbed by the reopening of hostility brought about by the Townshend Acts, especially in view of their trifling fiscal return. Already they were looking for a dignified way out of the renewed controversy, and they agreed that Lord Hillsborough, recently appointed to the new position of Secretary of State for the colonies, should address a conciliatory circular letter to the colonial governments. Hillsborough, however, was a stupid man, and the circular he sent was full of threat and bombast. He fulminated over the Massachusetts actions and ordered every governor to dissolve the assembly of his colony if necessary to prevent any similar action. A number of assemblies, however, had already endorsed Massachusetts' action, and others were spurred to it by Hillsborough's bumbling arrogance. New Hampshire, Connecticut, New Jersey, and Virginia were among the colonies that gave the Massachusetts action their formal support. Hillsborough went further and instructed Governor Bernard to reconvene the Massachusetts House and order it to rescind its action. The House, of course, by more than a five-to-one vote, refused to be dictated to, and Hillsborough was left with an embarrassing impasse for his pains.

Meanwhile the first tentative agreements on nonimportation were being enlarged into colony-wide "associations" having nearly the force of law. In Boston, New York, Philadelphia, and Baltimore the merchants themselves drew up more rigid nonimportation agreements by the spring of 1769, applying to nearly all British goods. This program was given a revolutionary impetus by Virginia in May, 1769. The House of Burgesses adopted the Virginia Resolves, drawn by George Mason, introduced by George Washington, and unanimously supported by the planter leadership of the colony. These asserted again the sole right of Virginians to tax themselves and attacked the British government for its efforts to suppress the Massachusetts circular letter and its proposals to evade colonial juries by removing colonists accused of treason to England for trial.

An address to the King presenting essentially these views, introduced by the more radical elements of the assembly, was adopted by the following day (May 17, 1769), whereupon the governor promptly dissolved the assembly.

It was then that the first truly revolutionary act occurred. The members of the House of Burgesses met the following day as an extralegal body and adopted the Virginia Association, which forbade all imports of dutiable goods except paper, along with many non-dutied British products. This was not a mere agreement among merchants regulating their own conduct. It was the action of a body of high officials of the colony, acting outside the law, but speaking in fact, if not in name, for the whole body politic. Their association could not be enforced through the courts, but by the pressure and threats of local committees it was to be carried into effect more thoroughly than ever the Crown had been able to apply the Acts of Trade. Not only had the authority of the British government been denied and flouted; there had been created the beginnings of a new authority that could take its place.

Throughout the summer and fall one colony after another followed Virginia's example, acting through the assemblies when they were in session and through extralegal bodies when the governors had prorogued or refused to call them. By colony-wide resolutions, or in a few cases by the action of special committees in the ports, at the end of autumn every colony save New Hampshire had taken measures to forbid importations from Great Britain in whole or in part. Coupled with these actions were frequent resolutions or committee programs to increase colonial manufactures in order permanently to lessen the dependence of the colonies on British imports.

The results were promptly felt. In 1769 alone, before the nonimportation program had been fully in effect for an entire year, imports from Britain fell by more than forty percent. In New York, where the agreement was adopted early and well enforced, the reduction was about eighty-five percent. In a rapidly expanding British economy, the loss of nearly one million pounds a year of exports to the colonies may actually have hurt less than the much smaller loss following the Stamp Act, which came in the immediate post-war depression; and British merchants did not besiege Parliament with their petitions as they had on the earlier occasion. But such a loss was obviously out of all proportion to the trivial few thousands of pounds of revenue from the dutiable commodities that evaded the nonimportation ban. As the ban became more effective, even this little income was likely to disappear. Obviously the Townshend program had been a total failure as a revenue measure and a disaster for the British colonial program. The ministry must extricate itself from this mess as best it could.

Since George III had come to the throne, one ministry had succeeded another with great rapidity. Six Prime Ministers had served during the first nine years of his reign. None had had the degree of support from the Crown and Parliament that could enable him to form a coherent and stable ministry or to plan and fully carry out a consistent colonial policy. Such governmental instability was the principal reason that Great Britain was unable, in the fluid post-war years, to construct any rational pattern for the government of her new empire. Fundamental decisions encompassing vast areas of policy needed to be made, and no one had the time or power to make them. The chaos reached its worst during the latter part of Chatham's ministry, while he lay ill and wordless and his cabinet officers pursued their individual and conflicting policies and their individual flirtations with the opposition. It continued during the months in which the Duke of Grafton took formal responsibility for the ministry. Order and the possibility of a coherent policy began to emerge with the appointment of Lord North as Chancellor of the Exchequer and subsequently, in January, 1770, as First Lord of the Treasury and Prime Minister. For all the obloquy to which North has been exposed by subsequent generations of patriotic American historians, he was an engaging man. There was nothing about him of fanatic zeal or of restless vision. Portly and slow of body, torpid of mind, he held no bitter rancor against the colonies and felt no rage to avenge insults to Britain's dignity. Nor did his eyes rest on any Pitt-like view of a globe-engirdling empire bringing unforeseeable glory to Britain's name. He merely wanted to get on with business, dealing day by day in an orderly and rational way with whatever problems came to hand, quietly and stubbornly persistent in the King's service, quietly and stubbornly loyal to the King himself. Britain's empire in America was lost in an unimpassioned, decent, humdrum sort of way.

One of the first pieces of tidying up North had to do was to be rid of the Townshend duties. A second retreat before colonial contumacy was unwelcome to Parliament and the country, and North had but narrow support even in his own ministry. As in the case of the Stamp Act repeal, the price of retreat was a truculent assertion of right to powers whose exercise was being abandoned, together with a formula for rationalizing the retreat as a concession to British rather than American interests. In the case of the Townshend duties the rationalization was that it was "uncommercial" to tax British exports and hence to encourage American manufacture. In lieu of a Declaratory Act the duty on tea was to be retained as an assertion of Britain's rights. Tea was chose in part because the "noncommercial" argument did not apply to duties on a commodity that could not be produced either in England or in America, but primarily because of North's thrifty desire to hang on to the only one of the Townshend duties that produced any appreciable revenue.

With this sweetening, Parliament reluctantly enacted the repeal of all the duties except that on tea, and the King gave his assent on April 12, 1770. This action signaled a general disengagement from the American controversy. The requirement for quartering British troops in the colonies contained in the annual Mutiny Act was quietly omitted from the next such bill. Cases were not taken to the new and feared Admiralty Courts, which sat in near idleness. Colonial offenders were not taken to Britain for trial; writs of assistance were not generally or offensively employed.

Irritants there remained. The Declaratory Act continued to assert Britain's complete authority over the colonies; the duties on tea and molasses remained in effect as an exercise of the taxing power Britain claimed. The Proclamation Line of 1763 continued to run along the mountaintops, barring—or attempting to bar—the land-hungry Americans from the golden time they looked for. The reinforced customs authority continued its heightened vigilance, and a bitter little running fight continued day in and day out between the colonists and the collectors.

This was to reach its height two years later, in June, 1772, when the customs vessel *Gaspee* ran aground in Rhode Island waters. A large party of colonists, under distinguished leadership, seized this chance to board the schooner, remove its officers and crew, and burn the vessel. Against the united support of the colonists, a subsequent royal commission of inquiry could gather no evidence. The ringleaders, though well known, enjoyed complete impunity in their insurrectionary act.

Another remaining irritant was the continued presence of British troops in the colonies. Insults, quarrels, and scuffles exhibited the tension from week to week. In 1770 there were two sizable riots between troops and colonists. The larger was the so-called Battle of Golden Hill in New York in January, 1770. Dozens of troops fought a pitched battle against gangs of Sons of Liberty after several days of minor brawls. Although a number on both sides were badly hurt, no one was killed. In a smaller and otherwise less important encounter in Boston two months later, the colonists were not so lucky. A beleaguered squad of redcoats fired into a heckling mob and killed five. Although colonial propagandists made much of both events, and especially of the "Boston Massacre," the more responsible elements in both colonies sought to check the rising violence. Alexander McDougald, the leader of the Sons of Liberty in New York, was imprisoned by the colonial authorities. Two patriot spokesmen, John Adams and Josiah Quincy, defended the British soldiers in their trial for murder in Boston and won their acquittal.

But in spite of continuing friction with troops and customs officers, in spite of the harangues of colonial propagandists, in spite of the growing burden of discriminatory laws of trade, the relations between Britain and the colonies were sliding back to their pre-war negligence and indifference. One by one the colonies drifted away from nonimportation, save for tea, which was generally forgone or smuggled from Holland. Rising prosperity both in Britain and in America lessened the tension over tax burdens. Nothing had been resolved, but much was being ignored. Most great political issues are no doubt outgrown rather than settled. It would have been impossible in 1770 to devise any formula for British-American relations to which both Parliament and the colonists could agree. Those relations could be sustained only by evading irreconcilable differences between the two until some new and mutually acceptable pattern of empire could in time evolve. North's good-humored lethargy toward the colonies and the very limited character of his policies gave promise of such a healing inattention.

It might well have turned out so, and a vaster decentralized British commonwealth might in time have emerged. But it was not to be. The seeds of disaster left planted in the Declaratory Act and the tea duty were to have their fruits. Other problems left unsolved in India were to start a half-accidental chain of events that would end evasion and bring both Britain and the colonies back face-to-face with the inescapable insolubility of the imperial problem.

6 ★★★★★★★★★

End of Empire

Many pages have been devoted to the events of 1763–1770, for it was in those years that Britain awoke, or half awoke, to its new imperial responsibility. It was then that the government at Whitehall tried to grasp the scattered assortment of trading posts, wilderness domains, and commercial ventures now grown to colonies and to shape them into some sort of ordered political commonwealth. It had tried under the worst circumstances, when vision and enterprise had been exhausted in the bloodiest war the world had yet known and when men, as after our Civil War and the First World War, were turning their backs on greatness and seeking their own enrichment. It was a time of political confusion, and Britain's efforts had to be carried out by a whole series of short-lived cabinets in which little men with insufficient backing fumbled briefly with great problems they did not understand.

It is not therefore surprising that Britain failed on almost every count. Her own machinery for colonial administration had been somewhat strengthened, but the new officials accomplished little save a tighter enforcement of the customs laws around Boston. British military force in the New World had been augmented, but only enough to anger the colonists without intimidating them. The bold ideas for rationalizing and making uniform the pattern of colonial administration had not been seriously pushed. The effort to remove Crown officials from the hostility, and colonial offenders from the protection, of local juries through transfer of their cases to England or to Admiralty Courts remained a dead letter.

The Western problem remained unsolved. The Proclamation Line of 1763 still ran along the crest of the Alleghenies. It had been drawn to give the British government time to make decisions that a decade later had still not been made. Should the West remain unsettled, left to the Indians as a source of furs, thus forcing settlers north to Nova Scotia and south to Florida? Or should the West be vigorously and systematically developed for British colonization? The question was still unanswered. The decision depended on whether Britain viewed America as an imperial extension of the British people—as a commonwealth—or whether it viewed the colonies as commercial outposts to be confined near seaports and cultivated only for their contribution to British mercantile policy.

In the outcome, neither view prevailed. The ban on settlement west of the line remained, but little was done to enforce it. Twenty thousand Americans had drifted west to the Ohio waters by 1770, but nothing had been done either to defend them or to govern them. The West would be neither protected as Indian country nor developed as British soil. Imperial agents continued to handle relations with the tribes, but the licensing of traders devolved again on individual colonies, opening the way once more to the disorder of the 1750's. Though there were British troops in the seaports, where the colonies had no enemies, there were only a handful to subdue the frontier wilderness. Canada and the Western lands alike still awaited a settled pattern of government.

Imperial plans had been abandoned largely because the problem of imperial finance had not been solved. It had become clear that the colonists would not yield up taxes to the demand of Parliament. That body in turn was unwilling to confine its taxing authority to Britain and thus leave the King free to develop an independent source of income from requisitions on the colonial assemblies. This series of impasses derived from the failure to conceive a pattern of empire in which the colonies participated equally with the homeland. The realm was Britain and Britain alone: the colonies were not that realm grown across the face of the earth, but rather subordinate possessions existing only for Britain's ends.

The imperial vision had failed in India as well. The vast theater of Clive's heroism and Pitt's dreams had become an arena of hectic stockjobbing and squalid avarice to which the interests of the Indian people, the British Crown, and the East India Company alike were recklessly sacrificed. So long as dreams of a speculative fortune dangled before the eyes of all the insiders in London, nothing could be done to bring order to that troubled country, for fear that with order would come the end of looting. It was, oddly enough, the failure in India that was to end the uneasy colonial truce of 1770 and bring down the American empire.

As it had after Queen Anne's War and King George's War, the fit of imperial reorganization stimulated by wartime frustrations had dwindled out. Once again the situation had seemed to return to its pre-war status, in which a mother country and colonies, remote from each other, maintained their separate pretensions unexercised and untested. But now there was a difference. The situation that had seemed to demand unity in the earlier wars had been peculiar to the conflicts themselves. With the end of each of those wars it had been possible for Britain and the several colonies to relapse into their isolation from each other. Nothing forced the imperial relation to be made explicit, and each could maintain his own view of it.

But now the empire had grown too close. The Western and Indian problems had been only deferred. Somewhere decisions would have to be made as to the organization, settlement, government, and defense of the Western lands and the method of financing these operations. With the rapid expansion of trade the commercial relations between Britain and the colonies were growing larger and closer, and the regulations governing them must from time to time be altered. The growth of the colonies would compel them in time, and soon, to break away from their subordinate position in British mercantile policy and develop their own manufactures and trading patterns. Decisions must be made either to permit this growth or to suppress it by force. Problems of imperial defense would be as pressing as problems of imperial organization, trade, and finance. France's ambitions had been only scotched, not destroyed, and she awaited an opportunity for revenge. All along the Mississippi and through the Caribbean there remained a zone of friction with Spain. In India, in the American West, and around the trading posts in Africa there were powerful and potentially hostile native populations.

Decisions truly imperial, involving the futures of all the residents of the empire, both at home and abroad, must somehow be made. A sovereign power must make them, and the location of that sovereignty remained the unanswerable question—the issue on which the empire was to fall.

The series of events that led finally to independence began, remotely enough, with the financial disintegration of the British

East India Company. The company had been plundered for years by its own employees, who seized for their private accounts the more profitable new trading opportunities. The decades of war and turmoil in much of India had put the company to great expense, compounded by grievous mismanagement. The boycott of British tea still partially enforced in the colonies had drastically reduced its American market. The company was unable to pay its contributions to the British Treasury, and its stock—the favorite speculative medium of British financiers—suddenly dropped almost half its value on the exchange. It seemed essentially to the North government to shore up this vast semipublic corporation, on which the Crown depended for the administration of its enormous Indian interests and with which all factions of British politics were intimately linked.

North sought to do this by an ingenious measure. The principal single financial embarrassment of the East India Company grew from the millions of pounds of tea locked up in its warehouses. To promote the sale of this, North proposed the rebate of all British duties on the tea upon its reexport to America. Moreover, the company, which had hitherto sold only at auction in England would be allowed hereafter to ship directly to the American colonies and sell there through its own agents. Although the threepence per pound duty on tea imported into the colonies would remain in effect, the remission of the much higher British duties and the elimination of middlemen would mean that the colonists could buy tea cheaper than ever before and much cheaper than it could be bought in London. The anticipated price, indeed, would be about half that previously in effect. This would drive from the market the tea smuggled from Holland, which now dominated it; stifle the trade of the smuggling merchants, damaging them severely in the process; and, hopefully, entice the Americans into the general acceptance of a tea duty. Coupled with this proposal were plans for direct financial aid to the company until it was back on its feet. The bill was passed on April 27, 1773, but shipments of tea to the colonies did not begin until the following autumn.

Possibly the scheme would have worked had there been only the duty to think of, and the thirsty colonists might well have swallowed the threepenny tax along with their cheap tea. But the British East India Company monoply of tea sales was a direct threat to the merchants who were the leading citizens of every port town. Tea was the most important single item of import, and the loss of the tea trade to a British monopoly was a direct and substantial threat to their businesses. Even worse measures might be in prospect. If tea, why not any other staple import? Could not British chartered companies by act of Parliament take over as much of the American trade as they chose? This immediate threat to their pocketbooks helped the merchants mightily in seeing the long-run danger to American liberties that would be raised by a total acquiescence in the tea duty. They were leaders in organizing the populace for action in every seaport.

Threats of violence like those that had earlier menaced the stamp distributors were made against the merchants selected as consignees of the tea. But this time the threatened men did not wait for violence and, except in Massachusetts, resigned promptly and peacefully. Old Governor Hutchinson, a stern and elegant Tory, son of one of the oldest Massachusetts families, maintained the law and even some of the majesty of England with a firmness not made less bitter by the destruction of his property during the Stamp Act riots. His sons were among the recipients named by the East India Company, and Hutchinson would hear of no weak resignations in the face of mob threats. Instead the Massachusetts consignees took refuge behind British bayonets in Castle William.

In late November and December the tea ships came to harbor in the major ports along the coast. From most of these ports the ships simply returned with their cargo in the absence of consignees to whom it could be delivered. In Charleston the tea was landed under bond and placed in a royal warehouse. Only in Boston was compromise impossible. The Bostonians would not permit the tea to be landed. Hutchinson would not permit the ships to leave without having paid duty on the cargo. After twenty days in port, the customs officers were charged by law to seize the cargo for nonpayment of duties and to hold it in the customs warehouse. The impasse continued until December 16, the last day the tea could remain aboard. On the day the Bostonians forestalled landing of the tea by boarding the three waiting vessels and throwing their cargo into the harbor. Other lesser "tea parties" took place elsewhere in the colonies, but it was the Boston uprising that forced the issue.

This was no mere idle gesture. The tea was valued at thousands of pounds, and there could be no question of the flat, deliberate lawlessness of its destruction. In the British view of the time, to hang the governor in effigy or tar and feather a customs officer could be thought of as mere exuberance; but to destroy valuable property was to call in question the fundamentals of society. And this was an act of the whole city of Boston, not of a handful of rioters. Eight thousand Bostonians had been at the town meeting on December 16 from which the "Indians" had emerged. Hundreds in slender disguise had boarded the vessels. John Hancock and Samuel Adams were believed to have organized the raid and were even rumored to have joined in it. Not one resident of all the city of Boston was willing to step forward and identify any member of the mob. The city was bold and united in its insolence.

British patience was at an end. Such an act, following on years of British retreat, inflamed even North's phlegmatic anger. Frustrated by the conspiracy of silence from seizing the actual vandals, the British were determined to punish the city and colony that harbored them. For the first time in decades of controversy with the colonies Britain responded to truculent resistance with force rather than with concession.

There were a few leaders in Britain who in the midst of fury over the destruction of the tea still kept their eyes fixed on the preservation of the empire and the restoration of good relations with the colonies. Chatham, though outraged by the Boston episode, counseled against reprisals upon the whole city or colony. So too did Edmund Burke. But to no avail were their Cassandra-like warnings. Parliament was first officially notified of the Tea Party when it reconvened on March 7, 1774. Within three weeks the ministry had drawn and rushed through Commons the Boston Port Bill. This was the immediate punishment of the city of Boston itself. It closed the port to all trade, inbound and outbound, except for military stores for the British troops and such shipments of food and fuel as might be specifically approved by the customs officers. This law was to go into effect June 1 and to remain in effect until the destroyed tea should be paid for, duty and all. Since Boston lived by trade, this law would be a death blow to the city. Suggestions that so drastic a penalty await further investigation and an opportunity for the city to make voluntary payment for the tea were brushed aside. Britain's long-simmering fury was now at full boil.

Once driven to decisive action, Parliament moved rapidly to reinforce its position in the colonies. Three additional bills were enacted on May 20. One carried into effect the long-discussed reorganization of the Massachusetts government. This Massachusetts Government Act was sweeping. After its effective dates, the council, heretofore elected by the lower house, would be appointed by the King to serve during his pleasure. The judges of the Supreme Court (the colony's highest) would be appointed by the King on the governor's nomination. All other judges, including the justices of the peace, and the attorney general and all sheriffs were to be appointed by the governor. All would serve during his or the King's pleasure. The sheriff, now the governor's man, would summon juries, thus controlling their membership. Town meetings were forbidden, except for one each year solely to elect town officers. Any other meetings could be held only with the governor's permission and could deal only with such matters as the governor had approved.

This act was far more sweeping in its implications than the act closing the port of Boston. It had hitherto been held that a charter issued by the King under the Great Seal was a solemn compact that could be voided or amended only by mutual consent or by an action at law based on a violation of the charter. In many of the colonies the residents relied upon a similar charter as the guarantor of their rights. Yet Parliament here asserted a right to amend or abrogate the Massachusetts charter at will. If this were tolerated, other charters as well were meaningful only to the degree that Parliament wished them to be. Moreover, the character of the amendments almost totally stripped Massachusetts of its long-held freedom. The assembly could still meet, but its power to legislate and to give or withhold taxes had little purpose if Parliament could legislate at will with respect to internal Massachusetts matters and could tax at will and use the revenue to pay local officials. Recourse to the courts was of little value if the Crown controlled judge and sheriff and jury. Even the slight protection of such courts was further lessened by a companion act that permitted any British or colonial official sued for acts performed in the execution of his duties to have his case removed to Britain for trial upon request of the governor and council.

In its burst of energy Parliament at the same time resolved the long-pending questions of the government of Canada and of the Old Northwest—the territory north of the Ohio and lying between the Appalachian Mountains and the Mississippi. The Quebec Act, approved on the same day (May 20, 1774) as the Massachusetts Government Act and the Administration of Justice Act, adopted and continued French patterns of government in Canada. The Catholic Church was recognized; legislative power was placed in an appointed, not an elected, assembly; French civil law prevailed, including trials without jury. More ominous to the older colonies was the definition of Quebec's boundaries to include the vast stretch of land north of the Ohio River and running westward from the mountains to the Mississippi. No doubt the British ministry thought of this act as essentially unrelated to the Boston tea controversy. No doubt it intended, in the references to the territory now comprising Ohio, Indiana, Illinois, and Michigan, only to provide a temporary pattern of administration until the country should be sufficiently settled to support a more regularly organized government. Indeed, the act itself contained a rather ambiguous clause disclaiming any intention of depriving existing colonies of their charter rights over the Western lands.

The Quebec Act, however, was not seen in this light by the American colonists. It seemed to them that most of what they had fought for and won in the French and Indian Wars was being surrendered. To open the Western lands to American settlement, to orient the rich fur trade toward Albany and western Pennsylvania rather than toward Montreal, to protect the West from the arbitrary government and the popery of French Canada, and to make it a free, Protestant, American land—these were the objects for which the colonists had fought for nine years, and, so it would seem, in vain. Instead the Western lands would be closed to them and would be placed under the control of a government at Montreal that continued the autocratic and Catholic traditions of the old enemy.

The determination that lay behind these acts was further shown by the dispatch of additional regiments of British regular troops to Boston, bringing the total to six. A Quartering Act, enacted June 2, 1774, revived the earlier provision of the Mutiny Act requiring the colonies to provide quarters for British troops, but added a requirement, infuriating to the colonists, permitting the billeting of troops in private homes if other quarters were not available.

Moreover, the commander of the British troops, General Gage, was commissioned as the governor of Massachusetts, succeeding Hutchinson. In a sense, this put Massachusetts under martial law. Henceforward the Bostonians, unlike the colonists at the time of the Stamp Act, would be dealing with no lone civilian governor whose only power lay in a dying respect for royal authority. They would be confronting a governor whose word could command a military force far more powerful than any that had ever existed in America in peace.

There was no doubt about it: the Boston Port Bill could be and would be enforced, as the Stamp Act could not.

It was North's strategy to single out the port of Boston and the colony of Massachusetts for punishment, hoping that the other colonies would not join to make a common cause as they had in 1765. If his expectations had been realized, Boston must have succumbed, and the whole history of the period might have taken a different turn. And well those expectations might have been realized. The New Englanders in general and the Bostonians in particular were not a popular lot in the other colonies. They had a reputation for killjoy Puritanism, for sharp dealing, for a querulous sea lawyer's insistence on the last detail of their rights, for an ungenteel and uncouth "leveling" of social class. Anglicans were vexed by their religion; the gentry were annoyed by their democratic manners; and men of property everywhere were shocked by their destruction of the tea. There was a considerable feeling that the Boston hotheads were getting what was coming to them and that their anxious communications were an effort to get other colonies to pull their own rashly thrown chestnuts from the fire.

This sentiment might have prevailed a half dozen, or even three or four, years earlier. But in the meantime two things had happened. Samuel Adams, the principal organizer of Revolutionary sentiment in Boston, had led the setting up of a Committee of Correspondence of the Boston Town Meeting in the autumn of 1772. This committee drew up eloquent, indeed fiery, statements of the rights of the colonists and of British violations of them. Though founded primarily to unite the Massachusetts towns on local issues—particularly the acceptance by colonial officials of royal salaries—the system of committees of correspondence rapidly spread on an intercolonial basis. Not only other towns in Massachusetts but also other colonies as well formed their own committees. By the time the Tea Party became known up and down the coast, almost every colony had its committee, engaged in busy correspondence with radical leaders throughout its own towns and counties and with those of every other colony. Although the leaders of the several colonies except those who had met as delegates to the Stamp Act Congress in 1765 were still largely unknown to each other, an intercolonial Revolutionary party was beginning to emerge by 1774, organized on the basis of these committees of correspondence and prepared to act in common.

The other development was the outpouring of propaganda

representing the views of the colonial radicals. The radicals, or Whigs, in the colonies were unlike most revolutionary parties in that they controlled rather than opposed all the local organs of government and society. They dominated the colonial legislatures, managed the principal newspapers, spoke from the pulpits of most of the churches. Radical ideas could and did find expression in resolutions of the assemblies and town meetings. Newspaper columns were filled with contributions signed with antique Roman pseudonyms—"Publius," "Agricola," "Audax" —setting forth patriotic views. These were repeated, at least from Congregational and Presbyterian pulpits, in many a fiery sermon. In every colony by 1774 a "radical," or Whig, position had been defined and was well known at least to the lawyers, merchants, clergymen, and large landowners who were the colonial leaders. Essentially this position was that the historic relation of Britain and the colonies as it had existed prior to 1763 could be altered only by mutual consent. The colonials were convinced that Parliament intended to alter this relation radically, first by taxing the colonies directly and then by using the proceeds for paying officials, for maintaining troops, and for carrying on other operations in the colonies not authorized by their assemblies. And they were determined that these parliamentary innovations must not be recognized or obeyed, even if that policy led to violence.

The view had also grown that this was an intercolonial problem, in which the residents of all the colonies shared the same rights and faced the same threats. The success of united action in meeting the Stamp Act and the Townshend Acts was remembered. At the same time, it was recognized that an aggressive British policy permitted to succeed in one colony would afford both precedent and encouragement for its extension to others.

The apprehensive leaders of the committees of correspondence had hitherto had little concrete evidence to justify their views to the populace. Whatever the British theories set forward in the Declaratory Act and attempted in the Stamp Act and the Townshend Acts, in practice the relations of the colonies and the mother country had been little changed. But the series of Intolerable Acts following the Tea Party forced the issue once and for all. Clearly, unmistakably, and with superior force to back its purpose, Parliament had determined sweepingly and unilaterally to alter the whole pattern of imperial relations with Massachusetts and with the West, and through the West with almost every colony. The problem was now so clear and so exigent that none could deny it. It had to be met, to be met immediately, and to be met jointly.

The way of meeting it was the Continental Congress, which convened at Philadelphia on September 5, 1774. Massachusetts had wanted more immediate action and had responded to the Boston Port Act, before the other Intolerable Acts were known in America, with an appeal for a prompt nonimportation agreement. The impulse to meet and confer before adopting any such measure was felt, however, throughout the colonies. Rhode Island, Pennsylvania, and New York issued unofficial calls for a congress even in May; the Massachusetts legislature formally proposed one in June. As news of the Intolerable Acts came in during the summer, all the other colonies save Georgia joined in and by either official or irregular action named delegates. The colonies had entered on the road to union as well as to independence.

The delegates who met in Philadelphia on September 5 were a remarkable group of men. Among their fifty-six members were many of the men who were to be the creators of the American nation—John Adams and his cousin Samuel, from Massachusetts; Silas Deane, from Connecticut; John Jay, from New York; William Livingston, from New Jersey; Thomas Mifflin and John Dickinson, from Pennsylvania; Caesar Rodney, from Delaware; John Rutledge and Christopher Gadsden, from South Carolina; Peyton Randolph, Benjamin Harrison, Richard Henry Lee, Edmund Pendleton, Patrick Henry, Richard Bland, and George Washington, from Virginia. They were sober and responsible men, most of them of extraordinary ability, leaders in their own colonies, many of them men who hazarded great wealth, and all of them men who hazarded high position on the outcome of their dangerous move. Nine of them had served in the Stamp Act Congress, but for most of them their sojourn in Philadelphia was their first chance to meet the like-minded leaders of other colonies, or indeed to confront any public problem beyond the internal administration of their own colonies.

It is fortunate that the Congress took place in so wealthy, urbane, and hospitable a city as Philadelphia. The sessions sat from nine until three daily, and the afternoons and evenings were given over largely to wining and dining among the delegates. They sat at formal dinners in the great houses of Philadelphia merchants, and two by two over ale and tobacco at the back tables of taverns. Connecticut dined with Carolina, and Massachusetts wined with Virginia. The Adamses and their colleagues made it a special object to come to know the Southern delegates and be known to them and to avert so far as possible the suspicion of their angular and Puritan radicalism. In the relaxed atmosphere of Philadelphia, not only were many of the issues confronting the first Continental Congress resolved in amity, but there began to be formed a loose fraternity of men who knew, understood, and trusted one another. In less than two years they would be willing to pledge to each other their lives, their fortunes, and their sacred honor in a hazard for independence itself; and this group of men, growing and changing in membership, but maintaining a continuity of association, would create the United States of America.

The issues that confronted the delegates gathered in Philadelphia were difficult, but essentially simple in conception. They all were agreed that the rights of the colonies were grievously violated by the Intolerable Acts and that the recent course of the British government threatened even more extensive violations. They were all agreed that they should join in action to stop this course. But how were the rights of the colonists to be defined? And did they enjoy these rights because the charters of the colonies guaranteed them? Or because, as Englishmen, they were protected by the British Constitution? Or because, as men, they enjoyed natural rights that were the proper due of all men? What measures should they take to persuade or compel Great Britain to cease violating colonial rights? What solutions, if any, should they undertake to offer of the very real problems of imperial organization? And if Britain persisted in her course, what then?

In the eyes of conservative patriots, who might be as indignant as the radicals over the recent British acts, the rights violated by those acts were rights the colonists enjoyed precisely because they *were* Englishmen and hence subject to the King-in-Parliament. The problem was not to sever or diminish the imperial connection but to fashion a better one that would enable the colonies and Great Britain to achieve a closer and juster union. The radicals, on the other hand, had come to believe that Parliament had no proper powers whatever over the colonies, which in their view were separate realms united only by a common allegiance to the King. They were determined to reject the parliamentary pretensions outright. In their own minds, and in their private confidences with one another, some of them were beginning to face the question of what they must do if the Crown chose to place its majesty and force behind the claims of Parliament and make it impossible to resist the Commons without warring on the King. But for the moment the radicals were as fervent as the conservatives in protesting their fidelity to George III.

The radicals gained an early advantage by laying before the Congress resolutions adopted by a meeting of the citizens of Suffolk County, Massachusetts—the county in which Boston lay. These were quite literally revolutionary in that they not only urged resistance to the Intolerable Acts as unconstitutional but also recommended that an essentially independent government be set up in Massachusetts that should collect the taxes and control the militia. The endorsement of these Suffolk Resolves by Congress set the tone for its later actions.

The crucial issue in defining the rights of the colonists was the extent of Parliament's authority to regulate trade. It was difficult to deny a power that had been exercised, and acquiesced in, for more than a century. It was doubly difficult in view of the fact that John Dickinson and other spokesmen for the colonial cause had always fully conceded Parliament's power to legislate for the general concerns, and especially the commercial concerns, of the empire. Yet the logic of Dickinson's position was uncomfortable. Almost all colonists, radical and conservative alike, agreed in denying the propriety of Parliament's taxing the colonies when they were not represented in it. But if there were no legitimate basis for taxation, whence did Parliament derive any power to legislate at all? Taxation had been singled out as an issue because it had historically been an issue between King and Commons in Great Britain. But then the question had been where sovereignty resided within the realm; now the question was the altogether different one of what were the boundaries of the realm over which this sovereignty extended. It could well be argued that in its relations with the Crown Parliament had certain powers and lacked others; but it could hardly be argued that some of the powers Parliament undoubtedly had within Great Britain stopped at the water's edge and others extended to the colonies.

The inconsistency of the colonists' earlier positions had been resolved in the thinking of the more advanced writers by 1774. James Wilson of Pennsylvania, later to be a Justice of the Supreme Court, had treated the subject most systematically in his pamphlet *Considerations on the Nature and Extent of the Legislative Authority of the British Parliament*, and Thomas Jefferson had done so even more eloquently in his *Summary View of the Rights of British America*. Both these writers concluded that Parliament had *no* powers with respect to the colonies. They asserted that the several colonies were in fact totally independent of Great Britain and constituted, like Hanover or like Scotland before the Act of Union, separate realms sharing nothing but a common allegiance to the person of the King. As Wilson put it, he had undertaken his studies "with a view and expectation of being able to trace some constitutional line between those cases in which we ought, and those in which we ought not, to acknowledge the power of Parliament over us. In the prosecution of my inquiries, I became fully convinced that such a line does not exist and that there can be no medium between acknowledging and denying that power in *all* cases."

The inconsistency of this position with the century-long acceptance of the Navigation Acts and other parliamentary measures regulating trade was resolved by regarding these as the expressions of a tacit agreement, an implicit compact, between the colonies and Great Britain by which the former agreed to the regulation of their common trade by the Parliament of Great Britain. This "agreement" was thought of as having the character of an unwritten commercial treaty between Great Britain and the various colonies. (The total absence of any evidence of an actual agreement to this effect troubled the writers not at all. For nearly a century English political thinkers had been schooled by Locke to believe that all legitimate government had been founded by compact. And since actual compacts were practically never to be discovered, they were regularly inferred from the mere existence of government. It was no more difficult to infer a hypothetical commercial treaty between England and the colonies than it was to infer the primordial agreement by which savages in a state of nature had first set up government and conceded to it certain powers over their persons and property.)

This position of Wilson and Jefferson was the one adopted, though less forthrightly stated, by the Congress. In the declaration and resolves finally promulgated by the Congress, Parliament was denied any power of its own over the colonies, but the latter, with a view to the common convenience, "cheerfully consented" to the operation of Parliament's acts for the regulation of trade. The colonists now thought not of the powers of the colonial assemblies as having been conferred by Parliament, but rather of Parliament's authority over trade as having been conferred by the colonies.

There was no dispute over other "rights" of the colonists: to be tried by jury in the colonies before judges who could not be removed by the King, to assemble and petition for redress of grievances, to have no standing army in time of peace without the consent of the assembly of the colony in which quartered, and in general to enjoy all the benefits of the common law.

As an Englishman entitled to the traditional rights of the British realm, one could plead the British Constitution to limit or define the powers of Parliament. It might appear inconsistent, however, to plead that Constitution in order to deny the rights of Parliament altogether and to support the view that the colonies were no part of the very realm whose Constitution was being invoked. Those who wanted to sever all connection with Britain save for a general allegiance to the King hence wanted to avoid a dependence on the British Constitution for the defense of their rights. It was the common conviction of Locke and his disciples that all men had a natural right to their lives, their liberty, and their property that could be taken from them only by their consent or by the operation of general laws to which they had previously consented. It was upon these "natural rights," enjoyed by all men, inside or outside the British realm, that the radicals preferred to base their defense, asserting that the colonists had never conveyed to the British Parliament any power over their own lives, liberty, or property.

The matter was of great moment, quite apart from the legal advantage of one argument or another. If the American Revolution were to defend only the rights of Englishmen within the empire, its significance, no matter how great for those involved, could only be parochial. To have a universal significance the Revolution must be based on principles that would vindicate the natural right of all men everywhere to government by consent.

On this issue the Congress again compromised. Just as it had conceded Parliament's power to regulate trade in practice while denying it in theory, it asserted the natural-rights argument without abandoning arguments based on the British Constitution, the common law, and the colonial charters. On this point the final language was: ". . . the inhabitants of the English colonies in North America, by the immutable laws of nature, the principles of the English Constitution, and the several charters or compacts, have the following rights. . . ." In practice, however eloquent the appeals to natural law, the specific rights that were asserted were rights of Englishmen, developed under English law, and were defended as such.

Having defined their rights, the members of Congress must decide what course of action might best preserve them. The conservatives wished to rely primarily upon argument and persuasion, the radicals upon direct action. Again, both courses were followed. A petition to the King and an address to the British people were adopted, moderate in tone and as persuasive as the pens of John Dickinson and John Jay could make them. The radicals had little hope for the favorable reception of these, but they recognized that the colonies would not support more vigorous acts until the possibilities of persuasion were more fully explored.

Meanwhile they would put to use the weapon that had served them so well in dealing with the Stamp Act and the Townshend Acts—a breaking off of trade. But this time with a great difference. The earlier efforts were undertaken by individual colonies or ports, and usually by agreements among the merchants affected. They could be only sporadically and informally enforced. Now there was to be a Continental Association. The members of the Congress unanimously agreed that imports from Great Britain should cease on December 1, 1774, and exports thereto on September 10, 1775. Special provisions barred the imports of slaves from any source after December 1, 1774; the import of East India Company tea immediately; and the use of tea from any source after March 1, 1775. As a concession to South Carolina, the export of rice to Europe would be permitted. Committees were called for in every county to enforce the "association," and penalties were provided for its violation.

Though still called an association, the new edict of Congress was not, like earlier provisions for nonimportation, an agreement. In all but form it was a statute to which obedience would be compelled without reference to any prior agreement to observe it. The Congress had assumed for itself a legislative and governing authority. The system of enforcement committees it called for was also not to be a group of volunteers; rather, each county committee was to be elected by those qualified to vote for delegates to the assembly, and hence would exist as a formal, quasi-official body. The embryo of an independent American government was already beginning to form.

With the completion of the association and of the various petitions and addresses, the work of the first Continental Congress was at an end. It left the problem of imperial organization no nearer solution. However stumblingly British policy had been developed, it had at least recognized the necessity for a more closely integrated empire. It proposed to center the control of this empire in a Parliament that, though representing Britain alone, would extend its authority equally throughout the entire domain. In totally rejecting this policy, the Congress had united the colonies more firmly and more completely than ever before. It had, however, proposed nothing save a return to a decentralization even more complete than that existing prior to 1754. The colonies were now insisting —though they joined together to do it—that each of them was a wholly independent realm owing no subordination to Parliament or to the King's British government or indeed to any authority save the King's person. Imperial problems of Indian relations or defense were not faced; those relating to trade were somewhat superficially disposed of by conceding to Parliament, as an act of grace on the part of the colonies and not as a right, a power to regulate the trade of the empire in the interest of its members generally.

This idyllic vision of many separate and equal realms only loosely associated by personal allegiance to the King was as impossible of realization in 1774 as the British vision of a centralized union achieved by a subordination of all the colonies to the unlimited authority of Great Britain. One effort was made in the Congress to move toward the obvious solution—a closer union, but one based on equality and consent. This was advanced by Joseph Galloway, a Pennsylvania leader of great ability whose devotion to the empire matched or exceeded his concern for colonial rights. Galloway's proposal closely resembled the Albany Plan of Union of 1754 drafted by his friend Franklin. It would have created an intercolonial government consisting of a Grand Council, or legislature, chosen triennially by the colonial asemblies, and a President General appointed by the Crown. Each colony would retain its authority over its internal affairs. Imperial and intercolonial matters would be dealt with by the new bodies. The consent of both Parliament and the Grand Council would be required for any legislation affecting the colonies jointly or their relations with Great Britain.

It was a clumsy and incompletely worked-out scheme, but it was a genuine effort to achieve by consent the kinds of changes necessary to meet new imperial problems that the British were seeking to enforce unilaterally and the colonies to resist entirely. It commanded considerable support and failed of passage by only one vote. Most of the opposition no doubt came, as in the case of the earlier Albany Plan, from colonial leaders who opposed subordination of their individual colonies to any central authority, either British or American. But much of it probably came too from an attitude expressed by Franklin himself in a letter to Galloway: a growing distaste, even a disgust, for the character of the British government and British society and a questioning of the wisdom of any effort to cement the union with the mother country. As Franklin put it, ". . . when I consider the extreme corruption prevalent among all orders of men in this old, rotten state, and the glorious public virtue so predominant in our rising country, I cannot but apprehend more mischief than benefit from a closer union."

This was a view to which Franklin had been slow to come. All his public life he had cherished and worked for a vision of a great English-speaking commonwealth. Other men, less thoughtful than he, had not made their shift of view explicit even to themselves and were continuing to protest their loyalty to King and empire. But the feeling was nearly gone. If independence had not been adopted as a goal, imperial union had been nearly forgotten as one. Inertia alone held the empire together for a few months more of drift.

Meanwhile the Congress, perhaps frightened by the considerable support the Galloway plan had received, voted to expunge from its records any reference to the proposal. Galloway himself sent it to a few liberal leaders in England, either directly or through Franklin, but it commanded no enthusiasm there either.

When Congress adjourned on October 26, 1774, it was with the understanding that it would reconvene on May 10, 1775, unless meanwhile the grievances it set forth had been redressed. Such a redress would have required a total abandonment of the British program of retribution for the Boston Tea Party, an abandonment of any claim of power to tax the colonies, and an admission of the total defeat of British colonial policy. The impasse was to prove complete. Over the next year and a half the colonies would become independent, and afterward they would declare themselves so.

7 ★★★★★★★★

Independence

British response to the declaration and resolves of the first Continental Congress was foreshadowed by George III himself, who wrote Lord North on November 18, 1774: "I am not sorry that the line of conduct seems now chalked out, which the enclosed dispatches thoroughly justify; the New England governments are in a state of rebellion; blows must decide whether they are to be subject to this country or independent." Part of the blindness of the King and the ministry was that they never doubted what those blows would decide. The Britain that had in recent memory made its arms prevail from the Ohio to the Ganges and had triumphed over the greatest military power of Europe could not fear the outcome of a test of strength with the colonists. The King and his followers did not see the events of 1774 and 1775 as steps, one after another, toward the irrevocable destruction of the empire. In their eyes, there was only an exhibition of truculent and insufferable disobedience on the part of the colonists that required disciplining. The punishment would be quickly and easily administered; and after it was over, the colonists, with all the nonsense knocked out of them, would return soberly to their duty.

Not all Englishmen saw it so. Chatham, now able to resume a sporadic attendance in the House of Lords, rose to his last brilliance. He foresaw that the continued presence at Boston of the large British force under Gage would inevitably lead to armed conflict with the colonists and that once violence had broken out, any peaceful resolution of the controversy would be made vastly more difficult. And he realized that the force of those troops and thousands more like them would be totally insufficient to support an authority the Americans did not voluntarily respect. The Earl of Sandwich and the other hotheads who would bully the colonists into immediate submission saw only the British regular infantry matched against a sneered-at-mob of American hayseeds. Chatham saw that same handful of regulars facing not a farmer militia, but three million freemen and a wilderness empire of endless forest, impassable streams, unconquerable distance. "What though you march," asked he, "from town to town, and from province to province; though you should be able to enforce a temporary and local submission, which I only suppose, not admit—how shall you be able to secure the obedience of the country you leave behind you in your progress, to grasp the dominion of eighteen hundred miles of continent, populous in numbers possessing valour, liberty, and resistance?"

Chatham made two separate proposals—one for the withdrawal of troops, one for a more general settlement. The latter would have involved a disclaimer of British intention to tax the colonists without their consent, a repeal of the Boston Port Bill and the Massachusetts Government Act, a restriction of the Admiralty Courts to their traditional jurisdiction, a reassertion of the right of the colonists to trial by a jury of their neighbors, an appointment of judges during good behavior rather than at the King's pleasure, a limitation on the King's authority to use troops in America against the liberty of the colonists, and legitimizing of the Continental Congress—all conditioned on an explicit recognition of the legislative supremacy of Parliament in other matters than taxation and on a willingness of the Continental Congress to consider in good faith the granting of a perpetual revenue to be devoted by Parliament to the extinction of the national debt. There is some reason to believe that Benjamin Franklin, who still sought some mode of accommodation that would preserve the empire, and with whom Chatham had conferred, may have influenced the latter bill.

Both proposals were overwhelmingly defeated in the House of Lords and hence never came before Commons. But they would certainly have been defeated, and probably even more decisively, in the lower House as well. A new House of Commons had just been elected in 1774. The use of the royal patronage to control elections had never been so open, widespread, and effective. Even in the relatively honest elections for knights of the shire, anger over the Boston Tea Party had helped sweep into office the narrowest and most uncompromising adherents of total British supremacy. It was not a House of Commons apt to think or to act either magnanimously or wisely.

Before this House a month later, in March, Edmund Burke delivered one of the greatest speeches in British political history, his address "Conciliation with America." In language even more moving than Chatham's and with an imperial vision as splendid, Burke appealed for a magnanimous surmounting of all the matters of contention with the colonies. Though he abandoned none of the sovereign authority of Parliament, he sought the use of that power to sweep away the fears and resentments of the Americans and to unite them and the British in a joint devotion to their common and traditional liberties. He was not ready to destroy an empire in the petulant proof of a point or to press home any legal argument, no matter how well founded, that tended to divide the colonies from their ancient allegiance. "The question," Burke said, ". . . is not whether you have a right to render your people miserable, but whether it is not your interest to make them happy."

The Americans' own insistence upon their rights Burke admired as a reassertion of English freedom. He would have welcomed it as a bond between Britons and Americans. But his appeal to the Commons to "elevate our minds to the greatness of that trust to which the order of Providence has called us" was scorned. His speech was in support of resolutions that would have repealed the Intolerable Acts, restricted the Admiralty Courts, forsworn the intention (though not the right) to tax the colonists, and made evident the purpose of the British government to re-create an affectionate union. They were defeated as decisively in Commons as had been Chatham's resolution in the Lords.

Chatham's and Burke's proposals represented at most the minimum concessions that might have averted, or more probably delayed, the secession of the colonies. That Parliament was not willing to entertain the bare idea of even so modest a concession was a measure of the irreconcilable differences that already separated Britain and America.

The official reaction to the declaration of the Continental Congress was brought forward by the ministry. It consisted not only of measures to strengthen the army and navy and add to Gage's force in Boston, but also of a New England Restraining Act. This banned after July 1, 1775, all trade from New

England ports except to Britain and the British West Indies, and after July 20 excluded New Englanders from the Atlantic fisheries on which most of New England depended, directly or indirectly, for a living. This act was passed on March 20 and two weeks later was applied to New Jersey, Pennsylvania, Maryland, and South Carolina as well. In effect it extended to most of the colonies the principal strictures of the Boston Port Bill. By forcing the neighboring colonies into the same situation as Massachusetts, this action tacitly recognized the failure of North's earlier strategy of attempting to isolate the Bostonians and subdue them separately. The tendency of Parliament's course was to force the more hesitant colonies out of the empire and into union with the more belligerent.

The one concession North was prepared to offer was embodied in a resolution brought forward by the ministry in February, 1775. This would have excused any colony from parliamentary taxation that by its own legislative action adequately supported the royal officials in the colony and contributed to Britain a sum Parliament considered satisfactory. As a matter of law and theory, such an act of parliamentary grace would in fact deny all the rights for which the colonies were contending; as a practical matter, it would exact from them as much money as direct Parliamentary taxation. Even so, it was only by the use of ministerial and royal pressure that North was able to bully the measure through a sullen Parliament reluctant to offer the Americans anything but force.

Meanwhile the ministry's policy was compelling the creation of Revolutionary governments in the individual colonies. Governors were instructed to prorogue assemblies that adopted measures or undertook action in the colonial cause—such as electing delegates to the Continental Congress, ratifying the association for nonimportation, or voting Whiggish resolutions. Most of the assemblies had offended in this way, and most had been dissolved. To fill the governmental vacuum thus created, provincial congresses or other unlawful bodies met, did what was necessary in support of the colonial protest, and while doing so began to take over the ordinary functions of government as well.

Virginia had set a pattern for this type of extralegal body as early as 1769, when the House of Burgesses, after having been dissolved, met as an unofficial body to draw up a nonimportation agreement in opposition to the Townshend Acts. Now again in May, 1774, when Governor Dunmore prorogued the assembly for having voted a day of prayer and fasting to mourn the Boston Port Bill, the Burgesses met privately and drew up another nonimportation agreement. During the following year similar provincial congresses or informal bodies took over the functions of the assembly in New Hampshire, Massachusetts, New Jersey, Maryland, and North and South Carolina; and in Delaware the lawful assembly met unlawfully without the call of the governor. In Rhode Island and Connecticut no extralegal assemblies were needed, since the elected governors placed no restraints on the functioning of the lawful legislative bodies. In New York, Pennsylvania, and Georgia the constitutional assemblies were not yet displaced, but mass meetings of citizens were taking over much of the authority of government.

The provincial congresses were primarily concerned with the election of delegates to the Continental Congress and the preparation of their instructions, and with adopting the nonimportation association and setting up machinery for its enforcement. But they went beyond this, to initiate military preparations and to supply an ordinary civil government. By the time the second Continental Congress met, in May, 1775, every colony except New York, Delaware, and Georgia had begun to arm itself outside the law and the King's authority. In most of the colonies the military preparation hardly went beyond a more frequent mustering and a more active drilling of the local militia. But in Massachusetts generals were appointed, responsible not to the governor but to a committee of safety named by the provincial congress. Similar committees of safety were set up in other colonies, assuming executive authority as the congresses themselves had assumed legislative power. Preparation passed into the beginning of action in South Carolina and New Hampshire, where powder was seized from the governor's control. The New Hampshiremen captured, along with the powder, the little fort where it was stored. In Massachusetts the provincial congress as early as the summer of 1774 was levying its own taxes, to be paid into its own treasury.

Throughout the colonies in the winter of 1774-1775, government hung in suspense. In parish and town and county the local officials performed their local tasks; but in the provincial capitals the assembly halls were empty, and the governors sat powerless or were already in flight. The lawful assemblies, in which all shades of colonial opinion were represented, were not permitted to meet and give voice to colonial discontents. In this emptiness the only organized authority became that of the extralegal provincial congresses, representing only Whig, and predominantly radical Whig, views. It is hardly too much to say that power was abandoned to the radicals because of the governors' unwillingness to countenance protests through constitutional channels.

During the tense winter of waiting, the one effective expression of royal power left in the colonies—Gage's force at Boston—had been held in an uneasy restraint, closed up in a half-beleaguered city amid a seethingly hostile population. For all George III's conviction that blows must decide, nothing had been done to administer them. While North's conciliatory motion was being debated in Parliament, the ministry was forwarding instructions to Gage to take the offensive and begin action to suppress the rebellion. He responded promptly on April 19, 1775, by sending a picked force on an expedition to Concord to capture Samuel Adams and John Hancock and a store of arms and powder.

The expedition was a fiasco, or worse. An attempt at secrecy was frustrated by Paul Revere's legendary ride. More by accident than by design, a little body of farmers and villagers awaiting the British at Lexington was fired on, and a number of them were killed. The countryside arose, and after a fruitless stay at Concord, the British were harried mercilessly on a long, bloody, exhausting retreat to Boston. At day's end, the column had been driven back into the town, having suffered seventy-three dead and two hundred wounded or missing. Boston was surrounded by the local militia, augmented within days by troops from all over Massachusetts and from the other New England colonies. The British were now firmly cooped up, and their problem became one of withstanding siege rather than suppressing rebellion.

When the second Continental Congress met on May 2, 1775, it was clear that there was to be no peaceful redress of grievances. The defeat of Burke's and Chatham's measures for reconciliation, the refusal to accept the address to the King, the New England Restraining Act, and now the blood shed at Lexington and Concord gave the British answer. Behind it lay the news of British plans to strengthen the army, rebuild the navy, and devote the whole might of England to the suppression of the colonists.

The Continental Congress in turn prepared to fight. Though its membership was largely identical with that of the first Congress, there had been a shift toward the radical side. Some conservatives, like Galloway, had left. Among the new members were men eager for action, like John Hancock, Benjamin Franklin, James Wilson, and, a few weeks later, Thomas Jefferson. In three short months, between May 2 and its temporary adjournment on August 2, the Congress transformed itself from a conference of delegates into a functioning government with legislative and executive powers. On May 15 it resolved to put the colonies in a state of defense. A month later it voted to create an army of its own and adopted the troops besieging Boston into the Continental service, drew up rules for their government, and appointed George Washington their commander.

It assumed other functions as well. On June 22, a week after Washington's designation, the Congress voted to issue paper money against its own credit to pay and supply its new army, and it set up the rudiments of a treasury. Other administrative offices were created in July to take over functions formerly exercised by the British directly; an Indian Commission on July 19 and a postal service on July 26. Foreign trade was resumed at the same time to permit the import of supplies for the army.

While preparing to fight, the Congress had to deal with proposals for reconciliation and declare the colonists' position to the world. North's offer to abstain, as an act of grace, from taxing a colony so long as it taxed itself to the satisfaction of Parliament was rejected with little ceremony. A report drawn by Jefferson for a committee consisting also of John Adams, Franklin, and Richard Henry Lee damned it as "unreasonable and insidious" and totally unresponsive to the real issues. The report was approved on July 31.

The Congress' position had already been made clear in its Declaration of the Causes and Necessity of Taking Up Arms, which the conservative Dickinson and the radical Jefferson had joined in drafting and which had been unanimously adopted on July 6. This vigorous statement again set forth the colonists' grievance at being taxed and governed by a Parliament in which they were not represented. It cut through all the legal artificialities of "virtual representation" by pointing out that the interests of those actually represented in Parliament were not only different from but often in conflict with the interests of America. It recited the unheard petitions: "We for ten years incessantly and ineffectually besieged the throne as supplicants; we reasoned, we remonstrated with Parliament, in the most mild and decent language." The ministry, it pointed out, had called their protest rebellion and had sent armed forces to silence it. The colonists had been left with a choice only between total submission to British will and armed resistance to British force. They chose the latter, confident in their own strength, resources, and military experience, and hinting at the possibility of foreign aid. It was a bold statement: ". . . the arms we have been compelled by our enemies to assume, we will, in defiance of every hazard, with unabating firmness and perseverance, employ for the preservation of our liberties, being with one mind resolved to die freemen rather than to live slaves."

But even in the declaration itself the Congress was at pains to define as its goal not independence but the restoration of the traditional relation between Britain and the colonies: ". . . we mean not to dissolve that union which has so long and so happily subsisted between us, and which we sincerely wish to see restored." This sentiment was more forcefully stated in the Olive Branch Petition adopted two days later. Dickinson and other conservatives in the Congress insisted on one last appeal to the King's wisdom and sense of justice and imperial unity, and Dickinson himself drafted the petition in which it was expressed. In the humblest and most affectionate terms, the Congress implored the King to set up some mode of redressing the colonists' grievances, meanwhile suspending hostilities and repealing the more obnoxious statutes. The Adamses and many other congressmen knew this was a futile gesture; but it was nevertheless probably a wise one, since its rejection made it finally clear that there was no door left open to reconciliation. Having expressed its wish for peace and its readiness for war; having adopted an army, named a general, printed a treasury, and set committees busy providing arms, the Congress recessed on August 2 to reconvene six weeks later.

Meanwhile the war that began at Lexington was continuing. A handful—or two handfuls—of irregular troops, one under Benedict Arnold commissioned by Massachusetts and one a group of Vermont frontiersmen under Ethan Allan, took the crumbling and barely held British fort at Ticonderoga early in May. This gave the colonies control of the key point on the route between Canada and New York and provided them with badly needed cannon. A month later, on June 19, 1775, there was an exceedingly bloody skirmish over Breed's Hill and Bunker Hill, overlooking Boston on the Charlestown peninsula.

The British drove the colonists out of hasty fortifications they had thrown up in an effort to seize a vantage point from which to shell Boston. But the British success was at so heavy a cost in dead and wounded as to demonstrate nothing but the impossibility of fighting their way out of the city.

Both the colonists and the British were beginning to realize by midsummer that they were facing a general war rather than a local action to enforce order in Boston. Neither had any carefully worked-out strategy. The American goals were simple: to drive the British troops from Boston and to capture the lightly defended posts at Quebec and Montreal. Control of the latter might bring the little Canadian settlements into the American union and would protect the colonies from attack along the Champlain-Hudson route so often fought over by the British and French in their imperial wars.

Two attacks were mounted against Canada. Troops from General Schuyler's northern New York forces under the immediate command of Richard Montgomery were sent against Montreal. Benedict Arnold with a thousand men set out on an expedition of almost incredible hardship, traversing the Maine wilderness of lake and river and tangled forest in order to attack Quebec from the rear. Schuyler's advance began in late August, 1775, Arnold's in mid-September. Montgomery's rapid progress led Sir Guy Carleton, the able British general, to abandon Montreal and concentrate his little force in Quebec. The Americans occupied the former post on November 13, just as Arnold, with seven hundred staggering, half-starved men left of his thousand, emerged from the wilderness and crossed the St. Lawrence to attack Quebec. The two commanders joined forces and made an assault on December 31. It was beaten back in a violent snowstorm; Montgomery was killed and Arnold badly wounded. Though the American troops continued a halfhearted siege for some months longer, the effort was given up in early May, 1776.

The few hundreds of men playing out this drama in the wintry Canadian wilderness affected history profoundly. Had the New Years' Eve assault on Quebec been successful, Canada might have been drawn into the American cause and been a fourteenth state in the new nation. Carleton's narrowly won victory was not only a substantial immediate setback for the Americans; in the long run, it turned out to have preserved the possibility of a separate Canadian nationality.

British efforts at an offensive turned out no better than the American. Obviously it was hopeless to launch an attack from

Boston itself. The royal governors of the Southern colonies believed that the Revolutionary infection in their provinces went far less deep than in New England and that thousands of loyal subjects were prepared to join the British standard if given encouragement and support. General Clinton, who had been added to Gage's staff along with generals Howe and Burgoyne, shared their view. He was ordered south in February, 1776, with a contingent of the Boston forces and with the support of a large naval detachment to attack the Carolinas. Loyalist uprisings were to be timed to coincide. This was basically a sound plan; but like many British military plans during the war to come, it failed from an excessive reliance on largely mythical loyalist forces, an unwillingness or inability to provide enough British ships and troops, and poor coordination between British generals and admirals.

In North Carolina, Governor Martin relied on the loyalty of Highland Scots newly settled in the area near what is now Fayetteville. The Scots were to rise and fight their way to Wilmington to join the British forces. Rise they did, but were soundly defeated by Whig militia at the Battle of Moore's Creek Bridge on February 27, 1776, with the result that the projected British landing had to be abandoned. The British fleet and troops then moved on Charleston. The Congress, anticipating this strategy, had already raised Continental troops for the defense of South Carolina and sent General Charles Lee to command them. The successful fortification of Sullivan's Island at the entrance to Charleston Harbor, erroneous charts, and blundering coordination of British military and naval elements enabled the colonists to beat back the British with heavy loss on June 26-28. The British assault on the South, like the colonists' on Canada, ended in complete failure.

But the Americans won at Boston. Over the winter of 1775–1776 the siege grew tighter and tighter. Daring American whaleboat raids took off the cattle from the harbor islands from under the noses of the British. The tight land blockade kept out fresh food, and the British troops were confined to a scant and monotonous diet. Wood was even scarcer, and houses had to be torn down to provide fuel for the meager fires of a bitter winter. Lexington, Concord, and Bunker Hill had proved that it was fruitless to try to break out against the Yankee fortifications barring the few exits from Boston. Only pride, not military judgment, kept the British army uselessly immured in Boston over the winter.

Pride itself received a blow at winter's end. A bold American scheme was made to use the guns of Ticonderoga. They were too heavy for wagon wheels and axles; but as soon as the snows covered the long roads through the Green Mountains and the Berkshires from Lake Champlain to Boston, oxen were lashed to heavy sleds on which the guns were mounted. Henry Knox, a man still in his twenties, led the appallingly difficult winter march. By early March the guns, unbelievably, were at Boston. With silent surprise the Americans placed them overnight on Dorchester Heights, where they commanded Boston and the British ships in the harbor. The game was up. General Howe, who had succeeded Gage upon the latter's recall in October, 1775, loaded his men and their loyalist supporters on British transports and on March 17, 1776, evacuated the city. At first it was feared that he had moved to attack New York, and hasty efforts were made to fortify that city. But in fact he had retreated to the British base at Halifax, there to rest, reinforce, and await orders.

While the principal campaigns were under way, the British engaged in harassing actions that embittered the colonists without otherwise affecting the results. The fleet bombed and burned coastal towns, of which the principal were Falmouth (now Portland, Maine) and Norfolk. In Virginia Governor Dunmore made a foolish effort to free slaves and arm them against their masters. In hundreds of local communities loyalists and rebels had begun the bitter struggles that flamed up destructively here and there throughout the following years. Rarely were there pitched battles like that of Moore's Creek Bridge. The conflict was fought out in barn-burnings and ambushes, property seizures and tar-and-featherings; but from them came the bloodiest hands and the deepest hatreds of the war.

The British aggravated the bitterness and the sense of decisive separation in other ways. In August, 1775, came a proclamation that the colonists were in rebellion, which amounted to a declaration of war. Along with news of this action the colonies learned that the humble Olive Branch Petition had not even been received by the King, much less thoughtfully considered.

Perhaps the most embittering experience was learning of the ministry's decision to hire German mercenaries—or more properly to buy them from their princes—to use against the colonists. This was a necessity to which Britain was put by the reluctance of Englishmen themselves to volunteer for service against their fellow countrymen. But it was a humiliating necessity. The King's approaches to Russia and the Netherlands to obtain troops were rejected with contempt. The more liberal and decent element in Parliament was revolted at the contract—little better than slave peddling—finally made with the ruler of Hesse-Cassel. And the Americans were shocked and deeply angered. The King himself, to whom but recently they had solemnly and almost reverently pledged their affectionate loyalty, had not only spurned their petitions but had hired foreigners, alien to every idea of English liberty, to assault them, his own subjects.

While the fighting was going on, independent governments were taking form in the individual colonies. Even before Lexington and Concord the royal governors were left with only a shadow of power, if any at all, and provincial congresses had almost everywhere succeeded the lawful assemblies. During the year following the outbreak of hostilities, however, the colonies were compelled to go much further and to set up executive departments, military forces, and treasuries to meet the daily necessities of government and in particular to defend themselves against the threats of invasion that menaced the entire coast. In the midst of actual or potential armed conflict, the remaining instruments of royal government were necessarily swept away.

During the six months following the battle of Lexington, almost every vestige of Britain's power beyond musket range of the troops at Boston simply collapsed. Governor Martin of North Carolina began the exodus of royal governors in April, 1775, fleeing first to Wilmington, then to a tiny royal fort, and thence to a British warship. He was followed during the summer by Dunmore of Virginia, Wentworth of New Hampshire, Tryon of New York, and Campbell of South Carolina. By the autumn of 1775 the only royal governors still at their posts were Wright, who remained powerless in the little frontier settlement that was Georgia, and William Franklin, Benjamin Franklin's son and governor of New Jersey, whose father's popularity protected him so long as he remained quietly at Perth Amboy and did not attempt to exercise authority. Wright was to flee just after the turn of the year, and Franklin to be seized by the colonial militia in the spring.

The proprietary governors—Penn in Pennsylvania and Delaware and Eden in Maryland—were able to remain until the formal declaration of independence, but only because both of them cherished a tacit sympathy and an affectionate relationship with the colonists and because neither of them made any real effort to stay the course of revolutionary developments. In the two charter colonies, Governor Trumbull of Connecticut put himself actively at the head of the Revolutionary movement; but Governor Wanton of Rhode Island, even though popularly elected rather than royally appointed, was suspended from office by the Revolutionary movement when he refused to sign commissions or execute documents that did not recognize royal authority.

The authority of the governors was taken over by the already established committees of safety. By the end of the summer of 1775 each of the colonies had a functioning Revolutionary government. Except where the assembly was still able to sit as an effective legislature for the Revolutionary movement, provincial congresses were now meeting regularly. Their election was becoming formalized, and they were assuming an even more general legislative authority. In North Carolina a system of district committees was set up to govern the colony, and local and county committees were created in other provinces.

By the autumn of 1775 the colonies were beginning to regularize these expedients. The Revolutionary organs that had been set up to deal with an immediate crisis were being reshaped to serve as continuing governments. Massachusetts, acting on the advice of the Continental Congress, resumed its government under the old charter, adopting the procedures normally followed when the governor's chair was vacant. By December New Hampshire had moved to adopt a formal constitution, and two months later South Carolina followed its example.

While new governments were forming in the individual colonies to fill the place of the old, the Continental Congress was taking over more and more of the intercolonial and imperial responsibilities of the Parliament. When it had adjourned in August, 1775, it already had an army, a general, a treasury, a currency, a post office, and an Indian Commission. When it reconvened in September it set to work to authorize a navy, at first only to provide a modest support to the army in combined operations. On November 9 it learned of the rejection of the Olive Branch Petition, and thenceforward it moved rapidly toward all-out war. Almost immediately the new navy was authorized to attack and capture British vessels, thus threatening an aggressive action beyond American soil. The following March, privateering was authorized. This act permitted the large New England fleet of fishing vessels and fast merchant ships and its vigorous population of seamen—all left unemployed by the British blockade and the closing of the fisheries to Americans—to find a new and profitable trade preying on British shipping. This action presented a far graver threat to the British than the earlier authorization of naval attacks.

The more noteworthy actions were political, however. On November 29 the Congress set up a "Committee of Correspondence" whose secret function was to open negotiations with France and with any other interested powers. This action was clearly treasonable if the colonists were still to be thought of as subjects, and was clearly in conflict with the last summer's unheeded protestations of loyalty to the crown. A week later the Congress formally disavowed its allegiance to Parliament, though not yet to the King.

A year after the battles of Lexington and Concord the colonies were in fact independent. No royal governor held office anywhere in their territories. Save in isolated frontier posts, no British troops were on their soil. Nowhere, from Maine to Georgia, was there an officer who could enforce the King's will. All the actual power of government was entirely in the hands of the colonists. British authority had been completely overthrown.

During that spring the colonists had to decide what to do with their unexpected success. They had meant only to reform the exercise of British power and had discovered that that power had existed in the colonies all along only by their acquiescence. The authority of Crown and Parliament was created by American loyalty, not by British force. When the loyalty was withdrawn, the authority vanished. With hardly an effort, the colonists had rid themselves entirely of the sovereignty they had sought only to limit.

They now faced a fundamental decision. Should they be prepared to accept the return of royal authority, subject to the limits that had existed prior to 1763, or should they assert and maintain their almost accidentally won independence? This was the question debated through the winter and spring of 1776. If the colonists had had a choice between a peaceful return to their earlier isolation within the empire and a war to sustain their independence, there can be no doubt that gladly and almost unanimously they would have chosen peace and union.

But that was not the choice Great Britain offered. Unless the colonists were prepared to surrender their claims of right abjectly and accept the total supremacy of an alien Parliament over their lives and fortunes, they had a war to fight in any case. If they lost, it would be Britain that defined the terms of its supremacy. But if they won, or if they forced such a stalemate that Britain abandoned the struggle, how should the Americans define their terms—autonomy within the empire, or independence?

The forces for autonomy within the empire were strong. They included, most of all, habit: the generations-bred loyalty of the English-descended to the Crown and to the name and ways of England. To the colonists, even the most radical of them, "England" meant not only the stamp tax and the Declaratory Act and the tea duty—not only Lexington and Concord and Bunker Hill—but the Magna Charta, the common law, the Protestant faith, the bulwarked freedom building from precedent to precedent down the centuries. It still symbolized the island unity, banded together against the Catholic French and the haughty Spanish. These bonds of tradition and loyalty were not easy to break.

There were those too who feared the isolation of a weak new nation on the wilderness edge, unprotected by the British fleet and arms amid the swirling imperial conflicts of the century. There were even those who found the constraints of the Navigation Act and other bonds of the mercantile system a reassuring guarantee of a fixed, if limited, place in the great European economic pattern.

Even more compelling were the fears of those who saw in British law and authority their protection against the leveling cupidity of the landless and the debtors. The mobs that tarred and feathered the stamp agents, ransacked the houses of the Boston great, poured good tea into Boston harbor, and even now, all up and down the coast, were beginning to confiscate Tory lands and goods were to many conservative souls the heralds of anarchy. What floodings of paper money to wipe out an honest lender's capital, what stay laws to halt the foreclosures and executions by which he might hope to collect, what evasive bankruptcy laws, what simple mob rule might not be expected once the colonies were cut loose from the restraints of Crown and Parliament!

And finally there was the fear of Britain itself. From their victories in the Seven Years' War, the British armed forces still retained great prestige. The more apprehensive of the colonists were appalled at the risks that had been taken in defying British authority and driving the King's troops from Boston. And there were probably few indeed who did not view somberly and anxiously the prospect of all-out war with Britain. If independence were the colonists' announced goal, every resource of the British Crown must be used to its utmost to crush them. If they maintained a struggle to achieve limited ends, perhaps it could be waged with limited means, and the ultimate horrors of an unrestricted war could be avoided.

But it was the necessities of the war itself that cut through these arguments. Whatever the colonists' goal, there was a major war before them. It could not be fought with vaguely defined purposes. Men and resources could not be mustered to fight through the bitter years with stalemate and negotiation the only object. The institutions to govern the country, mobilize its resources, recruit, train, and supply its armies, and organize its war effort could not be extemporized on a tentative basis. To work, they had to be the institutions of a government that had forthrightly declared its reality and perseverance. And perhaps most realistically of all, the French and Spanish aid that the colonists would need to win and for which they were already negotiating might well be given to a determined effort to sever the British empire, but not to an effort merely to gain freedom within it.

All these issues were clearly put to the Americans in a remarkable book published in January, 1776, *Common Sense,* by Thomas Paine. Paine was a previously almost unknown English radical in his thirties, a self-educated editor who had been only two years in America. He brought a wholly new point of view to the controversy over independence. Even the more radical colonists, when they spoke of independence at all, had hitherto set it forth as a last alternative to which they should turn only reluctantly and only after Great Britain's actions should have left them no other course. In Paine's view, however, independence was no evil to which the Americans might be forced, but a positive good that they should eagerly seize while they had the chance.

He boldly and buoyantly attacked all the sentiments that stood in the way of independence—filial loyalty to the King, anxiety for continued British protection, fear of British arms. Royalty itself, Paine held, was a fraud imposed on mankind, and George III but a crowned ruffian who had forced his ministers to their anti-American acts rather than having been misled by them and who by hostile acts against the colonists had destroyed his every claim upon their loyalty. British protection in the imperial wars he dismissed as having been useful only to British interests, and he asserted that the colonists had indeed been dragged into these wars in the first place only to serve Britain's imperial purposes, not their own. British power was in decay, he held, and in any event could never hope to triumph across a vast ocean against the united force of ardent American freemen, who, once they had claimed their independence, would undoubtedly have French and Spanish aid.

Independence was bound to come; it was impossible to conceive a vast and growing continent forever bound to a small and distant island. No time better to seize it than now, said Paine, when it was already half won and the colonies were united. Already lives and fortunes had been spent in resisting British tyranny, but a little more and independence would be won. To settle now for half concessions from a reluctant Britain would merely postpone a final reckoning, and the whole thing would be to do over. ". . . for God's sake, let us come to a final separation," pleaded Paine, "and not leave the next generation to be cutting throats. . . ."

And once independence came, Paine foresaw the brightest of futures for an America freed from the burdens of British economic and political control, no longer drawn into Britain's remote European quarrels, and able to make untrammeled use of its own abundant resources. Reconciliation having in any case been made impossible by the bloody encounters of the preceding months, the colonies should boldly seize the golden chance before them and press on to independence.

Here was none of the rather arid legalism that had characterized all previous colonial writing on the imperial controversy—no lawyer's distinction between taxation and trade regulation, no summoning of dusty precedents, no appeals to the British Constitution, indeed no argument as to legal rights. The plain common sense of the matter, Paine pointed out, was that the colonists had broken from Britain and willy-nilly had a war to fight. They would be freer, happier, and wealthier if they were rid of British rule entirely; and the war would be easier to win if fought for independence rather than merely for some improvement in the terms of the bond. Paine's arguments were not drawn from Coke or Locke, but from a practical weighing of advantages to the colonies.

Yet to this practical calculation he brought a noble fervor:

"The sun never shined on a cause of greater worth. 'Tis not the affair of a city, a county, a province, or a kingdom, but of a continent. . . . 'Tis not the concern of a day, a year, or an age; posterity are virtually involved in the contest, and will be more or less affected, even to the end of time, by the proceedings now." The response was electric. In the first dozen weeks of its issuance, one hundred and twenty thousand copies of the pamphlet had been sold and passed from hand to hand to reach a high proportion of all literate Americans. It brought the issue of independence clearly into the open and helped to force the several colonies to decision during the spring of 1776.

The first colony to act formally was North Carolina, whose provincial congress on April 12, 1776, authorized its delegates to the Continental Congress to vote for independence. On May 15 Virginia went a step further and directed its representatives to introduce a resolution declaring the colonies independent. On June 7 Richard Henry Lee obeyed that instruction by moving in the Continental Congress that "these united colonies are, and of right ought to be, free and independent states." The New England colonies had long been impatient for such action but had prudently awaited Southern leadership. South Carolina remained divided, but in March had adopted a new frame of government that implied independence; and the little settlement in Georgia had been spurred to complete support by the British bombardment of Savannah.

The difficulty was with the Middle colonies. Congress deferred action on the Lee motion until these commonwealths could reach their decision. The key was Pennsylvania, largest of the colonies and seat of the Congress. High property qualifications and a heavily disproportionate representation of the older eastern counties, coupled with the disfranchisement or political apathy of the large German population, left control of the assembly in the hands of conservative Anglicans firm in their loyalty to Britain and of pacifist Quakers who opposed independence as a step to war. Yet, probably because the proprietary governor had no power to prorogue or prevent the meeting of the assembly, it had managed to remain as the effective legislative body and had not been superseded by a provincial congress. The assembly was dominated by leaders like John Dickinson, the author of the *Farmer* letters, and Robert Morris, later to be the financier of the Revolution, whose devotion to colonial rights was unquestioned but who were strongly opposed to independence. The assembly in November, 1775, had instructed delegates to the Continental Congress to oppose independence, and on April 4, 1776, repeated the directive.

Whigs throughout the colony were incensed and moved to abolish the assembly as a relic of British government and as unrepresentative, in spite of concessions that the majority had made toward larger representation of the western counties. They were strengthened by resolutions of the Continental Congress urging the renouncing of vestiges of royal authority in the colonies. Mass meetings were held urging the overthrow of the assembly, and its leaders finally surrendered to the pressure. On June 14, as its last act, the assembly left the delegates free to vote on independence as their judgment decreed.

At almost the same time (June 11), a new provincial congress met in New Jersey. The shift in sentiment in the colony was reflected in the radical control of that body, which immediately sent to Philadelphia a new delegation ardent for independence. Delaware remained under the influence of its fellow proprietary colony, Pennsylvania, and like it, approached the crisis in a divided mind. In New York alone did instructions to the congressional delegates opposing independence remain in effect.

In the meantime Congress was hurried along by a massive tide of sentiment for independence. Newspaper correspondents, pamphleteers, and Whig parsons up and down the coast hammered home the arguments of Paine and others that the die had already been cast, that no return to the pre-1763 days was possible or desirable, and that the colonists had little to fear and everything to hope for from the independent status that had, in effect, been thrust upon them. By the time of Lee's motion Congress itself had declared independence in all but name. The previous winter it had formally renounced any obligation to obey acts of Parliament; in April, 1776, it opened the ports of the colonies to trade with all powers; on May 10 it advised the commonwealths that had not done so to establish their own independent governments; and on May 15 it urged the omission of all indications of royal authority from oaths, commissions, and other public forms and documents.

When Lee's motion was called up for debate, its approval was assured, though four colonies remained hesitant: Delaware, New York, Pennsylvania, and South Carolina. The South Carolina delegation reluctantly came around on July 2; Caesar Rodney made a dramatic night ride to break a tie in the Delaware delegation and permit its vote for independence; John Dickinson and Robert Morris absented themselves so that they

Faneuil Hall served Boston as a meeting-place for patriot groups throughout the Revolutionary period. This 1776 engraving is by John C. McRae.

(Culver Pictures, Inc.)

Federal Hall, New York, in the Lacour-Doolittle view. Formerly (and subsequently) New York's City Hall, this building was altered and decorated by Pierre L'Enfant for President Washington's first inaugural, April 30, 1789, here depicted.

(Courtesy of The New-York Historical Society, NYC)

Independence Hall in Philadelphia was built to be the Pennsylvania State House. It later housed the Continental Congresses and was for a time the capitol of the United States. This engraving, dated 1778, is from a painting by Charles Wilson Peale.

(Culver Pictures, Inc.)

A view from New York harbor in 1787. Trinity Church can be seen through the rigging of the ship at the left of the picture, the cupola of Federal Hall appears to the right of the mast, and the Federal Mansion (inhabited by President Washington) is at the center of the picture.

(The Bettmann Archive)

Charleston, the only large city in the Southern colonies, as it appeared in 1774. Engraving by Samuel Smith of the painting by Thomas Leitch.

(Courtesy of The New-York Historical Society, NYC)

Philadelphia from across the Delaware River, 1761. Philadelphia was the second-largest English-speaking city in the world at this time, and the many ships in the picture indicate her importance as a center of commerce.

(The Bettmann Archive)

Portraits by John Wollaston (active 1749—1767) of William Walton (1706—1768) and his wife, Cornelia Beekman Walton (1708—1786). The Waltons exemplify the solid, wealthy mercantile class who held important posts in colonial governments. William Walton was a New York merchant who served in the General Assembly and later was named to the Governor's Council.

(Courtesy of The New-York Historical Society, NYC)

This portrait of Paul Revere by John Singleton Copley depicts the famous patriot in his everyday attire—in shirtsleeves—as a silversmith. Craftsmen like Revere, along with lawyers and ambitious merchants, formed the nucleus of such groups as the Sons of Liberty and the Committees of Correspondence. *(The Bettmann Archive)*

“America in Distress,” a caricature by Paul Revere. A disheveled America (with Indian headdress and bow and arrows) is shown suffering the ministrations of evil physicians (to the left, with chains and a dagger) and being comforted by her friends (one of whom brandishes the ax of revolution, to the right). America’s petitions to King and Parliament lie ignored at her feet.
(The Bettmann Archive)

This caricature by Benjamin Wilson satirizes the disappointment of some of King George III’s ministers at the repeal of the Stamp Act in 1766. George Grenville is carrying the coffin of the infant “Miss Ame-Stamp” in the funeral procession, which also includes Lord Bute, Lord Halifax, and the Earl of Sandwich. Two bishops from the House of Lords follow the procession of figures, who were considered illiberal even by some English Whigs. The Whig leaders who brought about repeal are named on the ships in the background—Conway, Rockingham, and Grafton.
(The Bettmann Archive)

A patriotic American barber, Jacob Vredenburgh, objects strenuously to shaving Captain John Crozer, who commands H.M.S. *Empress of Russia,* then (1775) docked in New York harbor.

(Courtesy of The New-York Historical Society, NYC)

This cartoon of 1775 depicts America undergoing various indignities at the hands of the King's ministers, who have discarded the petition from the Boston town council and have answered it with the harsh Boston Post Bill. Their activities are guarded by a figure labeled Military Law. Brittania, following her better instincts, averts her eyes from the scene. The caption reads: "The able doctor of America swallowing the bitter draughts."

(The Bettmann Archive)

"The Bostonians Paying the Excise-Man, or Tarring and Feathering"—a caricature of 1774 that shows the famous Tea Party and the repealed Stamp Act hung upside down on a "Liberty Tree."

(The Bettmann Archive)

A nineteenth-century re-creation of the festivities in New York on July 23, 1788, celebrating the ratification of the Constitution. A "Federal Ship" float in the parade is named for Alexander Hamilton, co-author of the Federalist Papers.

(Culver Pictures, Inc.)

After independence was proclaimed, patriotic New Yorkers pulled down the equestrian statue of King George III that stood at Bowling Green (July 9, 1776).

(Courtesy of The New-York Historical Society, NYC)

An eighteenth-century view of Harvard College, entitled "A Prospect of the Colledges in Cambridge, New England." When the Revolution came, the oldest college in the colonies was already 140 years old.

(The Bettemann Archive)

Two eighteenth-century New York landmarks: the Park Street Theatre, built in 1798, and St. Paul's Church, built in 1764.

(Courtesy of The New-York Historical Society, NYC)

An engraving by William Birch of street life in Philadelphia in 1799—the corner of South and Market streets. *(The Bettmann Archive)*

8 ★★★★★★★★★

The War of Independence

As the Congress in Philadelphia concluded its debate on the Declaration of Independence, Admiral Lord Howe's men-of-war and the naval transports bearing the troops of his brother General Howe were sailing into New York Harbor to begin the first serious campaign of the war. It was not a war in which the Americans fought to overthrow entrenched British authority. That authority was already gone. Save for frontier posts in the remote West, there were no British troops on American soil and no vestige left of British power. The war was rather one fought by the British to reinvade from distant bases the American territory from which they had been expelled and to reconquer an already independent nation.

We have been accustomed to picture the Revolution as a matching of the American David against the British Goliath—the little band of untrained, poorly armed, half-clothed, ill-fed patriot troops against the vast and entrenched might of the world's greatest empire—and to assume that only a miracle of fortitude and courage aided by a divine providence could have brought victory. But in fact the odds were the other way, and the military problem that the situation presented to the British was in its essence an insoluble one.

That problem was not to defeat an army or to capture a fort or a city, but to return the colonies to a loyal subordination to the Crown. The possibility of success was conceivable only on the assumption that the majority of the colonists were in fact loyal or at least indifferent and hence ready to accept a restoration of British authority if the organized power of the insurgent elements could be broken. British planning was indeed based on just that assumption: that it would not be necessary to conquer the colonies in their entirety or to occupy them throughout, but only to break up the armed combinations by which—or so the British thought—the radicals had overawed and intimidated the loyal majority. Repeatedly campaigns were to be undertaken in the expectation that loyal subjects would rally around the British standard as soon as it was triumphantly displayed. Such expectations were not wholly without a rational basis. There were indeed many Americans who maintained a stubborn fealty to the Crown, especially among the wealthier classes of the Middle colonies. And, as in all the many wars of the eighteenth century, there was a far larger group that plowed its fields or followed its trade in indifference to or even in ignorance of the struggle.

A considerable number of loyalists did in fact enlist as individuals in the royal service and fought with courage and fidelity. But nowhere were the British forces greeted by the outpouring of supporters they had hoped for, and nowhere in the colonies were local Tories able to form a government or control a community except in the immediate presence of British guns. These failures of largely nonexistent loyal forces to respond as the British had expected frustrated campaign after campaign and were the most important factor finally assuring British defeat. If the colonies were to be brought again under the control of the British Crown, it would have to be by British ships and troops.

This task was formidable indeed. Even with support from the far larger number of English colonists, the conquest of little more than fifty thousand French in a handful of tiny settlements on the St. Lawrence had strained British resources heavily during the Seven Years' War. Now Britain confronted nearly three million Americans, spreading along more than one thousand miles of coast and reaching back 200 miles into the interior. Forces to subdue this enormous area must be raised in a country of six or seven million people and transported and supplied with tiny sailing vessels over more than three thousand miles of ocean.

Nor were the British military resources that could be brought to bear on this problem the most efficient. The British Army was typical of the European professional armies of the eighteenth century. It was an instrument of royal or dynastic purposes, by no means the popular, or citizen, army drawn from and fighting on behalf of the entire people, such as came into being with the French Revolution and was anticipated in part by the American forces. The officers of the British Army were professionals drawn primarily from the younger sons of noble or wealthy families, often with generations of military tradition. Commissions were a species of property, purchased rather than earned in service, each commission as it became vacant being offered for sale to the officers, in order of seniority, in the next lower rank in the regiment. Commanding a regiment was in itself something of a business venture, as the colonel was provided with a fixed sum from which to recruit, feed, and clothe his regiment and stood to profit or lose according to his thrift and skill. This system produced some officers whose principal qualifications were birth and wealth, but on the whole the consequence of promotion by purchase was probably not very different from the consequence of the promotion by seniority generally followed in modern armies. The fact that the officer corps was professional and normally engaged for life meant that most officers had a considerable experience and were sustained by traditions of courage and fidelity. On the whole, the qualifications of the British officers who served in America were good, and certainly were better than the average of those of their American counterparts.

There was no tradition of military service in the ranks by British subjects generally, and the enlisted men came usually from the poorest levels of society—landless farm workers, vagabonds, debtors, jail inmates, those starved out of the depressed areas of Scotland or Ireland. They were enlisted by bounties or duress or the seductions of drink, but once in, they usually stayed with the colors as lifetime career soldiers. They were well trained in the close-order drill and musketry of the day and harshly and thoroughly disciplined. For all his lowly origin, the eighteenth-century British soldier was a highly effective fighting man who stood to his task unfalteringly in the face of danger and slaughter. There can be no question that the British regular army in America was substantially superior to the Continental forces, and indeed it won almost every engagement in which they were matched.

The principal limitation of the British Army was its size. In spite of the great addition to Britain's imperial responsibilities after 1763, the army was radically reduced at the close of the Seven Years' War, and it had not been increased even during the period of rising colonial tension. A standing army normally of fifty-five thousand men, but by no means up to that strength, had to defend the home islands, man Gibraltar and the other island outposts in the Mediterranean, and meet Britain's imperial responsibilities in India, North America, and the Carib-

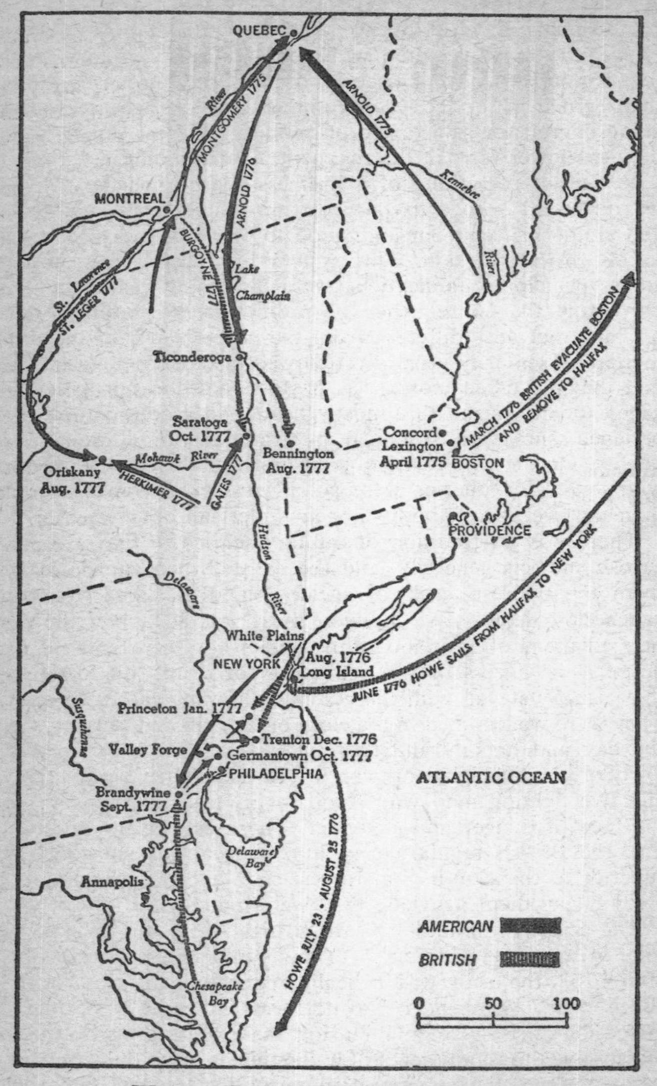

WAR OF INDEPENDENCE—1775-1777

bean. Obviously such a force provided no reserves from which could be drawn an expedition adequate for the enormous task of reconquering the former colonies. Nor could the army be quickly increased by new enlistments. Conscription was unknown, patriotism was an insufficient stimulus to enlistment, and available bounties were relatively unattractive at a time of prosperity. Especially was this true in view of the heavy emigration to America, which had already drawn off tens of thousands of displaced farm workers, Highland clansmen, Irishmen, and others who might otherwise have found enlistment attractive.

It was this difficulty that led to the use of German mercenaries, but even with the addition of these purchased troops the British forces available for service in America were never nearly sufficient to provide the strength rightly demanded by generals on the scene. Throughout the war the British were never able to mount more than a single successful campaign at a time, so that a major effort at one spot required the abandonment or suspension of activities elsewhere. The British could take one post or area only at the cost of giving up another.

The character of British weapons and training has been cited as a further limitation on the effectiveness of royal forces, but this is hardly true. The basic weapon was a heavy musket, cumbersome to carry, unworkable in rain or snow, slow to load, inaccurate beyond fifty yards, and useless beyond two hundred yards. Since the only effectiveness of such a weapon lay in massed firing, an intricate drill was used to maneuver the troops about in order to deliver such volleys and to follow them up with bayonet charges. This is contrasted with the much greater accuracy of the frontier rifle and the greater effectiveness under frontier conditions of a loose deployment of individual soldiers.

As a matter of fact, however, the muzzle-loading rifle, whose tightly fitted bullet had to be hammered down the barrel, was much too slow in loading for use in battle, and the few American companies of riflemen were far more spectacular than useful. Almost all the American troops were armed with muskets identical with or very like those of the British. And it was the highest ambition of the American command to develop an army drilled and disciplined like the British and hence as maneuverable in formal battle. "Indian," or "frontier," tactics were in practice used only by the militia and usually near the frontier. Nor were the British slow to adopt such tactics

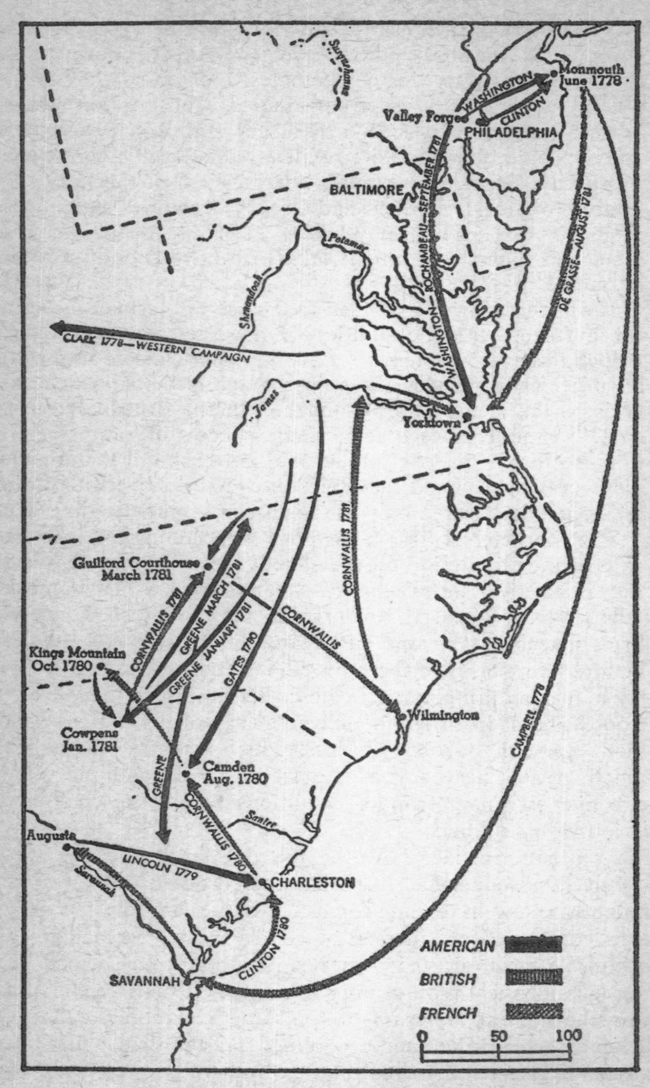

War of Independence—1777-1781

when they were useful. British commanders like Fraser, Simcoe, and Rawdon became masters of this type of fighting.

British power in the Americas was also severely limited by the unwonted weakness of the Royal Navy. After its brilliant performance in the Seven Years' War, paralyzing reductions in ships and manpower had drastically reduced its effectiveness. The bungling stupidity of the Earl of Sandwich as head of the Admiralty, political animosities within the high command, and the simple incompetence of some of the admirals cost it further. The newly thrown-together American Navy was too small to challenge control of the seas; but even so, poor naval cooperation hampered and delayed military operations and the navy was not effective in blockading American ports or stopping the liberal flow of arms and supplies from France and Spain. And at a crucial stage in the war, the French Navy was to wrest control of the coastal waters long enough to permit the final victory at Yorktown.

The most severe limitation of British strength was the inadequate management of the war in London. The loose coordination of the various ministries and offices described in Chapter 2 had by no means improved. Indeed the fifteen years of changing and insecure ministries that had made up George III's reign had undermined the slender traditions of cabinet unity and overall responsibility of the Prime Minister that had grown up in the days of Pelham, Newcastle, and Pitt. And where the blazing force of Pitt might be able to weld the loose elements of the British government into an effective whole, the dull and stubborn lethargy of Lord North could only lament their clumsy disorganization and defer to the King, in whom a special authority over the conduct of war was still believed to inhere. George III, in turn, brought to this task little more than a selfish persistence in wrongheaded courses.

Lord George Germain, the Minister of War, though not so deceived by delusions of British power and colonial weakness as the Earl of Sandwich, his colleague at the Admiralty, was an egregiously bad executive. He had risen from disgrace, more by royal favor than by merit, following a court-martial conviction of cowardice at the Battle of Minden in the Seven Years' War. In the sentence of that court, he had been declared unfit to serve the Crown in any military capacity; yet in sixteen years he had become, in effect, the commander of all the King's armies. An arrogant determination to dominate personally the conduct of the war possessed Germain, so that he was not prepared to confine himself to the raising, equipping, and training of armies, but must himself minutely direct their use in the field. No field commander was ever given free authority to plan and conduct the campaign to reconquer the colonies, and the instructions from England were too often late and confused if not contradictory.

Finally, until 1778 a substantial body of Whigs—small no doubt in total numbers, but including some of the ablest political leaders and most experienced army and navy officers—were opposed to the effort to reconquer America and openly rejoiced in American victories. Even among the great majority of Englishmen who supported the King's policies there was little enthusiasm for the conflict and no such outpouring of national effort as had brought victory in the Seven Years' War. The entry of France into the war in 1778 and Spain's subsequent participation united British support of the Crown by transforming a civil war into a world war, but at the same time sealed the impossibility of British victory.

The Americans also faced formidable difficulties. The resources of men and of most supplies available in the United States were far greater than Britain could ever hope to transport to those shores. That is to say, no matter how much larger the British empire as a whole, the power it could deliver to the scene of conflict was necessarily very much smaller than the potential of American power. The American problem was to transform that potential into actual power. And the great impediment to this was the very localism and separatism of the individual colonies that had underlain the resistance to British centralism. Congress, like Parliament, was able only to requisition grants of funds it needed. That these grants were regularly made late, or in depreciated or nearly valueless currency, or not at all meant that Congress could pay its own bills only late, or in nearly worthless paper money, or not at all. Its occasional acquisitions of hard currency from French subsidies and Dutch loans had to be hoarded for foreign purchases and interest payments or for the most exigent needs at home.

No more than the British could the Americans use conscription to build up an army; and though patriotism was a more compelling force than across the ocean, it was not alone an adequate inducement to enlistment. Thus bounties and pay were the reliance of recruiting officers in America as in Europe; but the absence of a pauper class meant that the offering had to be high indeed to be attractive, and Continental paper money quickly became quite unattractive. Congress and the individual states took liberal advantage of their one major economic asset by offering allotments of Western lands as enlistment bounties. But the financial weakness of the American government was so crippling that it was never able to assemble a regular army large enough or well enough equipped to meet the British armies in America on equal terms.

The same financial difficulties added to the problems of supply, so that the American Army was often ill-fed and ill-clothed even in the midst of a country with an abundant surplus of foods and of fibers. But supply would not have been an easy problem even if gold and silver had filled the commissariat chests. Transportation over the back roads was still wretchedly primitive, and except for a few weeks, the British controlled the sea throughout the war, effectively limiting intercolonial shipments by water. Hence the mere physical problem of assembling in one place, from innumerable and distantly scattered farms, the food and clothing for ten to twenty thousand men was a formidable one.

The supply of munitions constituted an even more acute problem. At the beginning of the war the colonists had no facilities for casting cannon, only scattered individual gunsmiths making muskets and frontier rifles by hand, and a very limited capacity for manufacturing gunpowder. Reasonably soon powder plants were developed, but the Americans were heavily dependent on France for imported muskets and especially for cannon. The muskets in time came to be adequately supplied, but throughout the war the American artillery was scanty and ineffective.

The American Army particularly lacked experienced officers. Washington himself had seen service in the French and Indian Wars and in frontier skirmishes, as had Putnam, Morgan, Ward, and others given high command at the beginning of the war. But this experience had been years ago and was limited generally to company and battalion command. At the beginning of the war almost no American had had experience even in brigade command, much less in the high command of armies. In part this lack was supplied by foreign officers. Two former career officers of the British Army, Charles Lee and Horatio Gates, served as generals in the American Army; but both ended their careers in disgrace. So many European officers volunteered, many of them penniless misfits, as to constitute an embarrassment; but there were a few who were invaluable. The young nobleman Lafayette, Washington's admiring friend and aide and for a time commander of American forces in Virginia; Du Portail, who became Washington's chief engineer; the gallant Poles Pulaski and Kosciusko, and above all the hearty, crusty, profane German Steuben, who enjoyed claiming that he was a baron and had been a lieutenant general under Frederick the Great and who was to become the inspector general, organizer, and drillmaster of the American Army—all these made indispensable contributions to the American cause.

Many of the most useful officers, however, were Americans with little or no prior military experience who learned their trade during the war: Nathanael Greene, the Quaker blacksmith of Rhode Island; Henry Knox, the fat bookseller of Boston; the demon-tortured Benedict Arnold, who before his treason was the most brilliant of all; William Washington, the cavalry commander; and such irregular or militia officers as Francis Marion and Thomas Sumter, whose guerrilla campaigns in South Carolina were to be of great importance.

In Washington himself, their commander in chief, the Americans were uniquely fortunate. Time has frozen into a marble image the tall, passionate man, often vain, always punctilious, who rode like a Centaur, thirsted for gambling and Madeira, danced all night when he could, and when angered flamed forth with a temper listeners never forgot—and who in quiet loneliness bore the American cause through eight years of war, through the writing and ratification of the Constitution, and through the forming years of the first Presidency. And yet the statue image is not wholly untrue, though granite would be a likelier material than marble. So disciplined were the passion and temper, so stern the devotion, so changeless the fortitude and unending persistence, that this very human man was in fact, as well as in legend, metamorphosed into a sort of symbol of incorruptible and selfless constancy. Not a brilliant or even a very good tactician, a thorough but not an inspired or original administrator, Washington's supreme value was in the soundness of his slowly formed judgments and in the sheer unswerving force of his character. It was upon this rock that the Revolutionary cause was built.

It was the more fortunate that the absence at the beginning of any bureaucratic machinery for the management of the war left in Washington's hands a large area of freedom in the determination of strategy, together with many responsibilities for recruitment and supply that would normally be handled by civilian officials. Though this meant that Washington was too often unsupported and overburdened, he was relatively free of the confused and incompetent management from above that so often crippled the efforts of the British commanders.

With all of these limitations and weaknesses, the Americans had other and on the whole more important assets. One was the quality of individual soldiers. The training, even of the Continental Line, never reached the level of that of the British regulars; but in health, energy, and capacity for independent action they were, on the average, considerably superior. Their quality was shown particularly in the militia units. When Washington was compelled to use the short-term and half-trained or untrained militia to do the work of regular troops, he was made desperate by their ignorance and undependability in set battle formations and by their unwillingness to remain in service beyond a few weeks or to campaign beyond their home areas. The militia pleased their own regular officers no more than they had pleased the British officers in the Seven Years' War. But they were unjustly maligned, then and later.

The great American resource was the land itself, stretching over its endless hundreds of miles. What the American cause required was a locally rooted force that could make every mile of that land a hostile threat to the British, that could compel the British to pay with regular troops for even the temporary jurisdiction over every acre, and that could melt into the land before a British advance and rise up again to reclaim the land after it passed. This force the militia provided. Almost every significant American victory before Yorktown was won in whole or in part by them. It was they who drove the British back from Lexington and Concord and besieged them in Boston, who took Ticonderoga and Montreal and threatened Quebec, who held Moore's Creek Bridge. It was to be the militia that crippled Burgoyne at Bennington and aided in his defeat at Saratoga, that won at King's Mountain, that harried the British from the swamps of South Carolina, and that made up the bulk of the forces under Greene that dogged Cornwallis into his final stand at Yorktown.

With this pattern of strengths and weaknesses, the outlines of American strategy were clear enough. They had little to fear from the British conquest of any single city. There was no American metropolis, no capital, that served either as a national symbol or as an indispensable center of finance, production, or administration. The capture of London or Paris would signal the final defeat of Britain or France; but Boston, New York, or Philadelphia could be held by the British without serious damage to the American cause. The American task was not, therefore, to defend cities or hold fixed positions. Rather there were two necessary American goals. One was to keep a central army in being—as large a one as could be recruited and supported—to keep it near the principal British army, but at all costs to prevent its total defeat or capture. The purpose of this army was to force the British in turn to concentrate their limited force in a single large army rather than to disperse it in small units that could operate broadly over the thinly held states. The other objective was to use militia and every other resource available to harry any British force that cut loose from its seaborne support and ventured into the interior—to harry it until it was reduced to surrender.

The combination of these tactics, pursued over six patient years, would confine British power to two or three nonessential coastal cities, save for occasional forays in the interior, which, like Burgoyne's at Saratoga or Cornwallis' at Yorktown, were to end in disaster. Though the American force would never rise to the level of capturing the principal British army, this strategy, carefully employed, would preserve the freedom of almost all of the country while awaiting the exhaustion of British energy and interest and the intervention of allies.

Britain's successes were most brilliant during the first six months of the fighting. Her initial plan was to secure a major base in New York, with a subsidiary one at Newport. Here her principal army could be based and could be supplied from Britain. The loyalist cause was known to be strongest in the Middle states, and especially in New York; the British forces there would provide a rallying point for the Tories. Forces moving down from Canada and up from New York, using the watercourses leading into the interior from each of these bases, could meet and cut off rebellious New England from the rest of America. Then perhaps the lukewarm—or so they were thought—Southerners might drop the struggle and the isolated New Englanders might be crushed at leisure.

The British naval commander, Admiral Sir Robert Howe, and the army commander, General William Howe, were brothers. They were Whigs, not unfriendly to the American cause, and they bore a joint commission as peacemakers, authorizing them to grant pardon and amnesty to Americans who would return to their loyalty to the Crown. A desire to explore the possibility of peace before testing the outcome of combat, coupled no dobut with a natural lethargy, led General Howe to wait for six weeks after his landing on Staten

Island before beginning his campaign to take New York. These six weeks were spent in a wholly fruitless effort to involve either Washington or members of Congress in negotiations. These would in any case have had no chance of success, since the Howes had nothing to offer save an amnesty to follow total submission with no redress of grievances. But the approval of the Declaration of Independence, coming just as Howe's forces landed, made meaningful negotiations impossible. The one conference with a committee of Congress, held some weeks later after Howe's military success on Long Island, proved to be pointless.

Finally, in August, General Howe began his attack. It was clearly impossible for the Americans to defend the islands of New York in the face of a far stronger British force that was in complete control of the waterways. Though Washington had brought down to New York all that he could hold together of the troops with which he had successfully besieged Boston, he still had only thirty-three thousand men, of whom two thirds were militia, to confront Howe's well-trained army of equal size, all of whom were regulars. Washington's force was, moreover, hazardously divided between the little town of New York on the tip of Manhattan Island and fortifications that had been erected near Brooklyn Heights on Long Island, with the East River dividing the two sections. A swift assault by the shipborne British against the narrow waist of Manhattan might have cut off the entire American army and permitted its capture or destruction. In the face of this danger the wiser course for Washington would have been that advocated by Nathanael Greene—to burn the city to the ground, abandon its ruins to the British, and remove the troops to the hilly mainland, where they could not be trapped. But Washington heeded the more conservative views of Congress and attempted the defense of the city.

Luckily for him Howe also pursued the more cautious course, and instead of attempting to cut off Washington's army on Manhattan, ferried his troops across the Narrows from Staten Island to Long Island on August 22. The Americans moved out of their Brooklyn fortifications to a line along a range of hills to the south. Attacking skillfully on August 26, Howe engaged the American troops with a part of his army while with his main force he swung around the eastern end of Washington's line, using an unguarded pass near Jamaica. The successful flank attack threw the Americans into confusion and drove them back into their Brooklyn fortifications. Here they were in imminent danger of capture or destruction, driven back in confusion against the East River, which separated them from the remaining forces on Manhattan Island. Howe was slow to pursue, fog covered the American movements, adverse winds held the British ships in lower New York Harbor; and by the use of a battalion of Massachusetts fishermen, Washington was able to extricate his men without further loss, though at the cost of abandoning Long Island to the British.

He learned little from his narrow escape, however, and again divided his remaining forces, this time between the defense of New York itself and that of the wooded northern section of Manhattan Island. He invited the cutting off and destruction of the force in the city. Howe predictably attempted just this, smashing ashore at Kip's Bay, not far from the present United Nations Building, on September 15, and pushing west across the waist of Manhattan. By the narrowest of escapes the forces in the city fled in frantic haste up the western side of the island and were united with the troops in the Harlem Heights. After a skirmish on the Heights themselves, in which the Americans performed creditably, the British again attempted to outflank them by sailing past to Throgs Neck in the Bronx. Though repulsed there, they forced Washington to evacuate Manhattan entirely except for a large force left in Fort Washington, a strong but incomplete fortification near the eastern abutment of the present George Washington Bridge.

Washington's army was then moved north to the hilly country of Westchester, where it was relatively safe from entrapment. Howe followed and defeated Washington again at White Plains on October 28. Returning to Manhattan, Howe easily captured Fort Washington and the troops foolishly left there, and swung quickly across the Hudson to capture Fort Lee on the opposite shore as well. General Greene, commanding there, barely managed to escape with the garrison. Howe then moved west across New Jersey toward the American capital at Philadelphia. Leaving generals Lee and Heath with a force to hold the highlands of the Hudson, where the river passed through a cleft in the low mountains, Washington hung anxiously but impotently on Howe's flanks. He desperately crossed the Delaware River into Pennsylvania, seizing all available boats to delay pursuit.

As Christmas, 1776, approached, the American cause was at perhaps its lowest point. Washington had made mistake after mistake, and the American forces had been humiliatingly outgeneraled and outfought. His half-disciplined army had dwindled in the successive defeats and demoralizing retreats. The enlistment of the one-year men expired with the year's end, and few showed a taste for reenlistment and further mauling by the British. Only the easily crossed Delaware and a thin, disappearing line of American troops lay between Howe and the easy conquest of Philadelphia.

At this drear point, courage, cunning, and the boldness of desperation relit American hopes. On a snowy and freezing Christmas night Washington silently recrossed the Delaware, smashed the surprised Hessians at Trenton, and recrossed safely, only to repeat his venture and, miraculously, his success at Princeton on January 3, 1777. Howe hastily pulled his advanced troops back to a line from Perth Amboy to New York, leaving all but a corner of New Jersey in American hands and abandoning his threat to Philadelphia. The victories were an enlivening tonic to the American cause and enabled Washington's forces to go into winter quarters at Morristown, in northern New Jersey, with hope for the New Year.

Meanwhile, far to the north, on Lake Champlain, Benedict Arnold, after his defeat in the gallant winter attack on Quebec, had checked the American retreat and built a haphazard fleet of little vessels thrown together with no more than green wood and courage. Fighting those ships with the same rash brilliance he employed on land, he had so slowed up General Carleton's advance as to hold Fort Ticonderoga and southern Lake Champlain in American hands when winter came.

The campaign of 1777 offered Britain her one real, if slender, chance of victory. Lord Germain decided on a conquest of the Hudson as the year's goal. A sizable army was assembled in Canada and was put under the command of the theatrically elegant General Burgoyne rather than the brilliantly skilled General Carleton, who had so ably defended Canada against Montgomery and Arnold. This force was to push down the Lake Champlain route to Albany while a small auxiliary force under General St. Leger was to land on the southern shore of Lake Ontario and move down the Mohawk Valley toward the same goal. Howe meanwhile was expected, but not ordered, to provide at least a diversionary attack northward along the Hudson from New York and to seize Newport, in Rhode Island. Germain confidently expected by year's end to control the mighty midriver of America and from bases in New York and Newport to be able to blockade and subdue

New England. With that head and center of the rebellion conquered, the rest would be easy.

It was not to be. A detachment under General Clinton had taken Newport easily enough in December, 1776. But General Howe, incompletely informed of Burgoyne's plans and of the degree of cooperation expected from him, was left free to choose his own goals for the year. He elected to leave garrisons in Newport and New York and use the principal body of his troops not along the Hudson but in an attack on Philadelphia. He no doubt reasoned that this maneuver would force Washington to move the main American army south as well, thus relieving Burgoyne from pressure as effectively as would a campaign up the Hudson.

Perhaps warned by the previous year's experience of the difficulty of moving an army and maintaining a supply line over the miserable roads across New Jersey, Howe chose to move his troops by water down the coast, around Cape Charles, and up the Chesapeake Bay to take Philadelphia from the rear. Not only would supply be easier, but the American capital would not have the Delaware River as a defensive moat. Calms and adverse winds made a long voyage longer, and Howe's troops, who embarked on July 23, did not land at the head of Chesapeake Bay until August 25.

Meanwhile Washington had indeed moved his forces south as Howe had expected and had placed them between the British army and Philadelphia. Howe moved up slowly and skillfully. In a major battle along Brandywine Creek on September 11, he outflanked Washington and cleared the road to Philadelphia, which he entered with little further opposition on September 25. Washington's forces this year, however, were larger and better trained than the year before, and Washington himself had greatly improved in generalship. He was not prepared to leave Howe undisturbed, and he attacked fiercely at Germantown on October 4. The Americans were initially successful in this engagement and nearly triumphed, but were finally driven back.

Across the Atlantic, Benjamin Franklin is said to have reassured French friends of America by explaining that it was Philadelphia that had taken Howe and not the other way about. As had been the case earlier in Boston and New York, a major British army was to be bottled up uselessly in a city without strategic value, while the American army remained intact and the vast countryside was untroubled. In another few months the British, seeing no point in holding the city conquered at such effort, would abandon it back to the Americans in order to free troops for employment elsewhere.

Meanwhile Burgoyne was running into steadily worsening difficulties. The wilderness miles swallowed up priceless days and weeks from his scanty store of time and irreplaceable dozens and hundreds of his already too few troops. St. Leger's column, consisting primarily of Indians, was halted as it moved in from the west and was dispersed or captured before it could aid Burgoyne. A large detachment of Hessians was surprised and captured as it raided into Vermont for cattle and supplies. While Burgoyne's force shrank, the American army confronting him grew with the daily addition of militia who were ready enough to fight determinedly for their home ground. By September Burgoyne was in a perilous situation: the wilderness behind him, a larger and growing American army before him, his supplies vanishing, the yellowing leaves of autumn warning of early northern snows, no definite help from Howe in sight. Clinton's forces were beginning to raid north from New York, but as Burgoyne knew, with no plan to advance farther north than Kingston. Burgoyne attacked savagely at Bemis Heights and Freeman's Farm, but each time was driven back by larger American forces, well led by Gates and his subordinates and in critical moments inspired by Arnold's impetuous and reckless example. Horatio Gates, the American commander, had been a former career officer in the British Army and fought with competence if not brilliance. Burgoyne's losses were ruinous. He could have been saved only by complete victory in these engagements, and on October 17 he was compelled to surrender himself and his army at Saratoga.

Burgoyne's surrender was clearly the turning point in the war. It became obvious to the British cabinet that the reconquest of the American states was impossible and that it was hopeless to attempt the reestablishment of British authority as it had been asserted in the decade before the Revolution. The only hope of retaining any formal link with these commonwealths would be to concede everything the Americans had claimed in 1775. Such a proposal could not be made without the consent of Parliament, which was in recess and was not to reconvene until January, 1778. Promptly upon its sitting, however, North initiated bills that would authorize a peace settlement based on autonomy for the colonies and the repeal of all the legislation enacted since 1763 by which the Americans had been aggrieved. Parliament, which earlier had grumbled mightily over the slightest concession, now did not delay in voting North the sweeping authority he requested. A bill enacted March 9, 1778, granted terms that three years earlier might have averted the Revolution. A peace commission under the chairmanship of the Earl of Carlisle was sent to America to negotiate the hoped-for settlement.

Meanwhile Clinton replaced Howe as the commander of the British forces and was ordered to abandon Philadelphia and concentrate his forces in New York and to avoid offensive action pending the outcome of the negotiations.

Even more fateful decisions were taken in Paris. The overwhelming defeat of France in the Seven Years' War had stripped it of its overseas empire and reduced it to second rank within Europe. The swift growth of power that had enabled Britain to dislodge France was attributed by many French statesmen to Britain's overseas possessions and especially to the flourishing colonies of North America. From the moment of peace in 1763 Choiseul, the humiliated French minister, looked to the growing discontent of the American colonies as a potential lever with which France might bring Great Britain low. The ministries in Paris followed the Stamp Act controversies and the conflict over the Townshend duties with the closest interest. Ministerial changes in France and the relative quiescence of the colonial dispute during the early 1770's relaxed France's interest for a time. But the renewed conflict following the Boston Tea Party and the rise to dominance in the French cabinet of the Comte de Vergennes, the foreign minister, reinflamed France's concern in 1774. The debates in the Continental Congress were followed closely; and as soon as actual hostilities broke out in April, 1775, the French began to explore the possibility of action to further the revolt. Caron de Beaumarchais—adventurer, playwright, intriguer, diplomat—was acting informally as a secret French agent in London. He was excited by the possibilities of disrupting the British empire by exploiting American difficulties and pressed Vergennes to even more vigorous action. At his urging, the French minister dispatched an agent, Achard De Bonvouloir, to America. Bonvouloir had no official status, but he was empowered to reassure the Americans with respect to Canada and to hint encouragingly to them of French goodwill and interest in trade. Bonvouloir's reports over the winter of 1775–1776 emphasized the colonists' steady drive toward independence. In the spring of that year the French court entered upon a definite resolve to use the American unrest as an instrument with which to attack Britain and avenge its losses in the Seven Years' War. On May 2, 1776, before the colonists had declared their independence or made any overt request for French aid, the King decided to transfer to the colonists arms and equipment valued at one million livres.

Meanwhile the Continental Congress had voted in March to send Silas Deane to Paris as an emissary. Deane did not arrive until July, and early negotiations about the supply of munitions were carried on in London between Beaumarchais and Arthur Lee, a colonial agent there without express Continental authority. After Deane's arrival a formal contract was made between the Congress and Hortalez et Cie., the firm that Beaumarchais used as a front for his ostensibly commercial transactions. Through this channel a steady flow of indispensable supplies reached the American forces, far exceeding the originally contracted sum. Without the uniforms, powder, cannon, shells, tents, and muskets that reached the troops in this way it would have been extremely difficult, indeed very likely impossible, for the Americans to keep a central army in being.

But the Americans needed more than this. They needed French naval support if they were ever to be able to trap a major British force along the coast. And they needed French troops to strengthen the Continental regular army before it could successfully engage and capture or destroy the principal British army. The British efforts at reconquest were in any case essentially hopeless; but without aid in these dimensions, the Americans lacked power to bring the struggle to a definite end. Without decisive French intervention it could continue in stalemate as long as British stubbornness might maintain it. But such overt participation on France's part would, of course, involve her in full-scale war with Great Britain. And this France was prepared to risk only with the support of Spain and with reasonable assurance that the colonists were indeed determined on independence and able, with no more aid than France could afford them, to achieve it.

The Declaration of Independence, coupled with Spain's interest in provoking a general war as a means of conquering Portugal, almost brought France to this point in 1776. But the easy British conquest of New York chilled French readiness for all-out participation. Instead, the nearly overt supply of munitions was stepped up, and indispensable aid was given the Americans in fitting out privateers in French ports, which effectively harried British shipping. Vergennes's interest in pressing matters to a conclusion rose steadily during 1777, spurred by French popular support of the American cause and the skillful diplomacy of Benjamin Franklin, who had arrived in Paris in December, 1776, to head a diplomatic mission consisting of himself, Deane, and Lee. France was restrained for a time by the fact that a new ministry in Spain and a settlement of Spanish difficulties with Portugal had by then cooled Spain's interest.

But the exciting news of Burgoyne's surrender, the first great American victory of the war, precipitated the decision. The tidings came in early December, 1777, six weeks after the surrender itself. Not only was Vergennes reassured as to the prospects of victory. The American success was so great that he anticipated, correctly, that the British would offer major concessions in the hope of ending the war on terms that would keep the American commonwealths at least loosely affiliated with Britain; and he feared that the weary Americans might accept such terms. Such a resolution, leaving the British empire intact, even though decentralized, would be fatal to Vergennes's plans. Therefore he moved with haste to offer the Americans an alliance that would both bind them to fight for complete independence and give them a reasonable hope of achieving it decisively and soon. He promised such an alliance to the American commissioners on January 8, 1778, and the formal treaty of alliance—together with a permanent treaty of friendship and commerce—was signed on February 6.

The terms of the treaties gave almost everything the Americans could have asked for. The treaty of friendship and commerce followed American proposals, recognized the independence of the United States, and gave its commerce protection and full equality with that of other friendly powers. The treaty of alliance bound the two powers to fight together and make common cause if the French recognition of American independence led to war between France and Great Britain. Each pledged itself not to make a separate peace. The full independence of the United States was agreed on as an indispensable condition without which neither would conclude hostilities. France forswore claims to Canada, Florida, and Bermuda and left the United States free to take them if it could. The silence of the treaty as to other areas left France free, however, to seek gains in the West Indies and other islands, or to attempt to reestablish herself on the mainland through the cession of Spanish territory. (This in fact occurred in 1800 with the retrocession of the Louisiana Territory to France by the Treaty of San Ildefonso, which was quickly followed by its sale to the United States.)

It should be added here that her anxiety to forestall an Anglo-American settlement led France to conclude the alliance without awaiting Spanish participation, and indeed to enter into preliminary commitments without first consulting Spain. A cautious and offended Spain saw the opportunity, by remaining aloof, to achieve her desire to weaken England without risk to herself. For the next year Spain endeavored to exact Gibraltar from England as her price for remaining neutral and mediating the struggle between that country and France and America. This failing, Spain finally entered the war in 1779 as an ally of France with a definition of war aims and other commitments in part inconsistent with the obligations France had already taken toward the United States. In particular Spain had no desire to see an example of American independence and insisted on a definition of the Franco-Spanish joint war aims solely in terms of European objectives. Spain's contributions to the war were in any case to be negligible, but her differing war aims were to complicate the ultimate peace negotiations.

Vergennes's speed enabled France to forestall the British peace offer earlier described. Any serious consideration that might have been given the Carlisle Peace Commission was totally dispelled by the arrival of the French treaty of alliance on May 2, 1778. It was received with profound rejoicing and was immediately ratified. Bound in a common cause with the great French monarchy, recognized by Louis XVI as a free and independent nation among the powers of the earth, assured of the support of France's army, navy, and treasury, the Americans saw certain and final victory within their grasp.

The mission of the unlucky British peace commissioners was hopeless once the treaty of alliance had been ratified; it was made ridiculous by the fact, unknown to them, that the same packet that brought them to Philadelphia on June 6 also carried orders to General Clinton, the new British commander in America, to abandon Philadelphia and concentrate his forces in New York. This feeble surrender of what had been so hardly won the year before reinforced the Americans' conviction that it was pointless to negotiate with a crumbling British government that could no longer successfully oppose total independence. The acute hardship of the wealthy Philadelphia Tories who had come out for the Crown in the assurance of continued British presence effectively checked loyalist sentiments elsewhere.

Tories with a little of their goods, a few troops, and heavy armaments were dispatched to New York by sea, while Clinton marched the main body of his army overland across New Jersey, departing on June 18, 1778. The elated Americans, who had moved out of their winter quarters at Valley Forge, skirted Clinton's flanks to the north, awaiting a chance to attack. The chance came ten days later on a blisteringly hot day at Monmouth Courthouse, New Jersey. General Charles Lee caught up with Clinton's rear guard, bungled a chance at decisive victory, and was relieved by a furious Washington. A bitter seesaw battle followed through the rest of the exhausting day. Clinton fought off the American attack and made good his orderly retreat toward New York, but at a high cost in men dead, wounded, and deserted.

When Clinton's men reached New York, it was as retreating defenders, not attackers. Washington's army crossed over from New Jersey well to the north of the city and encamped near his old position at White Plains. As he himself remarked, ". . . it is . . . wonderful to contemplate that after two years maneuvering . . . both armies are brought back to the very point they set out from." Nothing could more clearly have demonstrated the futility of the British effort at reconquest. Two years of vast expenditure of funds and efforts had, it is true, left the armies back where they were. But the British Army was no longer the fresh, strong, arrogant force of 1776, but a considerably depleted, weary, dispirited army. Nor were Washington's troops the raw assemblage of militia of two years previously. Hardened by Steuben's training and the ordeal of Valley Forge, they now made a capable and reasonably effective regular army. There existed in Canada no force that could replace Burgoyne's, and now France stood at the Americans' side. Neither side then knew it, but the war in the North was over.

The Carlisle Commission was refused an official hearing by the Congress and dissolved in frustration. Obviously it was pointless to attempt again the sort of conquest of the Middle and Northern states that had failed so humiliatingly under far more favorable circumstances in 1776 and 1777. British aims could be gained neither by victory nor by negotiation, yet George III was not ready to abandon his efforts and acknowledge American independence. A new strategy must be devised.

This was to hold New York and Newport as bases, in part

to pin down Washington's army, but to attempt no further offensive in the North save for harassing raids along the coast. Instead the principal military effort would be directed at the South, thus reviving Clinton's favorite project of 1776. The commonwealths south of Virginia were weaker and more thinly settled than those to the north, their devotion to the Revolutionary cause less evident, their loyalist population believed to be larger and bolder. George III retained a stubborn faith that somehow the Revolutionary effort as a whole must collapse and somehow his subjects return to their duty if only he would hold out long enough. His ministers were likely to take a more realistic if more limited view. They hoped at best to subdue the Southern colonies and detach them from the American union. Britain could thus retain a foothold among the former colonies, and the retention of New York would give a bargaining point in the eventual settlement. Even though the independence of New England and probably of the Middle states was no doubt inevitable, if the South could be held the new nation would survive only as a weak body, surrounded north, west, and south by British colonies or bases and to the east by the British-mastered sea. In time this encircled fragment might also be willing to return to its loyalty. It was no doubt as sound a strategy for the British as could be devised.

Washington, of course, had a different strategy. His efforts throughout the war had been frustrated by the lack of naval power. The Americans, especially the New Englanders, were a maritime folk, and the ports were full of seamen made idle by the war. But the impoverished American treasury could not hope to build a navy capable of contesting the command of the sea with the British. Individual American frigates had been gallantly commanded and had given a good account of themselves in individual ship actions; but no British fleet could be challenged. Useful American actions at sea had been largely confined to the assaults of privateers on British merchant shipping, and even these were being increasingly suppressed by the British navy. British armies holding any port could be reinforced and supplied indefinitely and were invulnerable to American attack. The destruction or capture of a British army could be hoped for only when, like Burgoyne's, it cut itself off from the sea. Moreover, British forces could be moved up and down the coast more rapidly than the Americans could march overland to counter them.

The entry of the French navy altered the balance. British naval escorts of merchant convoys and independent cruisers had to be withdrawn and gathered into fleets for protection, and American privateers were again emboldened. More important, if the French fleet, even temporarily, could gain control of coastal waters, it could blockade the British in New York. In such a case, reinforced with French troops, Washington might retake New York, capture Clinton's army there, and effectively end the war. For two and a half years after the French alliance was signed, this was the one goal of Washington's ardent hopes.

In this design he was repeatedly frustrated. In July, 1778, the French admiral D'Estaing arrived off New York with a fleet and army to begin the Franco-American collaboration. But the force did not seem adequate for the reduction of New York, and an attack on the British base at Newport was decided on instead. The arrival off Newport of a British fleet under Lord Howe and a violent tempest that disabled several of D'Estaing's ships led the French to withdraw. Newport was left safely in British hands, and under circumstances that embittered Franco-American relations and made future collaboration more difficult.

The French were not able to provide another fleet and army for more than a year, until the fall of 1779. This time D'Estaing was willing to operate only in the South, and his forces—about four thousand troops and thirty-five ships—were used with a small contingent of American Continentals under General Lincoln in an attempt to recapture Savannah, which was by then in British hands. This attempt also failed, in part because D'Estaing's forces were available for only too brief a time; and again the alliance proved a disappointment.

The following spring, in May, 1780, however, a French force of five thousand men was landed at Newport, which the British had abandoned in October, 1779, in order to release forces for the Southern campaign. This French army, under Rochambeau's command, was to remain in America indefinitely, and provided the first effective French force for Washington to use. Britain retained command of the sea, however, and for more than a year little use could be made of Rochambeau's troops blockaded at Newport. Finally, in the summer of 1781, Washington was able to unite them with his own forces hovering above New York. There they awaited a French naval force under Admiral De Grasse, which promised the chance to realize Washington's dream at last. But when the opportunity came, it was an unexpected one, and in another theater of war. Nevertheless, it was to prove as decisive as the fall of New York would have been.

For nearly three years Washington's army and Clinton's were to face each other silently across the no-man's-land between Manhattan Island and northern Westchester County. During those years the only serious fighting in the North took place in two frontier campaigns. One of them involved the Iroquois. Led by John Butler and the Indian chieftain Brant, and joined by loyalist rangers, these tribesmen had ravaged the Pennsylvania and New York frontiers in the summer and autumn of 1778 and into the following year. In August, 1779, a force of Continentals was detached by Washington and placed under the command of John Sullivan. Sullivan attacked the Iroquois in western New York and in a campaign of less than a month destroyed the Indian and loyalist power and left the frontier peaceful.

On a smaller scale, but far more important in the event, was the campaign of George Rogers Clark in the Northwestern wilderness. Clark was commissioned by the state of Virginia, which under its colonial charter claimed lands "northwest" as well as west of its coastal settlements. The Virginia claims included what is now Ohio, Indiana, and Illinois. There were growing American settlements in eastern Ohio, but otherwise this vast area was a wilderness save for tiny French settlements, now under British control, at such posts as Kaskaskia and Vincennes. Clark captured these two posts in the summer of 1778; lost Vincennes back to Hamilton, the British commander at Detroit, in December; and recaptured it, along with Hamilton himself, in February, 1779. This legendary campaign was fought by a handful of frontiersmen who could be counted by dozens rather than hundreds and who by simple audacity defeated not only a far larger Indian and British force but also a wilderness winter worse than any human enemy. The immediate military results were minor, but Clark's victories left a handful of Americans rather than a handful of British in possession of the unbounded West when their two delegations met to negotiate the peace. And this fact of possession was to be a mighty argument for the American claims to the region.

During these skirmishes and raids the major fighting was taking place to the south, as the British had planned. Once Clinton had consolidated his forces at New York and the failure of the Carlisle Peace Commission had become evident, he promptly began the Southern campaign. A force of nearly four thousand men was dispatched by sea to Savannah, Georgia, in late November, 1778. They landed at year's end and promptly captured the weakly held village. Within weeks the other settlements scattered up the Savannah River to Augusta had fallen and the little commonwealth returned for a time to royal control. American efforts to recapture Georgia during the spring of 1779 were easily repelled, including the major French and American assault described above.

With Georgia secured, the British moved next against South Carolina. Clinton himself, taking half or more of his army from New York, led a force of fourteen thousand men in a seaborne attack on Charleston in February, 1780. A long siege followed. Washington had sent south a substantial force of Continental troops to strengthen Lincoln's command. These were bottled up in Charleston on a long peninsula nearly defenseless against an attacker in control of the surrounding waters. On May 6 Lincoln was compelled to surrender the city with his entire force of more than five thousand men, and the South was left defenseless save for local militia and irregular troops. Clinton returned to New York with a part of his forces, leaving General Cornwallis in command at Charleston.

A harassing resistance was kept up in the swamps and the backcountry by guerrillas under Francis Marion, the "Swamp Fox," and other commanders so that the British were never able to establish effective civilian control of the commonwealth. But no regular army confronted the British until Washington sent south another contingent of Continentals to replace those captured at Charleston. These were commanded by Horatio Gates, the victor over Burgoyne at Saratoga. With a limited force Gates started from North Carolina in late July, 1780, on an aggressive march against Camden, South Carolina, the northernmost of the major British posts. When he met Cornwallis there on August 16, he had a superiority in numbers, including militia; but the Americans were poorly commanded, the militia broke, even the Continentals were disorganized, and Gates himself fled hastily across South and North Carolina almost to the Virginia border, leaving his entire army killed, captured, or dispersed.

For the third time the South was naked to the British, and the situation was fatally tempting to Cornwallis. After administering a further defeat to the guerrillas in South Carolina, he left that state thinly held and moved in September to invade

North Carolina. His position was hazardous because loyalist additions had not been sufficient to replace the drain on his forces of casualties and illness, and it had been necessary to reduce his central army substantially to garrison the posts farther south. Moreover, he was operating well inland, indeed just east of the mountains, and far from any port through which he could be supplied or reinforced.

His foray ran into an early check when the American militia trapped the loyalist force that made up Cornwallis' left wing, drove it to the crest of Kings Mountain, and there surrounded and captured the entire unit. This engagement, which took place on October 7, 1780, not only deprived Cornwallis of a thousand sorely needed troops; it effectively stopped any further loyalist enlistment. Cornwallis was forced to drop back across the border into South Carolina and await the spring to resume his campaign.

But he was not allowed to rest undisturbed over the winter. Washington's army was shaken by Benedict Arnold's attempt at a treasonable surrender of West Point in the autumn of 1780, and its men were pressed nearly to mutiny more than once by the complete collapse of American finances. Yet he managed to scrape together yet another little force, this time placed under the command of his ablest lieutenant, Nathanael Greene. With Greene went the finest American commanders of cavalry and light troops—Daniel Morgan, Light-Horse Harry Lee, and William Washington.

Greene moved promptly into South Carolina and scattered his forces to harass Cornwallis, not risking by head-on encounter a repetition of Gates's defeat at Camden. Morgan's riflemen, scouting to the west, crushingly defeated and nearly wiped out a large British cavalry force under Tarleton at Cowpens, South Carolina, on January 16, 1781. Even after this setback Cornwallis resumed his plan to press northward. His own army had recently been reinforced, and he knew that the British forces at Portsmouth and Norfolk, which had been seized in 1779, were also being strengthened by a detachment under Benedict Arnold, now serving as a British officer. He entertained hopes that by linking up with Arnold he could complete the conquest of the entire South.

Hence he promptly set out in pursuit of Morgan's victorious troops. Morgan and Greene, with the principal American force, moved rapidly northward, drawing Cornwallis after them and impeding his march by destroying boats at every river crossing. When Greene reached Virginia, Cornwallis turned back, aware that he was far from his bases and that his strength was being depleted every day while Greene's grew. Greene, by now considerably reinforced, moved south and challenged Cornwallis at Guilford Courthouse, North Carolina, near the present Greensboro. In the indecisive fighting that followed on March 15, Cornwallis won a technical victory, but at such a cost in killed and wounded and in supplies that he was compelled to fall back to the sea at Wilmington to refit.

Instead of following Cornwallis to the coast, Greene swept by him and reinvaded South Carolina and Georgia. A considerable British force remained on garrison duty throughout the two states, composed principally of loyalist militia. In a series of actions more thorough than brilliant, Greene drove them back to the coast. As a consequence, by the end of the summer the British were confined to Charleston and Savannah, and the rest of Georgia and the Carolinas had again been liberated. Once more the British forces had proved inadequate to control more than one substantial area at a time.

Cornwallis, meanwhile, instead of dropping back to protect the British posts to the south, pressed northward from Wilmington into Virginia. Once in Virginia, where he arrived in May, Cornwallis had no clear objective. The state government moved west to Charlottesville, out of reach. Raiding parties destroyed property here and there, but there were no cities comparable to Boston, New York, Philadelphia, or Charleston to be seized. Small detachments of Continental troops under Steuben, Lafayette, and Wayne were operating in the state. Though Cornwallis was able to strengthen his forces by uniting to them the troops under Arnold and General Phillips that were already in Virginia, he could not catch up with the American detachments or prevent their uniting or bring them to battle. With supplies and manpower dwindling as summer drew on, Cornwallis in July moved to the coast to set up a base at Yorktown. This was below Williamsburg, near the tip of the Virginia peninsula. His flanks would be protected by the James and York rivers, and he could easily be supplied, reinforced, or evacuated by sea.

He could, that is, so long as Britain maintained its control of the sea. But France was prepared to make another and major effort at collaboration with the Americans. When Cornwallis began his entrenchment at Yorktown, the French admiral De Grasse was already at sea with a large fleet. After a brief stop in the West Indies he headed north, promising to reach the American coast in August. It had been Washington's hope to use this fleet and the troops accompanying it to recapture New York, but he was persuaded that Cornwallis' force represented a more readily attainable goal.

Plans to move against Yorktown were swiftly concerted. Leaving a small force to watch Clinton in New York, Washington swung rapidly south in mid-August with all Rochambeau's five thousand men and two thousand of his own Continentals. Uniting with the forces under Lafayette already in Virginia, Washington's troops reached the peninsula as De Grasse's fleet arrived to close off Chesapeake Bay to the British and to land three thousand more French veterans. For once a complex American plan of campaign had worked beautifully. To bring together the several forces over many hundreds of miles, in spite of primitive methods of communication and transport, and to achieve perfect timing and effective surprise were nearly miraculous.

Yet it was done. The trap was closed. Cornwallis was cut off from supplies and reinforcement and left facing an army twice the size of his own. The Americans, moreover, could be supplied from the rich farmlands behind them and steadily reinforced with militia. Cornwallis, on the other hand, could only look forward to the melting away of both men and supplies. He was as firmly trapped on the peninsula of Virginia as Burgoyne had been four years before in the wilds of northern New York. He put up a correct, even a valiant, defense while Clinton anxiously sought some way to relieve him. But his situation was hopeless, and on October 17 he offered to capitulate. It happened to be precisely the fourth anniversary of Burgoyne's surrender.

A brave parade was made of the surrender. It was the first clear victory Washington had himself achieved in six and a half long years. The British arms were stacked, the British general's sword was offered, the British band played "The World Turned Upside Down." And the war was over.

Nobody knew it then. The British, after all, held New York, Charleston, and Savannah as well as Detroit and other posts in the West. Their navy was still matchless, and its loss of control of the American waters was only temporary. The war could still go on. But the British will was gone. Beleaguered around the world by France and Spain, plunged into vast debt, weary after profitless years of warfare, the British had no wish to organize another effort, which would have to be much larger than those that had gone before, and to fight through another term of years to master the American vastness.

For another year and a half the quiet armies continued to face each other, but the war at last was ended.

9 ★★★★★★★★

The Creation of a New Empire

We have pointed out that the American Revolution came because the closer military and commercial unity of the late-eighteenth-century world and the rapid growth of the colonies combined to make it impossible for those commonwealths to continue in separate and isolated independence. More minute commercial regulation became necessary—by eighteenth-century conceptions—to fit the growing colonies into the increasingly complex imperial economy. A unified command of military and naval forces was essential in an epoch when wars had become worldwide and were beginning to exploit a nation's whole resources. As the colonies spilled across the mountains that for nearly a century had been the barrier between them and the Indians and began to jostle the tribes into warlike reprisal, it became necessary to provide some central control over Indian relations and the patterns of settlement and trade. The determination of policy over all these matters needed to be vested in a central legislature and its execution in ministries of adequate scope and authority. And a method of financing these expanding operations must be provided.

The British answer to these problems was simple. Stricter commercial regulation would integrate the colonists into the imperial economy, checking their competitive manufactures and reorienting their trade as necessary. British regular troops, directly under British command, would take over from the decentralized and quasi-independent colonial forces the primary responsibility for the defense of America. The British Parliament would define the limits of Western settlement, and British officials would control Indian trade. Parliament would, without American representation, lay down policies in these areas and levy American taxes to provide partial financing for their execution. British officials would administer them and British ministries and courts would be extended as necessary for the purpose. And, of course, the Crown would continue to control all relations between the colonies and the rest of the world.

The colonial rejection of this one-sided solution of the problems of integrating the separate colonies into some larger framework did not dispel those problems or in itself provide a solution to them. On the contrary, the very necessity of collaborating in a major war against Great Britain forced more difficult decisions as to the nature of centralized authority above the individual commonwealths. In working out these decisions, the Revolutionary leaders devised many of the practical patterns of national government that were later to be embodied in the Constitution. Just as the debate over independence had forced the colonists to formulate a coherent and fundamentally important body of theory as to the nature, objectives, and legitimate bases of government, so the debate over the character of central government and its relation to the individual states hammered out many of the basic political theories of federalism.

In devising a central government the American leaders were caught between two opposing pressures. Circumstances relentlessly demanded effective national government. A national army was essential to win the war against Britain. The states had to speak with a single voice in asserting their place among the fierce military imperialisms of the late eighteenth century and in defending their claims to the navigation of the Mississippi and the Atlantic fisheries. The growing trade relations among the states and with Europe had to be defined. Western and Indian policies had to be settled and enforced. A new sense of national identity had to find expression. Most difficult of all, a means had to be found to finance these common activities.

But at the same time all the hostility to central control that had provoked the Revolution was directed almost as strongly against the government at Philadelphia as against the government at London. The individual commonwealths were willing to entrust the command of their troops to Washington as they had been to Wolfe and Amherst; but they were as determined in 1776 as they had been in 1756 to exercise their independent judgment in responding to calls for troops. They were as unwilling to concede a taxing power to the Congress at Philadelphia in which they were represented as to the Parliament at Westminster in which they were not. It was indeed to taxation by remote authority rather than to taxation without representation that the Americans really objected. They had seen, in their own experience and in their reading of history, how the power of the purse could be used to make a British King or a colonial governor dependent upon a legislature that could grant or withhold funds. Every colony or state wanted to be in a position to exercise this same power against any central government.

In the case of commercial regulation the individual commonwealths were in fact more jealous of a central American authority than they had been of British power. In the initial stages of their dispute with Great Britain the colonists had not questioned Parliament's right to regulate trade. And even in the latter stages of the quarrel, when it became necessary to deny that right in order to maintain a consistent rejection of all parliamentary claims of lawful authority over the colonies, they conceded the power in practice by stating that the long acquiescence in the Navigation Acts and other commercial regulations was evidence of a tacit contract by which the colonists had conveyed to Parliament an authority to act for them in such matters. Yet—except for wartime controls on imports and exports—they repeatedly denied to Congress authority to regulate trade or shipping in any form or to impose duties for whatever purpose.

In a sense all the issues and conflicts between local and central authority that had precipitated the Revolution were merely transferred to a new arena after the successful rejection of British claims. Had the central government in Philadelphia, like that in London, attempted to enforce its authority over the states, there can be no doubt it would have been similarly resisted by arms. The Congress, however, lacking the pretensions and traditions of power and having no resources save those granted by the states themselves, could extend its jurisdiction only by persuasion and consent.

In this second decision between central and local authority centralization was ultimately to win. In part this was because the actual unity among the neighboring American commonwealths was far greater than within the sea-riven British empire. In part it was because the American government represented all its parts, as the British government did not. But perhaps primarily it was because the Revolutionary generation was able to create a novel form and theory of federal government that could resolve most of the conflicts between national and state authority. This was the most creative political achievement of the era.

In the present chapter we shall explore the ways in which the problems of central government were dealt with during the period from the second Continental Congress to the adoption of the Constitution.

The second Continental Congress met on May 10, 1775, as an informal gathering of representatives of the colonies to consider what joint action they might take in view of the impasse. It remained in existence for six years, during which it declared independence, regulated trade, maintained an army and navy, commissioned privateers, dealt with Indians, printed and borrowed money, negotiated a foreign alliance, received and dispatched ambassadors, operated a post office, and fought a war to the eve of victory. It called a nation into existence and became at once its legislature and its executive. Yet during all those years it had no real legal sanction for its existence and remained in theory no more than a conference of ambassadors of the several states, having in itself no powers independently of the commonwealths it represented.

The delegates to the Congress were well aware of the need for some permanent frame of government. As independence approached, a committee was appointed, on June 12, 1776, to draft articles of union. This committee, under the chairmanship of John Dickinson, was busily at work during the same weeks in which Thomas Jefferson's committee was drafting a declaration of independence. The two projects were jointly conceived and undertaken, and whether the members of Congress thought, as did some, of the new union as an heir and replacement of the central government hitherto provided by Great Britain, or whether they thought of it, as did others, as simply a confederation to unite the new states' efforts in the war, all were agreed that union was the concomitant of independence.

But while Jefferson's draft of a declaration was adopted within two days after the final decision to secede, five years were to pass before the colonies could agree on a plan of union more definite than their informal association in the Continental Congress. A part of this long delay was due to causes that delayed all important business in the Congress: the absence of members, the pressure of wartime emergencies forcing the Congress to drop all else, the great difficulty in communication between the delegates and their state governments. But there were real issues of substance as well. These included the questions of apportioning representation and financial burdens among the states. Should each have one vote, as in the Continental Congress, or should states vote in ratio to their population? Should the financial quota each state was to contribute to the common purse be fixed by value of lands and buildings or by population; and if the latter, were slaves to be counted? Though there was general agreement from the first on a relatively loose federation of sovereign states as opposed to an independent national government that could act directly upon individual citizens, long debate was necessary to determine the exact boundaries of power between the Congress and the states. These matters engaged the Congress and various committees for more than a year, and it was not until November, 1777, that the completed articles were submitted to the states for ratification.

Here the process was even longer. The same issues were redebated in thirteen state capitals, where national viewpoints rarely tempered local prejudices. In the ratification process, another issue became more difficult even than it had been in Congress: the control of the West, that persistent problem of the Revolutionary period. It was not until that question had been resolved in favor of a nationalization of the Trans-Appalachian lands that the last ratification could be obtained—that of Maryland—and the Articles of Confederation could come into force, in March, 1781.

Thus it was that for six years of critical warfare—life and death years in the history of the country—its national government existed by sufferance and without legal warrant. Its form and scope during those years developed from experience rather than from the prescription of a constitutional convention. In general its powers were those the colonists would have been prepared to concede to Parliament and the Crown. There was a tacit recognition of the unity of the new states before the world. Congress declared their independence, advised on their constitutions, and conducted their foreign relations. It commanded their ships and armies and controlled the conduct of the war. Indian relations fell within its jurisdiction. It administered the post office. During the war years it controlled foreign commerce. It had a national treasury and borrowed and printed money on behalf of the United States. In general the division of responsibility between the central and the state governments that was formed by experience in the earliest years of the Continental Congress has, with one major exception, been little changed in all the succeeding decades. That major exception was the Constitution's later grant of authority over interstate commerce, which over the years has given the national government vast power over the whole domestic economy. What the Continental Congress—and the later Congress of the Confederation—lacked was not an ample and recognized sphere of responsibility, but rather the two powers essential to the exercise of that responsibility: the power to tax and the power to act directly on individuals.

The constitution and powers of the central government were formally determined by the Articles of Confederation, finally ratified in 1781, near the close of hostilities. In form the Confederation was a perpetual alliance among sovereign states, each of which retained all powers of an independent nation except those specifically granted to the central government. It was governed by a Congress, in which each state had a single vote, regardless of its population or wealth, but at least two delegates from the state had to be present to cast it. The affirmative votes of nine states were required for any important action, and the Articles could be amended only by a unanimous vote. Citizens from each state were allowed to migrate freely to any other, and each state was required to give full faith and credit to the actions of the courts of all others. Responsibilities vested in the central government included foreign affairs in all their aspects, the maintenance and recruitment of a navy and the appointment and commissioning of naval officers, the summoning of quotas of troops from the states, the appointment of general officers and the commissioning of all officers, the control of Indian affairs, the coinage of money, the emission of bills of credit, and the appointment of courts to deal with cases arising on the high seas and with controversies between the states and between private individuals with respect to the validity of grants issued by two or more states to the same land.

The Congress lacked the power to define the western boundaries of the states claiming land beyond the mountains, which the Dickinson committee draft had proposed to give it; but this had become academic since most of the Western lands had been ceded to the Congress or the boundaries had otherwise been settled. The power to regulate trade, which the Continental Congress had assumed as a form of economic warfare, was denied the Congress of the Confederation save as it could make treaties limiting the power of the states to levy tariffs. Nor did the Congress have any independent means of raising revenue. Like the Crown prior to 1763, it must requisition funds for its support from the individual legislatures. Hopefully the process would be made more reliable by the establishment of systematic quotas based on the assessed value of real property in each state.

In spite of the large area of responsibility vested in the Congress, jealousy of central authority was clear in every line of the Articles of Confederation. In the early years of the Revolutionary struggle there had been a surge of national sentiment as the rebels against British authority saw in a strong and centralized American authority their greatest strength in the struggle. In those days it was radicals like Samuel Adams who pressed for national unity, and a small-farmer democrat like Patrick Henry who could say in the first Continental Congress, "The distinctions between Virginians, Pennsylvanians, New Yorkers, and New Englanders are no more. I am not a Virginian, but an American." What the radicals were seeking in those days was the support of other colonists in their struggle against the local manifestations in each colony of British authority.

By the summer of 1776 that authority, as represented by royal governors and troops, had been driven out; and the local Revolutionary leaders had untrammeled control in each colony. Thenceforward a strong central government, even though American, was no longer an aid to achieving local autonomy but rather, like the central British government, a limitation upon it. From that time forward there was a strong trend among the more radical Revolutionaries to confine the central government to a narrowly defined league for the mutual defense and the conduct of international relations, which would derive all its authority from the individual states and be totally dependent upon them for troops, funds, and the execution of its decisions. There were conservative groups who had seen virtue in the protection against the democratic excesses of colonial assemblies given by British authority and who tended to seek the same protection in a strong central government in America. But it was the localist view that prevailed in the Articles of Confederation. It was precisely the powers over the economy formerly exercised or claimed by the British and opposed by the colonists that were denied the Congress under the Articles of Confederation: the power to regulate trade and navigation, to give bounties, to restrict or prohibit manufacture, to prevent the local issuance of paper money, or to veto local "stay" laws preventing or delaying suits for the collection of debts.

The hostility to executive power developed in decades of

resistance to colonial governors and other servants of the Crown was shown in the failure of the Articles of Confederation to make any provision for a national executive. They abandoned even the "Council of States," consisting of one delegate from each state, that the Dickinson draft had proposed as a sort of executive committee of the Congress. Instead, there was substituted a "Committee of the States," which sat only while Congress was in recess and which had only such powers as Congress might specifically delegate for the periods it was not sitting. The consequence was that in the Congress of the Confederation, as in the Continental Congress, members had to spend endless hours in committees performing executive and administrative functions, frequently at a level of quite petty detail. Absorption in such activity seriously limited the ability of the Congress to deal with the questions of policy that should more properly have been its concern.

Under the pressure of work and of sheer necessity, however, there were developed the rudiments of an executive arm. For some functions boards were created, part or even all of whose members were drawn from outside the Congress; and for others a single executive was named. Each of the departments began with a committee of Congress that tried not only to establish policy but also to supervise the details of administration. Thus from the earliest days there were a Board of War and Ordnance, a Naval Committee, a Committee on Secret (i.e., foreign) Correspondence, and a Treasury Board, all of which had been created even before independence was declared.

Each of these created a little bureaucracy under itself. Washington's headquarters staff did most of the central administrative work in recruiting and supplying the army, but the Board of War had its clerks. The Naval Committee, or Marine Committee as it was later called, had a substantial staff. Navy boards at Boston and Philadelphia oversaw the building, fitting out, and provisioning of ships and recruitment and payment of crews. Each board had a Continental Agent in every major port who acted for it in day-to-day dealings with masters of vessels, ship chandlers and suppliers, and shipyards. The Committee on Foreign Affairs, which succeeded the Committee on Secret Correspondence, had an interpreter and translator as well as clerks.

The most elaborate bureaucracy naturally grew up in the Treasury, with the necessary volume of paperwork. In July, 1775, nearly a year before independence, two treasurers were appointed. In the spring of 1776 an Office of Accounts was created, to be headed by an auditor general; and in the following autumn a Continental Loan Office was set up in each state. The Treasury staff was further reorganized and enlarged in 1778, and again in 1779, when six field auditors were appointed to deal with army accounts.

The appointment of clerical and administrative staff, however, did little to ease the nearly intolerable burdens on the members of Congress who served on executive committees. Long delays in the business both of the individual committees and of Congress itself resulted. In an effort to relieve this burden Congress provided in 1778 and 1779 that its executive committees, except that on foreign affairs, should be transformed into boards, with a majority of the members drawn from outside Congress. The congressional members could continue to coordinate policy with that of Congress as a whole, while the outside members would be free to carry most of the day-to-day administrative burden.

A further step in the emergence of an organized executive branch came in 1781, when it was resolved to appoint a single secretary to head each department. There had already been a postmaster-general, a position inherited in fact from the British colonial administration. New posts were authorized for a secretary of foreign affairs, a secretary of war, a secretary of marine, and a superintendent of finance.

Robert Livingston became the first secretary of foreign affairs and held the position throughout the peace negotiations. His role was limited, however, by the independent position taken by the negotiators in Paris. His successor, John Jay, achieved a position of real leadership in the complex efforts to establish America's diplomatic position at the war's end. He continued in charge of the department even after the adoption of the Constitution until Thomas Jefferson, Washington's first secretary of state, could take office.

The position of secretary of war, though authorized in February, 1781, was not filled until after the Battle of Yorktown, when General Benjamin Lincoln was appointed. He resigned with the demobilization of the army in 1783, and for two years there was no effective administration of military affairs. In 1785 Henry Knox, the artilleryman of the Revolution who had remained in command of the handful of troops that continued in the Continental service, was made secretary. He held together the few units of troops and the meager stores of war and maintained the frontier posts and the central command at West Point until both he and the department he headed became a part of the new federal government in Washington's administration. Though a secretary of marine had also been authorized in 1781, Congress was never able to agree on an appointee who would accept the position. After Yorktown the problems of the navy were in any case primarily fiscal rather than operational, and it became logical to make the superintendent of finance responsible for the liquidation of its complex accounts.

The most important executive office that emerged during the Revolutionary era was indeed that of the superintendent of finance. The rather elaborate organization of auditors and clerks serving the Treasury Board had been formally organized as a Treasury Department as early as 1778. But its efficiency was crippled by lack of authority and by internal friction between the Treasury Board and the officers of the department. Matters were brought to crisis by the total collapse of the national finances in 1780, when the paper currency so profusely issued by the Congress became worthless and it had nowhere else to turn for funds. In this emergency a new treasury organization was established in February, 1781, under the one-man rule of Robert Morris as superintendent of finance. By a number of expedients, including foreign loans and the chartering of a bank, Morris restored a measure of order to the national finances. Since money was the central factor in all problems faced by the new confederation, especially after the end of hostilities, Morris' abundant energies overflowed into other activities affected by finance. He administered the navy directly, and he assumed a general executive leadership. When he resigned in 1784 he left gratitude for his services, but also resentment of his aggressive course and reawakened fears of executive dominance. This was the one area in which the steady movement toward semi-independent departments headed by a single executive was reversed. The office of superintendent of finance was abolished and replaced in 1785 by a board of three commissioners. The working staff of the department remained, however, to serve as the nucleus of the Treasury Department under the Constitution.

In summary, the structure of central government as it developed during the period 1775-1789 bore the heavy impress of the Revolutionary controversy with Great Britain. In it were embodied the Revolutionary convictions that the individual colonies were separate and independent commonwealths subject to no higher lawmaking body; that any central government should be merely a confederation to deal with external threats and dependent on the individual commonwealths for both military forces and money; that executive authority was to be feared; that central authority over trade, navigation, the emission of currency, manufactures, or other aspects of economic life could and would be used to subordinate the economy of the less powerful commonwealths to that of those controlling the central government; that standing armies in peacetime were not needed; and that the surest method of limiting the power of the central government was to make it wholly dependent for income on grants from the local governments.

The separatist and local views that Britain had tried in vain to override were clearly dominant. Their validity would now be tested against reality. Without a central government capable of regulating trade, protecting property rights, making law, maintaining a standing army, and levying taxes, could the separate, loosely confederated commonwealths survive or prosper? Could they successfully meet the problems of defense, economic growth, and western expansion with which they were confronted?

It will be illuminating to explore the ways in which the new government under the Confederation undertook to meet those continental problems over which the empire had been divided.

The first of these was to establish the national status and security amid the imperial rivalries of the eighteenth century. The British had asserted in the years from 1763 to 1775 that the colonies needed the British regular army and navy, in part stationed in America, for defense against the French, the Spaniards, and the Indians; and the fearful agreement of the conservative colonists with this view had been a major argument against independence. The test now came after Yorktown. Could the colonists stabilize and maintain the independence they had won?

The first steps were to win a formal recognition of independence from Great Britain, to define the vague national boundaries in ample terms, and to secure certain rights along those borders, including the navigation of the Mississippi and access to the Newfoundland fisheries. George III, stubborn beyond all reason and out of touch with reality in America, would still have fought on and on after Yorktown, never acquiescing in the loss of the rich possessions alienated by his own blindness. But his subjects were ready to call it quits. Yorktown had been preceded by the loss of Pensacola and western Florida to the Spaniards. It was followed in the next four or five months by sweeping French victories in the West Indies, the Spanish capture of Minorca, and British reverses in Ceylon. To persevere in the hopeless effort to recover the American commonwealths might be to lose the rest of the empire, as well as to bankrupt an already shaky treasury. It was enough. In March, 1782, the Commons voted that anyone who should attempt, or even advise, the continuance of the war in America as a means of reconquering the colonies was an enemy of the country; and on the twentieth of that month Lord North was compelled to resign as Prime Minister. The Earl of Rockingham, the old Whig and repealer of the Stamp Act, was recalled to preside over a government committed to the abandonment of the former American colonies in revolt and to the liquidation of the world war in progress. Lord Shelburne, as Secretary of State for the Southern Department and as the minister personally closest to the King, had a special responsibility for the American settlement. A few months later he was to become Prime Minister upon Rockingham's death and hence to assume ultimate responsibility for the negotiations with France and Spain as well.

It is unnecessary here to trace the complex patterns of the three-way negotiations that followed North's resignation. The primary responsibility for representing the United States fell upon John Adams, who had been named as the American plenipotentiary for the peace negotiations, and Benjamin Franklin, the regular minister in Paris. Though Congress had variously instructed them from time to time, the distance and their own standing as major leaders of the Revolution left them in practice relatively independent of the Congress and of Robert Livingston, its secretary of state. This was fortunate, because Congress, remote from the actualities and overinfluenced by Luzerne, the French ambassador at Philadelphia, would have tied the delegates too closely to French leadership.

Throughout the seventeenth and eighteenth centuries the diplomatic and military history of North America had been determined by the links of the various colonies to their European homelands. Raids and ambush on the dark frontier were but little reflections of the massed encounters of forces on the European plains. Just as the need for British protection in this imperial warfare had been an argument against independence, one argument for it had been the need of the colonies to isolate themselves from those rivalries so that they could live in peace, distant from and undisturbed by European conflicts. Once independence had been declared, such a diplomatic severance from Europe became an American objective, and in 1776 Congress had drawn up a plan for a series of treaties of amity and commerce that would establish for the United States a friendly and neutral position in the imperial power system of the time.

But to achieve this position of independence, the new states had found it necessary to ally themselves with France and thus become in a sense once more an instrument to be used in the centuries-old conflict between England and France. When it came time to negotiate the peace, it found this alliance an entanglement, primarily because the French were in turn allied with Spain. The latter regretted American independence; feared American power; and, having common boundaries with the new power in Florida and along the Mississippi, wished to confine its expansion. Spain's price for her entry in the war was Gibraltar; and France was obligated not to make peace until that was won, while the American delegates were bound by treaty and instructed by Congress not to make peace separately from France. Even France, though herself no longer having a stake in the New World that would be threatened by American strength, had no wish to enlarge the boundaries or power of the new country she had helped bring to being. She wanted America independent only of Great Britain; she would have preferred to see it remain somewhat dependent on France herself.

In another way these same European rivalries aided the Americans, however, since Britain was anxious to make a quick peace with America in order to turn her entire strength against France and Spain. There was no question that the peace would be based on a recognition of American independence, but there was a controversy over timing and the order of events. The Americans wanted that recognition to come first, before negotiation on any other points, and to be embodied in the credentials of the British representatives; Britain wanted it to come in the treaty itself, as part of the price of peace. This was compromised in a formula that could be interpreted by each side as it chose, and negotiations were able to proceed in the fall of 1782.

The remaining issues were these:

1. *The American boundaries*. The boundaries had never been clearly defined by colonial charter or by Britain's treaties

with France and Spain. On the north there was no great disagreement, but there was real difficulty in defining a line through a wilderness whose geography was largely unknown. In the South the borderlands between Georgia and Florida were vaguely defined, and it was yet uncertain whether Britain would be able to hold the Floridas or must yield them to the Spaniards, who had seized Pensacola. Most crucial was the western boundary. Britain would like to retain the fur-rich lands of the old Northwest; Spain wanted to hold the Alabama and Mississippi country to the north and east of New Orleans and to assert a monopoly over navigation on the Mississippi, foreseeing the ultimate loss of her North American empire to the westward sweep of the Yankees if they were not somehow checked. France viewed the Spanish hopes benignly. To many Americans in the northeastern states as well, the western boundary seemed distant and unimportant. To settle the lands from the coast to the Alleghenies had been the work of a century and a half—why worry now about the distant Mississippi, which lay a far greater span beyond the mountains? They were willing to consider offering their claims to the remote area in exchange for immediate benefits to the commercial interests of the coast.

2. *Navigation of the Mississippi.* Related to the western boundary was the right of navigation of the Mississippi and of export through New Orleans. This was the only feasible channel of trade for the Western settlers. If it were barred to Americans, Western settlement would be blocked or would come under Spanish control.

3. *The future of Canada.* To bring the settlements in Quebec into the American union had been a project of Franklin's from the beginning of the conflict. In spite of the American failure either to conquer the territory or to win the support of its inhabitants, Franklin laid the question again on the conference table, though with no real chance of success.

4. *The removal of British posts in the West.* Though George Rogers Clark had freed some of the former French settlements in Illinois and Indiana from British control, there were still British posts at Detroit and elsewhere in the old Northwest. These represented the only forces in the area to protect fur traders from Indian attack. Even if the territory were clearly defined as American, the timing of their removal would remain an issue.

5. *The Atlantic fisheries.* The colonists had freely caught cod off the Newfoundland banks and dried their catch along

the shores of Newfoundland and nearby islands and of Labrador. The economy of New England and especially of Massachusetts was heavily dependent upon the access to these areas that its residents, as members of the British empire, had enjoyed. To win its continuance was more immediately important to the New Englanders than the navigation of the Mississippi to the Westerners.

6. *Trade privileges.* Were the Americans to continue to enjoy the free access to British ports and the West Indian trade they had enjoyed as colonials? Again, this was especially important to the mercantile and shipping interests of New England, but also to the Middle states, whose horses, lumber, wheat, and flour found their principal market in the British West Indies. It was less important to Southerners, whose tobacco had a substantial monopoly of the European market, whatever the trade regulations.

7. *The status of prewar debts to British merchants.* Southern planters in particular had been heavily in debt to British merchants and factors at the war's beginning. They were reluctant to have these obligations restored, especially as they may have been nearly doubled by accrued interest, and as they had felt many of them unfair to begin with. Also during the war states had often taken over these debts as enemy property and had given the debtors certificates of release upon their paying the appropriate sum—usually in depreciated currency—into the state treasury. But American merchants shared the desire of their British colleagues to establish the sanctity of debts.

8. *Rights of the loyalists.* By formal, or at times highly informal proceedings, the lands and other belongings of the loyalists had been confiscated in most of the states. This property had usually been resold to produce revenue for the American cause, and the consequence had been a major redistribution of wealth, particularly in states like New York, where there had been large loyalist estates. The British felt keenly the losses that had been endured by those Americans who had remained loyal to the Crown and were determined to do their best to achieve some recovery.

In the initial negotiations, handled with superlative skill by the American commissioners (Adams, Franklin, and Jay), the Americans seemed likely to get everything they wanted except Canada, and without paying any price in terms of concessions on debts or loyalist claims. At this time Britain's back was nearly to the wall, financially and militarily, and a formidable Franco-Spanish attack on Gibraltar was being prepared. In

September and October, 1782, however, this attack failed, and it became obvious that France was nearer bankruptcy and more anxious for peace even than Britain. The tone of the British negotiators immediately stiffened. Only in relatively minor points, however, was the final treaty materially changed from the tentative agreements earlier discussed.

The Americans gained only the "liberty" to dry on British islands the catch they were conceded the "right" to fish for off the Newfoundland banks, and in later years were to discover that "liberties" could be withdrawn. They did not guarantee the pre-war debts, but did promise that no legal impediments would be put in the way of their collection. More to save the face of the British negotiators than to achieve any real effect, they agreed that Congress would recommend to the states the restoration of loyalist property and rights, a recommendation that both they and the British knew would be generally ignored. Britain refused to consider commercial provisions in the treaty, reserving them for separate and later negotiation.

But the Americans got everything else they sought: a complete and unqualified recognition of independence, a clean sweep of territory to Canada, the Great Lakes, the Mississippi, and the southernmost of the boundaries with Florida that had been debated, together with a promise to remove the British posts in the West "with all convenient speed," and a recognition by Britain of American rights to free navigation of the Mississippi. Samuel Flagg Bemis, the distinguished diplomatic historian of the Revolution, has called the results "the greatest victory in the annals of American diplomacy."

France did not want, and Spain violently opposed such extensive boundaries for American power, and Vergennes would have discouraged the American negotiators from insisting on them. But, seeing their chance in England's distress, the Americans had broken their instructions to place themselves under Vergennes's guidance and had pressed their negotiations to a conclusion without his knowledge. They had, however, respected the letter of their treaty obligation not to make a separate peace by providing that the Anglo-American treaty would come into force only upon the completion of an Anglo-French treaty. Vergennes was not as indignant as might have been expected. He was no doubt relieved that the Americans had got what they wanted without pressing him to continue the war; he was probably pleased to have an additional means of pressure upon Spain to agree to peace without having won Gibraltar.

The treaty was agreed to on November 3, 1782, and formally signed November 30. It came into effect when the Anglo-French treaty was signed on November 20, 1783, and was finally ratified the following September.

The Americans had staked out an enormous claim to national sovereignty, but it was another thing to sustain it. Along none of the frontiers were the adjoining powers willing in practice to yield to the American claims. Alleging that the Americans had not fulfilled their treaty obligations with respect to the restoration of loyalist property or the collection of pre-war debts, the British refused to fulfill theirs with respect to the Northwestern posts. They continued to maintain troops at Detroit and other Western posts and even established a customhouse on New York territory, at Oswego, on the banks of Lake Ontario. They meant to control the fur trade as long as they could and to maintain a force in the great unsettled West against whatever contingencies might come in the unforeseeable future of the shaky republic.

More serious was the Spanish hostility along the southern and western borderlands. Spain felt in no way obligated by the definitions of American boundaries set forth in the treaty between Great Britain and the United States. She claimed for herself the strip of land along the northern boundary of west Florida, which the United States would have been willing to concede to Britain, and maintained a post at Natchez in that area. She endeavored to close the Mississippi to American shipping and to deny any rights of access to that stream.

For a withdrawal of American claims in the West, Spain was prepared to concede to American merchants certain commercial rights in the Spanish empire. This was attractive to many in the Northeast, who would benefit from the immediate concessions and who felt neither able nor anxious at the moment to assert American rights on the distant Mississippi, rights that they thought would not become meaningful for generations. At one time the Congress, by a narrow vote, actually authorized Jay (at that time secretary of foreign affairs) to agree to forbear to exercise the rights of navigation on the Mississippi for twenty-five to thirty years in negotiating a commercial agreement with Spain. Violent protests from Westerners and Southerners forced Congress to rescind this authorization, however, and no such agreement was reached.

All the borderlands—north, west, and south—hence were still in dispute when the Constitution came into effect in 1789. In the 1780's neither the British nor the Spaniards nor the

Americans had the power to make good their claims in that distant wilderness. The American inability to secure these borders may have been in small part due to the weakness of the central government under the Articles of Confederation, but it was primarily a consequence of simple uninhabited distance. They remained in dispute for years after the Constitution was ratified, and the situation was resolved only as the later western surge of population defined its own boundaries.

In its military policy the Confederation adhered to the colonists' theory of reliance on a local militia. The end of the war saw the rapid demobilization of the Continental forces, in part because of a deep-seated fear of standing armies in peacetime, in part because of a simple inability any longer to pay and maintain an army. French subsidies were discontinued with the peace treaty, and the states, most loath to contribute money, men, or supplies even when the British invaders were actually present, were totally unwilling to make such contributions against merely hypothetical dangers. Like the colonists in the pre-Revolutionary period, they could see no object against which a standing central army could be used except the liberties of their own individual commonwealths.

The process of demobilization was complicated by the bankruptcy of the Congress. If it could not afford to keep the army in being, neither had it the funds to pay off its heavy indebtedness to officers and men. To dismiss the troops penniless, far from home, and with not even a clear statement of the amounts due them would have been intolerable both to the conscience of the Congress and to the army itself. In this dilemma there were half-mutinous officers at Newburgh, New York, the headquarters of the dwindling force, who were prepared to use their military strength to seize control of the government and compel payment of the arrears of their salary. And there were men with their own claims against the government —for lands, for bonds perhaps bought at a fraction of their price, for the face value of worthless currency held—who would be willing to use the army for such a purpose. There were also honorable men who deeply felt the need for a strong and respected central government and who wanted to maintain a standing army, not as a mutinous threat, but as a legitimate support of the national sovereignty.

But the antiarmy forces won. By the late spring of 1783 the Treasury scraped together enough to give the soldiers three months' back pay, which might suffice to get them home and to help restore their farms or shops. On May 26, 1783, Washington was instructed to furlough those serving for the duration, and by the end of June the army had all but disappeared. After the peace, when the British garrison at New York turned over the control of the city, it was hard to assemble even a skeleton force to receive it. There remained after 1783 only a battalion at West Point and a handful of local militia at some of the Western posts. Trusting the barriers of ocean and wilderness and the strength of the people themselves as a militia, the new republic was ready to begin its existence otherwise unarmed.

The United States had to define its independent role not only in the imperial and military rivalry of the eighteenth century but also in its intense commercial competition as well. As a part of the mercantile system of the British empire, America had had a protected, if subsidiary, status. Now it could compete, and must face competition, in a world market. Britain was no longer able to restrict American manufactures or to confine American exports to Great Britain. On the other hand, it was under no obligation any longer to grant American products, like tobacco, a monopoly of the British market, or to give American ships a preferential access or indeed any access to the internal trade of the British empire, or to pay bounties for American products, or to grant tariff preferences, or to protect American ships on the seas.

The Americans fared well with their freedom. The British were the more anxious to hang on to their trade for having lost their sovereignty, and the other trading nations of Europe, especially France and the Netherlands, were hungry for a share. A few more farsighted British statesmen were indeed eager to preserve commercial relations just as they were, including Lord Shelburne, who had become Prime Minister in the summer of 1782, and who hoped for a close and amicable commercial relationship between Britain and the United States. The preamble to the preliminary treaty negotiated by Oswald as Shelburne's representative affirmed a joint intention to provide for reciprocal commercial rights. However, Shelburne fell from power in February, 1783; and Charles James Fox, the new Secretary of State, rejected the policy in a wave of reversion against Shelburne's liberal settlement. All references to commerce were omitted from the final treaty.

Instead, the Privy Council was given by statute a sweeping authority to regulate trade with the former colonies; and the upshot of its several edicts was to put the direct trade between

Great Britain and America—which was very profitable to British merchants, and on which the British had a favorable balance—on essentially its pre-war basis. American ships and goods continued to enjoy imperial preferences. The conditions of access of tobacco to the British market were even improved, in the hope of continuing the monopoly that could no longer be compelled. But American ships were totally barred from the British West Indies, and American dried meat and fish could not be shipped to those islands even in British vessels.

Meanwhile French and Dutch ports, both at home and in the Indies, were opened to American ships and products; and every effort was made to attract American trade. A commercial treaty accompanying the Treaty of Alliance of 1778 defined their trade relations, which were quite free except for minor restrictions on the importation of American dried fish. Similar commercial treaties were signed with the Netherlands in 1782, with Sweden in 1783, with Prussia in 1785, and with Morocco in 1787.

Thus by 1787 the United States had established free commercial relations with most of the major trading nations of the world. The effects of these laws and treaties upon the actual flow of commerce were not as great as might have been surmised. Smuggling made trade restrictions largely ineffective in the post-Revolutionary period as it had in the pre-Revolutionary years. Commerce with the French and Dutch West Indies was somewhat greater than before 1775, when it was illegal; and trade with the British Caribbean islands was doubtless somewhat less than when it had been authorized. But all the West Indian islands were heavily dependent on North America for lumber, foodstuffs, and other supplies that could not be adequately provided by their respective European homelands, and trade met this need, whatever the regulations.

Though French and Dutch exports filled a somewhat increased proportion of the American market, British exports quickly regained and then surpassed their prewar level. British merchants, aided by language, habit, experience, and established connections, retained their dominance over the American market. American exports, however, and particularly American tobacco, no longer had to be sent to Britain to be resold to the Continent, and a substantial direct trade to France and the Netherlands quickly developed. One consequence of these changing patterns was that the American balance of trade with Britain became even more heavily unfavorable and with France and Holland heavily favorable.

The new freedom of the Americans was exploited in another way. As soon as hostilities ceased, American ships began to fit out for the voyage to China. The *Empress of China* made the first voyage, 1784–1785, with enormous profits, and many other ships followed her. A vastly successful triangular trade was developed, taking metal tools and other showy items to the Pacific coast, where they were bartered to the Indians for furs, which were taken to China to be traded for Oriental goods. The great early fortunes of Salem and other ports were based on this exotic commerce.

It was in the interest of the United States to break up the mercantile patterns of trade that had dominated eighteenth-century imperial policy. The world commerce of that century was based on the exploitation by the several major Western European powers of the rich opportunities afforded by the newly opened lands of Asia, Africa, and the Americas. For the first time a major area outside Europe was able to enter fully into that trade as an independent power. To succeed, it must be able to trade across all the artificial barriers the European powers had erected to fence off their respective colonial possessions for themselves. The nearly complete success of the Americans in achieving this owed something to the new liberally of economic thought that was growing in Europe. But primarily it was because all the European powers, needing American markets and American products, realized that it was to their advantage to welcome the new republic to their trade rather than to exclude it.

Meanwhile the United States itself was precluded from establishing its own mercantilist policies because the Congress had no power to lay tariffs or to pass navigation acts. The Northeastern states pressed Congress for the grants of authority over navigation so that American shipping could be given advantages in American ports and so that threats of retaliation against British shipping could be employed to open the British West Indian trade to American vessels. The power to levy tariffs was sought primarily to raise money but also to encourage manufacture by the exclusion or penalizing of British and other European products.

None of the various proposals to endow Congress with authority in this area, even for limited periods, was ever enacted. The states of the lower South did not want an exclusion of British ships to force them into a helpless dependence on New England shipowners, nor did they want a tariff placed on their imports in order to benefit manufacturers in other states. On the other hand, many of the manufacturers in the Middle states opposed a central control over tariffs lest it result in lower duties than those already levied in their state tariffs. The fear of central authority over trade hence resulted in a policy of laissez-faire so far as the central government was concerned. A libertarian economic policy, such as Adam Smith would have applauded, was the half-accidental consequence of the absence of authority to establish any other.

Other fundamental policy decisions had to be made about the West. The distractions of the war and British-encouraged Indian hostilities had for a time impeded, but had never stopped, the flow of settlers across the mountains. A new policy had to be developed with respect to this Western area. Should it, as the British had insisted in the Proclamation of 1763 and the Quebec Act, be a central responsibility, or was it to be left to the individual states? Should rapid settlement be encouraged or discouraged? What should be the status of the new settlements, and how were they to be governed? Were Eastern speculators or Western settlers primarily to benefit from this vast domain? In what way, if any, was the national treasury to benefit? These were essentially the same questions the British had faced in 1763.

These issues were most acute with respect to the "old Northwest"—the land north of the Ohio River running west from the mountains to the Mississippi and comprising the present states of Ohio, Indiana, Illinois, Michigan, and Wisconsin. The lands now lying in Alabama and Mississippi were still a wilderness fought over by Creek and Chickasaw and Spaniard. No one questioned the claims of North Carolina and Virginia to Tennessee and Kentucky respectively. There were sizable settlements in both territories, and it was well understood in both cases that the new settlements would soon be given their independence and could seek admission to the Union on their own.

But in the old Northwest the conflicting land claims of Virginia, Pennsylvania, and Connecticut and of rapacious land companies claiming titles under state grants produced confusion. French hostility, British policy, and Indian warfare had left the territory with only very scant white settlement. A rich for trade vied with millions of acres of potentially rich farmlands as a magnet.

It has been pointed out that the "landless" states, and especially Maryland, had refused to ratify the Articles of Confederation until the competing claims to this empire had all been ceded to the Congress. When this process was completed in 1781, however, Virginia's cession imposed conditions Congress was prevailed on not to accept. The most important of these required the invalidating of all claims of land companies to the territory. Many members of Congress and their friends had interest in these enormous if tenuous claims, and it was not until 1784 that the Congress and Virginia were able to agree on terms that saved Congress' face and won Virginia's point. From that time forth it was clear that the control and settlement of the West would be under central, not local direction, just as the British at the close of the French and Indian Wars had seen it must be. A form of government for the new territories was provided in an ordinance drawn by Jefferson and enacted in 1784. This was never applied in practice, however, and was almost completely rewritten in the famous Northwest Ordinance of 1787. Meanwhile provisions for the disposal of land had been set in another ordinance in 1785.

The Ordinance of 1784 provided that the old Northwest should be divided into ten rather arbitrary and geometrically defined districts. The first settlers of each were to be free to organize a temporary government of their own. As soon as there were twenty thousand of them, they could hold a convention, adopt a permanent constitution, and send a delegate to Congress. Each such territory was to be admitted to the Confederation as an equal state as soon as it equaled in population the smallest of the existing states. The Ordinance of 1785 provided for the survey of the Western lands into neat thirty-six-square-mile townships. After the reservation of certain mile-square lots in each section for the support of schools and other public purposes, the remaining lots were to be auctioned off to the highest bidder, but at a price of no less than one dollar an acre. Jefferson had wanted the lands to be offered free to actual settlers, but the financial needs of the central government were too great to permit this, and his ideal was not to be realized until the Homestead Act of 1862.

A major exception to the Ordinance of 1785 was allowed almost immediately, when about one million acres of unsurveyed land in south-central Ohio was conveyed in a special grant without auction to a New England group organized as the Ohio Company, including many former army leaders in its membership. With this exception, however, the pattern of land sales and settlement proceeded in swift and regular fashion, disturbed only by the flow of unruly squatters who refused to await the Land Office's sales or who could not or would not pay the dollar-an-acre minimum price.

The appearance of these squatters in such numbers as to threaten control of democratically organized territories was doubtless the principal reason for the major difference between the Ordinance of 1784 and the Northwest Ordinance of 1787. The provision in the Ordinance of 1784 that territorial governments were from the beginning to be freely and locally elected was replaced in 1787 by a provision that the governor, secretary, and judges were initially to be appointed by Congress. Not until there were five thousand people could there be a locally elected assembly, not until there were sixty thousand a locally drafted constitution, and not until admission to statehood a locally elected governor. During the early and turbulent days of settlement the property rights granted by Congress were to remain under congressional protection.

In spite of this reservation to the Eastern-controlled Congress of a temporary power over newly settled areas, the net effect of these ordinances was to establish a pattern for the rapid settlement of the West by individual landowners, who would be quickly organized into new commonwealths equal in rights and status to the original states. This pattern, strengthened from time to time by such legislation as the Homestead Act of 1862, was to govern the entire sweep across the continent of the American people until the last public lands were granted in the 1890's.

Perhaps no legislative acts have had a more fundamental influence on the course of American history. The decisive policies that the West would be opened freely or nearly freely to all comers and that it would be governed by and for the benefit of those who settled it and not by and for the benefit of the Eastern states from which it was settled marked a sharp break from British policy, which had wanted to restrict and delay settlement and which had wanted to maintain the territories settled by Englishmen in permanent subordination to the interests of the homeland. A consequence was that the frontier that had taken nearly a century and a half to reach the Appalachians and a long generation to cross them leaped to the Mississippi in twenty-five years and in fewer than seventy-five years more was at the Pacific coast. Spanish, French, Mexican, and Indian claims to the West were simply overwhelmed in the outpouring. And just as the Atlantic voyage had left behind most of the European burdens of status and privilege, so the repeated creation in the West of new frontiers of individual settlement based on free individual landholdings was to wipe out inheritances of class and fortune that had developed in the older coastal cities and plantations. The Western policies hammered out in these years made it certain that the United States would quickly become a vast continental power and that the characteristic pattern of its political, social, and economic life would be one of sweeping and fluid equality, embracing change and offering its greatest rewards to individual drive and force.

Most difficult of the problems of central government was that of finance. This had been the irreconcilable issue that had split the empire. Would the Confederation be able to survive it? The colonies had firmly asserted that Parliament needed no authority to tax them and that their own assemblies would respond to requisitions by granting whatever funds were truly needed for defense and other imperial purposes. They were later, as states, to maintain this position even against their own Congress, and were never willing to give it authority to levy taxes or imposts directly. Save for loans and for subsidies from France, the Congress, during the war and during the Confederation, had to depend for its income on requisitions to the individual states and on the printing press.

The initial source of income was the printing of Continental currency, which was begun as early as 1775. This would probably have been necessary even if the Congress had had adequate taxing authority, since the country was perpetually drained of gold and silver and there was simply not enough specie available to provide a currency for the economic transactions involved in the mobilization of a continent-wide war effort. The initial issues were modest in size and served so useful a purpose that the new currency was widely accepted at or near par. As the years passed, however, and the Congress continued to depend on the printing press for funds, the Continental paper money began to plunge in value; and with each descent in value, larger issues were required to meet expenses. Meanwhile requisitions upon the states had begun, but these were responded to scantily and tardily. Moreover, such states as paid their quotas usually paid them in Continental currency. This provided some check on the precipitate decline of that currency in value, but provided the Congress with no hard income.

Domestic loans were an equally inadequate source of revenue. Little could be borrowed from a citizenry skeptical of

Congress' finances, except its own currency, which they were glad to give back to be consolidated into interest-bearing loan certificates. Meanwhile the insolvency of Congress was manifested in other kinds of evidence of debt. Quartermasters and commissary officers issued certificates in payment for supplies and quarters used by the Continental troops. The states made expenditures directly for the Continental cause, principally by paying and supplying troops of the Continental line from their states, and presented their claims to the Congress. Pay certificates and land warrants were issued to soldiers in lieu of pay. This chaos was compounded by the liberal issuance of paper currency by the states themselves.

A raging inflation accompanied these financial developments and was in large part due to them. The general commercial disorganization produced by the war, the disruption of transport, and the cutting off of nearly all imports would, however, have produced an inflation under the soundest of fiscal systems, and these developments contributed much to the financial disorder of the period. In fact this disorder did not reflect any fiscal recklessness on the part of the Congress or even the Congress' basic lack of authority, so much as it did the real difficulties of mobilizing the resources of the dispersed agrarian economy and organizing them in a centralized war effort. Even had Congress had a full taxing power, there was during the war years little foreign trade on which customs duties could be levied, nor were there nationally equalized tax rolls of real property on the basis of which a land tax could be assessed, or any bureaucracy that could levy and collect it, or specie in which it could be paid. Almost all that could be done was to use whatever devices were at hand to induce people to serve in the army and to provide equipment, food, and supplies. Paper evidence of this service, whether currency, loan-office certificates, land warrants, or quartermaster certificates, could provide a basis for a later rough adjustment of rights and burdens. It is not easy to see how any better arrangement could have been worked out in the circumstances.

By late 1779 and 1780, however, this feeble financial structure had collapsed. Continental currency passed into nearly total worthlessness and inflation got wholly out of hand. But for French aid, the whole American military effort might have collapsed, as the unpaid, underfed, half-naked troops were near mutiny. By this time, however, the French alliance had come into full action, and one of its most important elements was a flow of gold and silver in the form of loans and subsidies to the Congress. All told, about nine million dollars was supplied in this form, including a small sum from Spain. Almost equally important was the flow of hard money into the economy resulting from French purchases for the army and naval units stationed in America and from the pay of French soldiers and sailors. Increasing amounts of specie were hence available as a medium of currency for the last two years of the war, and Congress was enabled—indeed it was forced—to discontinue its printing of paper money. With French aid as their principal support, the finances of the Confederation were able to stagger through to the peace.

The end of hostilities and the demobilization of the American forces of course greatly eased the financial problems of the Congress. But with the peace came not only a sharp reduction in expenditures but also the end of French subsidies. Congress must now turn its attention to constructing an orderly and enduring financial system. It made considerable progress toward that end, at least to the extent of clarifying and systematizing its chaos of debts. But the lack of any power to tax or to compel the states to honor its requisitions prevented any fundamental solution to its problems.

The first need was simply to find out who owed whom, and how much. The Continental and most of the state paper money was already worthless and was simply repudiated. But there were loan-office certificates and a wide variety of other evidence of debt described above that had to be consolidated, placed on a consistent basis, and valued in terms of hard money. Most complex of all was the settlement of accounts between the Congress and the individual states. The states all owed arrears on requisitions due the Congress, some in money, which varied in value, depending on the year; some in goods, which had to be assigned a money value. On the other hand, every state had undertaken expenses in the common cause, primarily in providing supplies and equipment for Continental troops, for which it was entitled to reimbursement. Most states, indeed, thought the balance heavily in their favor.

Auditors and committees labored continuously over these accounts for the entire life of the Confederation and still had not completed their task when the government under the Constitution came into being in 1789. The indebtedness of the Congress to individuals for loans, supplies, and military service had been almost entirely determined and recorded in certificates of indebtedness, and the bulk of the work of settling accounts with the states had been completed.

To learn what the Congress owed was itself a task of enormous complexity and difficulty; to pay those debts and to establish a dependable income for future operations was a far greater one. Congress could look to three sources: requisition upon the states, the sale of Western lands, and the hoped-for acquisition of the authority to levy carefully limited taxes.

Requisitions upon the states proved to be even less productive than during the war. In the immediate postwar years a commercial and financial crisis and a rapid outflow of currency to Europe to pay for long-awaited imports made it difficult if not impossible for the states to meet the demands upon them. Even after this crisis was over many of the states were reluctant to make further payments to the central government while the wartime accounts remained unsettled, since they believed that the settlements would show the Congress to be heavily in their debt. The reluctance of some became the excuse of others. Only a small fraction of the postwar requisitions were met promptly by the states.

The states did, however, move to meet the critical financial problems of the Congress by taking over some of the national debts owed their citizens. This process began with a number of states redeeming the pay certificates of soldiers from their respective communities. This was in large part a patriotic and humanitarian gesture to meet the immediate and often desperate needs of men who had already made great sacrifices for their country. Congress later voted to allow credits to the states for such payments in the final settlements of their wartime accounts. Later, and somewhat similarly, the states began accepting in payment of state taxes the certificates of interest due on loans to Congress. Congress in turn accepted these in partial payment of requisitions upon the states.

A more serious issue arose on the question of the state assumption of the principal of the national debt. This had important political as well as financial implications. Those who favored a strong central government viewed the national debt as a unifying force, since it would be to the interest of the wealthy and influential creditor class to support a strong central government able to pay it off. The creditors themselves, however, were demanding early payment, which the states were able to make and the Congress was not. The states' rights advocates, seeing a chance to attach the wealthy interests to their respective states, pressed for state assumption in an unusual alliance with the merchants and moneyed men who were the principal creditors. Beginning with Pennsylvania, many of the wealthier states, whose citizens held most of the national debt, began buying certificates of indebtedness from their citizens and holding them as claims against the central government or using them in meeting congressional requisitions. As the process of assumption proceeded, the depreciated value of Continental securities rose rapidly, and they became an object of speculative buying by investors and by other states. As a result, by 1789 a major part of the domestic debt had passed into the hands of a few states, principally New York, New Jersey, and Pennsylvania.

Though this process deferred somewhat the clamor of individual debtors, it did not meet the need of the Congress for the modest sums required for day-to-day operations of the government. The Western lands were to be the ever-flowing treasury that provided this income, perhaps averting the need for taxes and requisitions altogether—or so the congressmen hoped. But it was 1785 before a procedure for land sales was established, and years more before any regular or dependable flow of money came from this source. By 1789 less than one million dollars had been received, and almost all of this was in warrants, loan certificates, or other obligations rather than in cash.

Meanwhile Congress borrowed from the Dutch to meet the interest on the foreign debt and the unavoidable minimum of expenses that had to be met in hard cash. Dutch bankers had a farsighted confidence in the future solutions of American financial problems, spurred by a keen appetite for a larger share of the newly opened American trade. By these hand-to-mouth methods the most urgent needs were temporarily met.

All the while, Congress had been pressing, with general support, for the power to command an independent income. Even before the Articles of Confederation had been finally ratified, an amendment was proposed, in February, 1781, to allow Congress to impose a five-percent duty on all imports. Such an amendment required the unanimous consent of the states, and it all but got it. Within eighteen months every state except Rhode Island had agreed. Rhode Island's objections were due in part no doubt to a rather cranky localism that dominated its politics, but primarily to the fact that its own state finances were based on duties levied on the thriving commerce of Newport. Since many of the goods coming in at that port were reexported to eastern Connecticut and neighboring areas in Massachusetts, Rhode Island's tax burden in this way could be passed on in large part to residents of those states. Special efforts to persuade Rhode Island to agree were abandoned when Virginia unexpectedly withdrew its ratification.

The almost successful effort to obtain this limited authority to levy a tariff had been spurred by the desperate need for funds to finance the closing campaigns of the war. A new effort was forced in 1783 by the crisis following peace, when it was necessary to pay off the army and give some assurance to wartime creditors. In April of that year a comprehensive plan was proposed by Congress. It would have changed the basis of the states' quotas from unascertainable land valuations to population, counting only three-fifths of the slaves. Congress would again be authorized to levy a five-percent duty together with certain specific duties, but only for twenty-five years, with the income pledged only to payment of interest and principal on the national debt. Moreover, collectors would be appointed by the respective states, and the duties collected in each state would be credited to its quota for national contributions. In addition, the states would undertake to make cash contributions totaling one and a half million dollars a year, apportioned among them according to the population formula and after allowing for the duties collected.

At one time or another in the following three years, every state agreed, some with reservations, to part or all of this proposal. Unanimous consent, however, was never gained on any single provision. The nearest approach to complete concurrence came on the familiar proposal for import duties. By 1786 all the states except New York had agreed to this in one form or another. After a long struggle New York also agreed in the spring of 1786, but with such reservations and limitations as to make its action ineffective. This ended years of effort at negotiation and persuasion. The movement toward a new constitution altering the whole basis of the union was already under way, and further efforts to improve the Articles of Confederation were abandoned. The problem of financing those governmental activities that must be carried on at a level above that of the individual states was almost as far from solution in 1787 as it had been in 1763.

For decades historians of the period from Yorktown to the ratification of the Constitution depicted it as a time of feckless confusion and collapse leading to the brink of a disaster from which the new nation was saved only by the Constitution. In doing so they were following the lead of John Fiske, an enormously popular writer whose history of those years, *The Critical Period of American History,* appeared in 1888. Later, when historians had become impressed with the significance of economic classes in history and when the Great Depression and the New Deal had given an antibusiness and agrarian cast to their thought, there was a tendency to swing to the opposite view and to consider the Articles of Confederation a reasonably satisfactory adjustment to the needs of the time, under which the states were in fact able to thrive and prosper.

The truth no doubt lies between these views. In the 1780's most Americans continued to live a simple farm and village life, unchanged since the early eighteenth century. For their needs, the separate governments of individual states served well enough, as they had for a century past. Once the economic dislocations that followed the war and demobilization were surmounted, the agrarian economy quickly recovered and indeed began to flourish. The standing armies, the maintenance of force along the frontiers, the regulation of commerce among the states and with foreign powers, the support of a stable and uniform currency throughout the country, provision for the effective collection of debts throughout the several commonwealths, the establishment of a bureaucracy to carry out these objectives, and central taxation to finance them—all the measures that were resisted with arms when the British proposed them—continued to be unnecessary to the welfare of most Americans. For their needs the Articles of Confederation provided all the central government that was necessary, and few of them felt a sense of urgent need for a stronger unity.

The American society and economy were, however, expanding rapidly in three ways. One was the westward surge of settlement. With growing wealth and population and with the removal of imperial restraints, families would pour across the forests and prairies to the Mississippi with almost explosive rapidity. The new government was speedily being required to exercise not merely titular claim to, but actual administration over, an empire far vaster than the total of the original thirteen states. Within a decade and a half this empire would be nearly doubled again by the Louisiana Purchase, extending the national domain to the Rockies and even beyond. The sheer size of the West transcended and indeed overwhelmed the parochial concerns of the little statehouses along the Atlantic coast.

The coming of peace left a brief and exhausted truce between the Americans and the trans-Allegheny Indians, the British in their still-held Northwestern posts, and the Spanish along the Mississippi. While this undeclared truce persisted, the military and fiscal helplessness of the Congress was not critical. But the renewed western flow soon revived conflict and tension, and it was obvious that the United States, in order to protect its interests, would soon need the capacity to maintain and use substantial forces along the frontier.

The American economy was growing outward as well as westward. With the end of the Navigation Acts, American ships and cargoes were entering every port of the world, penetrating the Baltic and the Mediterranean, cruising the African coast, rounding the frigid barrier of Cape Horn, trading to world-distant Canton. In this vast and growing traffic they no longer enjoyed the protection of British warships or British treaties. To bargain for rights in foreign ports, Congress needed control over the reciprocal rights in American ports. Naval power was needed even in peacetime to meet the threats of the Barbary pirates of the Mediterranean and other lawless forces on the seas. Moreover, the little time of peace among the great powers that followed the signing of the Treaty of Paris in 1783 and that allowed the Americans the luxury of almost total disarmament was to last for less than a decade. Few of the international tensions had been resolved, and bitter new ones were about to be created by the surging forces of the French Revolution. The Atlantic would offer no effective isolation from the tempestuous decades of war about to come, and only an armed and potent state would be able to maintain itself.

Finally, the economy at home was maturing. Subsistence farming eked out with neighborly barter was becoming rapidly less important. Merchants, always a vital element in the economy, were increasing the range of their trade. Robert Morris' Bank of North America was a precursor of continent-wide financial operations. A surge in manufacturing, now freed of British restraint, was hoped for. The exigencies of the war itself, requiring a traffic in arms and supplies up and down the continent, had helped to stimulate an interstate commerce. The issuance of a wide variety of state and Continental obligations had greatly increased the impersonal investment in securities as opposed to investment in personally managed farms or shops. A financial class was emerging.

A national economy was coming into being. Its health would demand a national control over foreign trade and navigation, a uniform and stable currency, well-secured bonds to provide a fluid and efficient means of mobilizing savings, a power to stimulate manufactures and other new enterprises with tariffs and bounties, and a sure and uniform means of enforcing contracts and collecting debts throughout the states.

The men who demanded a national government with all these powers and with the strength to control the West and protect American interests abroad of course spoke for their own self-interest, but they also spoke for the new American society and economy that were emerging and that could not have survived without an effective national government.

10 ★★★★★★★★★

Liberty and Equality

When the rebels declared that all men are created equal they were trying to find a general argument to support a very specific case: that Americans were created equal to Englishmen and hence equally entitled to govern themselves. But the argument outran its goal. If Americans were created equal to Englishmen, were they not created equal to each other? If it was no longer tolerable that Britons through their representatives in Parliament should have an unearned, inherited privilege to tax the property of unrepresented Americans, was it tolerable that disfranchised Americans should be taxed by the legislatures of their own states, in which they were equally unrepresented? If all men are equal, was it just that members of a dominant faith have advantage over those of other sects or that a rich man should have greater political rights than a poor man? If all men are created equal, what justification could be found to divide them into freemen and slaves and to allow men of one group to buy and sell those of the other?

Though the American colonies in pre-Revolutionary days were freer from structured privilege than any other commonwealths in the world, inequalities nevertheless existed; and for decades before the Revolution there had been struggles to reduce or to perpetuate them. The conflicts of low countryman and frontiersman, of rich man and poor, of the established churches and the dissenters, had gone on side by side with the controversies between colonial assemblies and royal governors. These two sets of conflicts sometimes coincided, sometimes cut across each other. Sometimes the same men were fighting both for equality within the British empire and for equality at home, like the Whig leaders in New York or

Massachusetts. More often, perhaps, the American leaders were members of oligarchies within their own colonies who sought to win from the distant British a greater power for those local oligarchies and at the same time to preserve their power from dilution at home. In North Carolina, for example, the Revolutionary leaders were the same men who half a dozen years before had supported the royal governor in suppressing the Regulator movement among the disadvantaged frontiersmen; and the Regulators of 1771 for the most part either supported the Crown or were indifferent when the Revolution itself came.

Carl Becker once characterized these two issues as the issue of home rule and the issue of who should rule at home. At the moment of independence, these two movements tended to coalesce in a surge of support for the concept of equality, drawn from the philosophy of the time and given shape by the rhetoric of the Declaration of Independence. In our own time we have seen a similar phenomenon, when both the logic and the emotion of our attack on Nazi racism during World War II overflowed into a pressure for Negro equality within the United States. Then, as now, the first enthusiasm of the idealistic goal receded; and then, as now, the accomplishments were far from complete. But nevertheless, the years from 1774 to 1789 saw not only the coming of American independence but also a considerable progress in democratic egalitarianism within the United States. We became not only free of Great Britain but also freer within our own society and government.

The manifestations of inequality and privilege against which the more egalitarian rebels struggled were numerous. One of them was a universal limitation of suffrage to persons of some property. In most colonies this limitation followed the British precedent of confining the votes to those holding a freehold in property worth forty shillings a year or more in rent. In view of the wide dispersion of real property and the ease with which land could be acquired, this limitation was not so restrictive as in Great Britain, where it confined the suffrage to a tiny minority. But even in America the exclusion of the landless—the farm laborer, the footloose itinerant, the urban workman—narrowed the franchise to a point where the number of voters was rarely so much as ten percent of the free adult male population. The total exclusion from the vote of women and slaves was a matter of course.

Even among those who could vote there was a further inequality in terms of representation. In almost every colony the older settlements along the coast, usually dominated by the wealthier and more conservative elements, hung on to an unequal voice in the legislature. Sometimes, as in North Carolina and Pennsylvania, this was achieved by giving the older counties more delegates than the new, regardless of population. In other colonies there was a refusal to create new frontier counties, leaving the very large populations of enormous western counties with the same representation as the tiny counties of the east. This imbalance reached perhaps its extreme form in South Carolina, where the upland settlements were not organized into counties at all and hence went entirely unrepresented.

Property qualifications were even more rigid with respect to officeholding, and the assemblies were in consequence likely to be made up of men of very substantial means. The large-propertied and professional classes were given a further privilege through their dominance of the appointive or indirectly elected governors' councils, which shared legislative power with the elective assemblies.

Except for the town meetings of New England—which were even more democratic than the relatively democratic assemblies of those colonies—local government was a stronghold of privilege. County government in most of the other colonies, as in England, was in the hands of a Court of Pleas and Quarter Sessions, which served as a trial court as well as the governing body of the county. It was made up of justices of the peace who individually exercised a large judicial and administrative power within their respective neighborhoods. Though officially elected by the assembly or appointed by the governor, the county court was likely to be a self-perpetuating body in practice, immune from popular control, and representing the large-property interests of the county. Insofar as the cities outside New England had been incorporated, their governments were likely to be legally, as well as practically, self-perpetuating "close corporations" in which a named group of burgesses made up the corporation and had power to fill vacancies in their number, or in which the burgesses were elected by a very restricted suffrage. City governments outside New England were likely to represent the larger merchants in the same way that county governments represented the larger landowners.

The opportunity to acquire land easily and cheaply had been the principal dynamic force driving toward equality in the colonies. Individual ownership of small farms was in itself an assurance of relative equality in an overwhelmingly agricultural society. But the influence of cheap land extended further. It strengthened the position of artisans and laborers, who could take up land as an alternative to continuing an oppressive or unrewarding employment. So long as land was easily come by, the limitation of the suffrage to property owners was not so harsh a restriction. To the extent that the opportunity to own land was freely and equally available, freedom and equality flowed out to all other aspects of colonial life. But in the years before the Revolution this opportunity was narrowing. Because of the primitive state of roads, only lands near water transportation were valuable for anything but subsistence farming, and most such lands had passed into private hands by the mid-eighteenth century. The remaining ungranted lands were, as Curtis Nettels has pointed out, vested in the Crown and in five proprietors: two Penn brothers, Lord Baltimore, Lord Fairfax, and Lord Granville, who owned lands in Pennsylvania, Maryland, Virginia, and North Carolina and Tennessee, respectively. All of these proprietors were interested in exploiting their property for a maximum return under quasi-feudal tenures, which normally meant large grants to wealthy purchasers. The line of settlement was pressing against the mountains, and the Crown in 1763, by drawing its Proclamation Line along the crest of the Appalachians, closed off to legal settlement the great reservoir of fertile land in the West. Negotiations were under way in the following decade, with several wealthy syndicates seeking to monopolize princely grants in the Ohio and Indiana areas. In 1774 the Quebec Act placed lands west of the mountains and north of the Ohio under the French feudal forms of land tenure used in Quebec. A pattern of restrictive and oligopolistic land ownership seemed about to replace the relative equality of the earlier days.

Legal patterns in some of the colonies further reinforced this trend. In New York the Dutch practice of granting vast patroonships with the characteristics of feudal estates was continued by the English, with the result that most of the valuable land in that province was vested in a few families like the Philipses, the Van Rensselaers, the Van Cortlandts, the Schuylers, and the Livingstons. Royal governors in other colonies, like New Hampshire and Georgia, were enabled to endow themselves with vast estates. Of special importance in the Southern colonies were the British practices of primogeniture and entail. Primogeniture assured the inheritance of landed estates by the eldest son in the absence of a specific will to the contrary. Entail was a legal procedure under which an owner could assure that his estate would pass down the male line of his heirs intact from generation to generation without being sold or divided. Both practices encouraged the formation and perpetuation of great landed properties after the British and European form.

Though a diversity of sects and the high degree of lay control of most of them made the churches much less an instrument of privilege in America than in Europe, Congregationalists in New England and Anglicans in the South did enjoy special privileges. Their clergy and churches were supported by the income from church lands granted by the colony and by taxes levied on all residents except for active members of certain recognized dissenting sects. Religious qualifications for officeholding in many colonies gave a further advantage to the adherents of the traditional faiths. The establishment of the Congregational Church in New England and of the Anglican Church in the Southern colonies had a political and economic as well as a religious significance in that these were the churches of the older, well-established, prosperous settlers of the coastal areas. The less well-to-do frontiersmen, already suffering from underrepresentation and inability to acquire fertile and well-situated land, and frequently deprived of the vote, suffered another handicap from the inferior status of their Presbyterian, Baptist, and German churches.

A further barrier to equality existed in the character of the educational system. Except in parts of New England, the school system was entirely private, and a child's education depended on the willingness and ability of his parents to pay for it. Moreover, there were few or no schools in the more thinly settled frontier areas, even for the parent who could afford to school his children. Again, the prosperous resident of port towns and the tidewater could pass on to his sons a more privileged opportunity of success than could the poor man or the frontiersman.

The traditions of the common law, as amplified in colonial statutes, had a care for the security of the well-to-do rather than for the suffering of the poor. Only the meager bounty of the parish fund protected the poor from catastrophe, and even this shelter was available only to settled folk, who were rarely those who needed it most. Rigorous sanctions of the law, however, protected the well-to-do in their right to collect debts due them, including the power to imprison a debtor unable to pay. In a day of very poor credit arrangements, without banks or other organized sources of loans, and with a limited and rigid money supply, perhaps most farmers and many small businessmen were dependent at one time or another upon loans from individual men of wealth. These loans were often difficult to repay promptly because of a shortage of hard money in the community generally, crop failures, the loss of ships at sea, or any one of dozens of unpredictable disasters that might befall in an economy far less well cushioned against misfortune than ours. Hard money and rigid collection, enforced by foreclosure and debtors prison, were the security of the well-to-do and the terror of those less fortunate.

But all of these inequalities among white Americans were as nothing compared with the gulf between white Americans and black. By all except a few eccentrics, the four hundred thousand African slaves were simply considered to be outside the community altogether, not part of the equal creation, nor possessed of any of those rights to life, liberty, and the pursuit of happiness that had been declared for all men. Instead, they were bought, sold, used, disciplined, and considered as a species of more intelligent and more dangerous cattle.

The opportunity to attack these elements of privilege in American society came in writing the constitutions adopted by almost all the states in the early years of the Revolution. The Stamp Act Congress and the two Continental congresses had legislated and made declarations on the fundamental problems of imperial organization and had philosophized about the theoretical basis of government in democratic consent. But it was in the drafting of the state constitutions that the Americans for the first time had to formulate in detail their ideas as to how government should be organized and administered at home. Except for the continuation of the colonial charters in Connecticut and Rhode Island, new constitutions had been adopted in all states by 1780.

The remarkable thing about them was not that they set up radically new forms of government, but that they so faithfully reproduced the old. The principal necessity faced by the new constitution-makers was to replace the royal governor and his council. Except for Pennsylvania, where executive power was vested in a committee, all the states provided for a single governor elected in some cases by the people and in others by the legislature. In most states the fear and distrust of the governor's office growing out of decades of controversy with its royally appointed incumbents was reflected in a marked curtailment of its powers. The principal issues were over the governor's appointive power and his authority to veto bills. In a number of the new constitutions the appointive power was severely restricted, either by making many of the more important state offices popularly or legislatively elective or by requiring the participation of a committee or a legislative group in the appointing process. Since many of the controversies between colonial assemblies and the Crown had involved the suspension or disallowance of colonial legislation, it was to be expected that in the new constitutions the veto power would be either denied the governor entirely, as in North Carolina, or limited in a variety of ways.

The council in most colonies was appointed, and hence represented a very small elite of wealth and power associated usually with the interests of the Crown. In every state except Pennsylvania some form of upper house of the legislature was provided as a substitute for the council. Usually, however, it was dissociated from the governor and from the executive functions exercised by the colonial councils and became purely a legislative body. The senates, as these houses were usually called, were given a more democratic basis, being elected either by the people or by the lower house. They continued, however, to represent an elite.

Except for the necessary reconstitution of the governor and council, who had been specifically royal officials, few changes were made during the Revolutionary era in the structure of the provincial governments as they had existed in the colonies. Almost no changes were made in local governments. The management of most cities remained in the hands of more prosperous merchants, that of most counties in the hands of the landed gentry.

More vigorous debates were over suffrage and the apportionment of representatives. Even here progress toward complete democracy was very slow. No state adopted universal manhood suffrage. Only New Hampshire, Pennsylvania, North Carolina, and Georgia—and later, upon its admission to the Union, Vermont—went so far as to admit all poll-tax payers to the vote. In all of the other states the franchise, with minor exceptions, continued to be confined to landowners. The usual colonial requirement of fifty acres or of land worth forty shillings a year rent remained generally in effect, being somewhat lowered in Virginia and actually considerably increased in Massachusetts. It remained true, as it had been throughout the colonial period, that those who owned the land governed the commonwealth. In a sense the Revolution was fought to protect those landowners in that power; and for all the declarations of the equality of men, they showed little more disposition to share it with their landless fellows than with the distant British.

Somewhat more progress was made in reducing the extremes of inequity in sectional representation in the state legislatures. This was most marked in Pennsylvania, where the small minority who lived in Philadelphia and the nearby counties had two thirds of the seats of the assembly. In an unsuccessful effort to forestall its own displacement by a provincial congress, the legislature in March, 1776, voted to divide its membership almost equally between the Philadelphia area and the rest of the colony. Even this allotment, however, was grossly unfair to the central and western counties, which by that date had nearly three fourths of the population. Substantial equity was achieved in the first state constitution, which gave the west two thirds of the seats.

Similarly, in South Carolina the upland settlements were almost entirely unrepresented in the colonial legislatures. In the first provincial congress they were given 40 out of 184 seats, and in the constitution of 1778 this proportion was increased to nearly one third. Even at this time, however, the uplands had the overwhelming majority of the white population; further concessions were made in the removal of the capital from Charleston to Columbia and in a provision for reallocations of seats in 1785 and at fourteen-year intervals thereafter. By 1790 the West, which then had nearly eighty percent of the white population, had achieved forty-five percent of the representation. In other states, such as New York, there were less sweeping readjustments of representation; and in nearly all states the creation of new counties along the frontier, each automatically entitled to seats in the legislature, somewhat improved the balance between east and west even in the absence of changes in the representation formula itself. As in the reduction of property requirements for voting, however, the movement toward equality of representation was carried forward slowly, reluctantly, and without fervor, and only the more extreme inequities were corrected.

The foregoing limitations applied to the lower house of the state legislature, which was intended as the voice of democracy. In creating the new upper houses and governorships to replace the old royal institutions, even more restrictive measures were adopted to assure that they, like their royalist predecessors, would continue to represent property and the status quo. Higher qualifications were often imposed for voters for governor or senator, and representation in the senate was even more unbalanced in favor of the older and wealthier sections. And even the most democratic states continued—some even increased—the property requirements to serve as assemblyman, senator, or governor. The constitution of 1778 in South Carolina, for example, required the governor to own real estate worth ten thousand pounds and senators to own land worth two thousand pounds. Though requirements were not so high in others, the constitutional requirements of nearly all of them made it certain that the commonwealths would be governed by men of substantial and settled property.

Since most of the restrictions on voting and officeholding were expressed in terms of the ownership of real property, their actual significance depended on the distribution of land. Here the consequences of the Revolution were truly revolutionary. The ownership of hundreds of millions of acres passed from the Crown and from various lords to the people of the United States or of the individual states. We have already pointed out that the long policy debate over the Trans-Appalachian West was finally and definitely resolved in favor of its rapid settlement by individual farmers to whom the land would be given cheaply. Gone were all ideas of preserving the area for the Indians or of restricting the flow of settlement to facilitate British control or to continue the dominant position of the Atlantic states. By the ordinances of 1785 and 1787, already described, the Western lands were thrown open on a democratic basis, and with the relatively easy ownership of land would flow a comparably easy access to full political status.

A similar democratization took place within the individual states. In the Southern states and in New York and Pennsylvania there were princely domains taken over from the Crown, or in Pennsylvania the proprietor, and not ceded to the Confederation. All of the states adopted relatively liberal policies in disposing of these possessions. A very large part of the state lands were used as bounties to encourage enlistment in the Revolutionary armies, thus speeding up its dispersion into private hands.

A third process important in democratizing land ownership was the confiscation and resale of loyalist estates. The states generally, by legislative acts early in the war, authorized the seizure of the property of those who remained actively loyal to the Crown. Enormous estates were involved. Many of the royal governors, like Wentworth in New Hampshire and Wright in Georgia, had managed to gain large domains for themselves; and these were, of course, among those confiscated. The largest loyalist estates were in New York, where most of the great landholdings along the Hudson were seized, along with nearly a quarter of a million acres held by Sir John Johnson in the frontier areas of the state. All told, more than two million five hundred thousand acres, including some of the best land in the state, was taken from fifty-nine loyalists who had monoplized these thousands of square miles. Though many of the loyalist lands were bid in by wealthy men who were themselves already large landowners, there can be no doubt that the breakup of these domains markedly changed the economic constitution of such states as New York.

Moreover, the legal structure was itself changed throughout the states to discourage the future creation or maintenance of estates of this size. The new land policies were aimed at granting family-sized holdings rather than the patroonships and quasibaronies of the colonial period. An attack was also made on the laws of primogeniture and entail that helped to hold the great estates together. Virginia abolished entails in 1776, and within a decade all other states had also done away with them or so modified them as to make them meaningless. Primogeniture was more stubbornly supported, but by 1789 it too had been abolished in Georgia, Maryland, New York, North Carolina, and Virginia. In other states, such as most of those in New England, the rights of the eldest son had been confined to a double portion, but this too was abolished in the Revolutionary period. By 1789 primogeniture survived only in Rhode Island and South Carolina, and it was on its way out there.

All told, the changes in the legal structure of land tenure that took place during the Revolution may have been the most significant of all the democratizing trends of the period.

The special privileges of established churches were also sharply curtailed during the Revolutionary period. The era itself was a skeptical one, and deistic ideas were predominant among thinkers in Britain and on the Continent. The intellectual leaders of the Revolution—men like Jefferson, Franklin, and John Adams—themselves held pronouncedly skeptical views. It is significant that the Constitutional Convention itself rejected a motion to have its sessions opened with prayer. The hostility to the political influence of churches on the part of such men as Madison and Jefferson gave leadership to a movement that found its principal support in the resentment of dissenter groups, especially Baptists and Presbyterians. Usually poorer than the dominant Congregationalists and Anglicans, and also discriminated against as residents of the underrepresented western sections of their respective states, these and other minority sects joined in abolishing the establishment of religion in most of the states.

The precise details, however, varied from state to state within broad regional patterns. In the Middle states, where the wide variety of faiths had never permitted the meaningful establishment of any one, an almost complete religious liberty was easily won. It existed already, in effect, in Pennsylvania and Delaware as a result of the policies of the original Quaker proprietors. In New Jersey, which had had no formal establishment in the colonial period, the constitution of 1776 forbade any requirement of church attendance or support or the establishment of any particular denomination. A somewhat similar provision in the New York constitution of 1777 ended the rather nominal Anglican and Dutch Reformed establishment in that state.

The story was quite different, however, in New England, where—except in Rhode Island—the Congregational Church was firmly established not only in law but also in the respect of the majority of the people, and where its relatively democratic control made it less vulnerable as an instrument of privilege. Massachusetts and New Hampshire, in their constitutions of 1780 and 1784 respectively, provided that no one sect should be subordinated to another by law, and allowed each town to select its own minister and hence, in effect, its own denomination. Each town was required to support some church, however, and as the overwhelming majority continued to support Congregational churches, the practical situation was little changed. Indeed it was made somewhat more, rather than less, difficult for dissenters to obtain exemption from church taxes levied by the towns in order to support their own churches.

Even fewer concessions were made in Connecticut, the most conservative of the Congregationalist states. The definition of dissenting groups who could have their taxes applied to their own churches was broadened in 1777, and in 1784 the right of internal self-government was granted to all religious bodies. Nevertheless, the Congregational Church remained the established church of Connecticut, and everyone had to pay taxes to it who was not regularly attending and supporting some other recognized church.

The most important struggles for complete religious freedom came in the South, where the Anglican Church had a firm legal establishment but lacked the popular support of the Congregational Church in New England and moreover had suffered from its identification with Great Britain. The establishment was most easily overturned in North Carolina, where it was weakest. There the constitution of 1776 forbade the preferential establishment of any denomination and any requirements for church attendance or support. All ministers were given the right to perform marriages, and other restrictions were removed. It was almost as simple in Georgia, where the establishment was also weak and where the constitution of 1777 had similar provisions. In South Carolina, where the Anglican Church was stronger and more popular, an attempt was made to continue the establishment in the temporary frame of government of 1776, but public pressure led to a provision in the permanent constitution of 1778 abolishing the establishment and according equal rights to all Protestants.

In Virginia, where the Anglican Church was deeply entwined with the aristocratic traditions of the state, the struggle over the establishment took on a special significance. As a first step, the constitution of 1776, though maintaining the establishment, gave all men the right to the free exercise of their religion. Subsequent legislation implemented this provision by the repeal of laws making it a crime to maintain certain beliefs and religious practices and by relieving dissenters supporting their own churches from taxation for the support of the Episcopal Church. Efforts permanently to eliminate all taxes for church support failed at that time; but the taxes were suspended for a year, and this suspension was continued from year to year until they were finally abolished in 1779.

A counterattack came in 1784, when Patrick Henry introduced a bill for the tax support of all Christian churches on an equal basis. He was able to rally to its support many Methodists and Presbyterians who had opposed the sole establishment of the Anglican Church, and the bill commanded a large majority in the legislature. Madison and other opponents were, however, successful in having it referred to the people for discussion. An intense statewide campaign followed, and in response to the public sentiment aroused, the bill was defeated in 1785. This finally paved the way to reintroduction and passage of Jefferson's famous bill for religious liberty that had been unsuccessfully presented in 1779.

This statute, finally enacted in 1786, Jefferson himself ranked with the authorship of the Declaration of Independence and the founding of the University of Virginia as one of three achievements by which he wished to be remembered. Going far beyond the statutes and constitutional provisions of other states, it provided for complete religious liberty for the citizen and a complete separation of church and state. It is one of the fundamental documents of American history, and its tenets were written into the federal Constitution when the First Amendment was adopted. Its key sentence reads: "No man shall be compelled to frequent or support any religious worship, place or ministry whatsoever, nor shall be enforced, restrained, molested, or burthened in his body or goods, nor shall otherwise suffer on account of his religious opinions or belief; but that men shall be free to profess, and by argument to maintain their opinion in matters of religion, and that the same shall in no wise diminish, enlarge or affect their civil capacities."

So sweeping a victory for religious freedom was won in no other state, and in most, officeholding remained confined to Protestants. Catholics and Jews and in some cases Quakers continued in a number of states to suffer, at least nominally, from a variety of disabilities. But the spirit of religious freedom seems to have outrun the statutes, and many restrictive laws that were not repealed were nevertheless ignored. In the post-Revolutionary decades, for example, North Carolina was to have a Jewish legislator and a Catholic Supreme Court justice, though nominally both offices remained open only to Protestants.

The more thoughtful Revolutionary leaders realized that a democratic government could be safely based only on a democratic educational system. To vote intelligently, a citizen must have the minimum of literacy that would enable him to use newspapers and books to form his own opinions. If officeholding were to be truly open to the people, then opportunities for higher education must be open to the abler children of whatever social class.

In the New England states this ideal had been approached. The Calvinist religion, with its emphasis on the responsibility of every man to read and interpret the Bible for himself, had provided a powerful sanction for universal education, which in turn accorded with the democratic organization of society in that region. Moreover, each of the New England colonies had a college, again intended primarily for the production of learned clergymen but serving the lay needs of society as well. The Middle colonies as well boasted a college each—two in New Jersey—and although education was almost entirely in the hands of the churches and private charities, the region was wealthy enough to provide a fairly general access to elementary education. The South, however, lagged far behind. There was no public or regularly organized church or charitable provision for elementary education, and William and Mary was the only college in the entire region. In consequence of these regional differences, literacy was nearly universal in New England, and the son of a plain farmer like John Adams, if his abilities permitted, could readily obtain an excellent classical education. In the South, in contrast, over half the white men, most white women, and substantially all Negroes were illiterate; and a college education was usually reserved for the sons of wealthy planters. This educational system—or lack of it—reflected and powerfully reinforced the aristocratic structure of Southern society. The situation in the Middle states lay between these extremes.

As early as 1765 John Adams, speaking of a common school system, had pointed out that "the preservation of the means of knowledge among the lowest ranks is of more importance to the public than all the property of all the rich men in the country." Jefferson emphatically shared this conviction and indeed proposed to the Virginia legislature a scheme by which all children other than those of slaves would receive a tax-supported education through the third grade, that is, through the basic skills of reading, writing, and common arithmetic; the more gifted would receive secondary training, still at public expense; and the ablest of all would receive their education free at a state university. Numbers of other leaders of the time had similar views, and it was a part of the standard beliefs of the time that political and educational equality must go hand in hand.

The Revolutionary epoch saw little done to achieve these ends. The war years themselves were, in fact, almost disastrous for education. The disorders of war and the preoccupation with the war effort closed hundreds of schools. The small endowments of the nine colleges that existed at the beginning of the war were dissipated by inflation, the buildings of several were occupied by British and American troops, and faculty and students were drawn into the war. Nevertheless, the devotion to educational ideals in the period was not wholly wasted; and if little was accomplished, much was planned and a good deal was begun.

John Adams, in his *Thoughts on Government,* written in 1776 as a guide to the making of new constitutions for the soon-to-be states, renewed his earlier appeals for public education. "Laws for the liberal education of youth, especially of the lower class of people, are so extremely wise and useful that to a humane and generous mind no expense for this purpose would be thought extravagant." His words found a definite, if modest response. New Hampshire (in its second constitution), Massachusetts, Pennsylvania, North Carolina, and Georgia in their new constitutions all made provisions of one kind or another for publicly supported education, as did Vermont on its subsequent admission to the Union. Connecticut and Rhode Island continued their colonial provisions for town-supported schools along with their colonial charters. In New York, though the constitution was silent on education, immediately after the end of hostilities Governor Clinton made an eloquent appeal to the legislature for a statewide educational program. As he put it in 1782, ". . . it is the peculiar duty of the government of a free state where the highest employments are open to citizens of every rank to endeavor by the establishment of schools and seminars to diffuse that degree of literature which is necessary to the establishment of public trusts." His appeal led to the passage of acts in 1784, 1785, and 1787 that created a "University of the State of New York," responsible for all education in the state, and a Board of Regents to govern it, and that set aside certain public lands for the support of education. Delaware's legislature made a more modest commitment to public schools.

In 1785 Georgia passed legislation somewhat similar to New York's, and both that state and North Carolina made provision for state universities. Though these institutions were not in fact to open until 1795 in the case of North Carolina and 1801 in the case of Georgia, they were the first two state universities in the country.

Poverty was to prevent any very realistic effort to carry out these ambitious projects, and a genuine system of public schools providing universal primary education would have to await the mid-nineteenth century. But by 1789 most of the states by one means or another had made a commitment to the ideal of free, tax-supported, education as an essential basis of democracy. The idea became part of the foundation of the American political philosophy.

Meanwhile private efforts were doing a good deal to enlarge educational opportunity. Dozens of "acadamies" were opened in the postwar decade, of which the most notable were those endowed by the Phillips family at Andover, Massachusetts, and Exeter, New Hampshire. Numerous colleges were also started, including Dickinson and Franklin colleges in Pennsylvania; the forerunner of Union College in New York; Washington, Saint John's, Cokesbury, and Georgetown in Maryland; and Hampden-Sydney in Virginia. In the twenty years after Yorktown, the number of colleges in the United States more than doubled.

There was also a more serious effort to engage the new academies and colleges more directly with the problems of democratic citizenship. Courses in science were enlarged, and new ones introduced in modern languages, political science, and economics.

The long relation between democracy and education in America had barely begun, but it had begun.

The common law of England, modified somewhat by statute, had provided the civil and criminal law of the colonies. It was a legal system designed to protect the liberty and property of men of substance against both the arbitrary exactions of the Crown and the grasp of the propertyless. It was ruthless in asserting the right of the creditor to exact the last pound of his claims and in protecting the man of means from crimes against property. Colonial bills to mitigate this severity by making paper money legal tender for the payment of debt or by staying suits or executions through the courts were stopped by royal veto. During the period 1776–1789 from the coming of independence until the adoption of the Constitution, which forbade the passage by the states of legal-tender laws and laws impairing the obligation of contracts, the states were free to experiment with measures to reduce or postpone the obligations of debtors. Such measures, on balance, would have worked in favor of the poorer men of the western sections of the states and against the interests of the generally privileged.

Perhaps surprisingly, most of these proposals failed. There was, of course, an inflationary issue of paper money during the actual Revolution, and a number of acts were passed making it legal tender in an effort to support its value; but these were measures aimed at financing the war rather than at strengthening the position of debtors in relation to their creditors.

In the mid 1780's there was a rash of bills for the issuance of paper money, for making it legal tender, and for staying legal actions for the collection of debts. These gained wide support from the sharp deflation and stringent currency shortage of the time; and in Rhode Island, Pennsylvania, New York, New Jersey, North and South Carolina, and Georgia bills for printing currency were approved in 1785 and 1786. In some cases these were reasonably carefully controlled issues; in others they were reckless. Ultimately, however, most of these issues were limited, redeemed, or canceled; and even before the ratification of the Constitution put an end to such legislation, the creditor class had been able to reassert its position.

There was, however, some amelioration of the provisions of the criminal law protecting property rights. Influenced in part by the widely read work of the Italian penologist Beccaria, the legislatures of several states drastically reduced the number of crimes for which the death penalty could be imposed, including such offenses as forgery and theft. There was also a strong movement to forbid the imprisonment of honest debtors, but it had only a very limited success.

Most significant in the development of the law toward the establishment of liberty and equality was the adoption by the states of bills of rights. A substantial protection of individual rights was embodied in the common law. The Magna Charta, in 1215, had provided an early codification of some of these rights; they had been further clarified in the English Bill of Rights of 1689. In the charters or the statutes of most of the individual colonies substantially the same catalog of rights had been set forth. There was, hence, a long tradition of the recording of individual rights in documents of enduring significance outside the patterns of regular legislation.

The traditional rights were, however, for the most part procedural rather than substantive. They defined the due process of the law: the right to freedom from unwarranted searches, to trial by jury with all its normal procedural appurtenances, and to protection from cruel and unusual punishments. Substantive freedoms, such as those of the press and religion, had only shadowy protection if any.

During the Revolution there was a strong impulse to clarify and record the political beliefs on which Americans acted. The Declaration of Independence itself expressed that impulse. In addition to restating the traditional British liberties as expressions of universal natural law, the Americans pressed further to assert a number of rights that had never been defined in Britain or the colonies. Following a precedent set by Virginia in June, 1776, they did so by including a separate bill of rights in their new constitutions or by expressing the same rights in the body of the constitution itself. Virginia's bill of rights, adopted on June 12, 1776, was the prototype of the others, not only as the earliest but also as the clearest and most comprehensive. Notable as new, enlarged, or more clearly defined rights in the Virginia constitution are: freedom from hereditary officeholders and hereditary privileges of any kind; a right to suffrage for all "having sufficient evidence of permanent common interest with, and attachment to, the community"; a protection from general warrants; freedom of the press (though still not clearly defined); and a free exercise of liberty for all men.

It was not to be clear for a long time whether such constitutional provisions were mere admonitions to the conscience of legislators or whether they were indeed a part of the law of the land, enforceable through the courts and having such superiority over statute law as to invalidate the latter in case of conflict. But in time the latter view prevailed, and the state and federal bills of rights of the Revolutionary period significantly enlarged the area of individual liberty in American life.

The greater liberty and fluidity of American society that emerged from the Revolution was not a matter of law and religion only. Perhaps equally important was the multiplication of economic opportunities that opened to citizens an increasing variety of paths to modest well-being or even to wealth. Attention has already been called to the confiscation and redistribution of loyalist estates, the liberalization of state land policies, and above all the opening of the West, which had continuing revolutionary effect in giving a truly democratic substance to the legalistic formulas of liberalism. Less immediate in its impact, but perhaps even more important in the long run of American history, was the birth of a national mercantile and industrial economy.

Prior to the Revolution, American economic life was almost wholly agricultural. The commercial apparatus of the country existed primarily to collect and forward to Britain or the West Indies the surplus agricultural products and to import and distribute British and West Indian products. The modest manufacturing enterprises were of a very small scale indeed, scarcely above home handicrafts, and with very few exceptions sold only to local and neighborhood markets. There was little commerce among the North American colonies, and land routes of transportation among them hardly existed.

The Revolution itself broke through these limiting patterns of trade and agriculture. Legal barriers were lifted, and the Americans were now free to buy and sell throughout Europe, and not merely in Britain. They could manufacture the once forbidden ironware and hats and establish corporations at will. The demands of the war gave a tremendous impetus to commerce on a national basis. Food, uniforms, shoes, tents, wagons, guns, powder, and other supplies had to be assembled for the armies from the length and breadth of the continent. The states, cut off from British and often from European trade, had to expand their manufacturing enterprises and use them to supply a national rather than a local market. Because the seas were so generally made dangerous to American traffic by the British Navy, it was necessary to improve roads. With better roads came improved postal service, and the inauguration of through stagecoach service from Portsmouth, New Hampshire, to Savannah.

Means of mobilizing money as well as credit were devised. The widespread use of paper currency during the war and even more importantly the issuance of tens of millions of dollars' worth of both Continental and state securities laid the basis for a more fluid organization of finance. The incorporation of the Bank of North America in 1780 and the subsequent organization of several other banks added to this fluidity. The advantages they offered may—as was charged at the time—have been available to only an inner circle of prominent businessmen, who thereby gained another competitive resource to be used against smaller businessmen. Nevertheless, they played an indispensable role in the rapid growth and diversification of the economy that followed the Revolution and that in turn created countless opportunities for small entrepreneurs, skilled artisans, managers, and clerks to find rewarding roles for themselves.

Even more important to the development of this more varied and open economy than the legal and institutional developments already mentioned was the emergence of a new group of lively and enterprising businessmen accustomed to thinking in national terms. These men grew out of the war itself, learning their skills and accumulating their capital in privateering, in opening new channels of commerce, in manufacturing for the army, and in many cases through service in the army commissariat or the Continental Treasury. This was the generation of men who were to found and lead the new economy.

By 1789 the country had not yet truly begun the remarkable economic growth that was to follow the inauguration of the new government. The disturbances of the war and the uncertainties of the following years had been too great to permit a real leap forward. But in those days the economy was organizing itself and developing the tools and skills that growth would require. Opportunity of the most diverse sort was ready to open itself to American youth, and the chance for jobs and business success would in time replace free land as the symbol of American egalitarian opportunity.

To one large group in American life all the larger liberties gained by the Revolution remained denied. These were the Negro slaves. Here and there a voice was raised to inquire whether the declaration that all men were created equal and were equally entitled to liberty was not inconsistent with the enslavement of human beings. In Massachusetts the courts went so far as to declare that the bill of rights adopted in the state constitution of 1780 did in fact abolish slavery. But with rare exceptions, even in the minds of the most liberal of the Revolutionary leaders, Negroes were considered to be outside the political community to which the tenets of the Declaration of Independence and the state bills of rights applied.

But if Negroes were beyond the reach of the new constitutional principles established by the Revolution, they were not altogether beyond the reach of the liberal sentiments of the era. Most of the Revolutionary leaders—including such Southerners and slaveholders as Washington, Jefferson, and George Mason—found slavery morally repugnant and deeply regretted that it had ever come to exist on American soil. In the Revolutionary debates only representatives of South Carolina and Georgia were likely to defend slavery as desirable or morally acceptable. The more liberal sentiments led to a considerable movement for Negro freedom as a measure of grace and humanity if not of legal right. The second New Hampshire constitution, adopted in 1784, specifically abolished slavery in that state, and during the 1780's gradual emancipation was provided by statute in Pennsylvania and the remaining New England states. No serious effort at emancipation was made, however, in any state in which there was any considerable number of slaves, and even in Virginia efforts to moderate the institution brought severe attacks upon their sponsors. In part the failure of any significant movement for emancipation to develop in the Southern states was due to the honest bewilderment of even such deplorers of slavery as Washington and Jefferson when confronted with the problem of how emancipated slaves, illiterate, largely untrained, many recently from Africa, and often unequipped for independent life, could survive if thrown on their own. Even so ingenious a mind as Jefferson's could think of no better solution than a gradual repatriation to Africa of manumitted slaves.

There was more success in the suppression of the slave trade. Though the opposition of South Carolina and Georgia was to withhold from the federal government until 1808 the power to prohibit the slave trade, all the other states had acted to suppress it in their own territories even before the adoption of the federal Constitution. Although the movement to suppress the slave trade had a genuinely liberal and humane motivation, its relative success, as contrasted with the almost total failure of the movement toward emancipation, was no doubt in part due to the fact that all the states except South Carolina and Georgia had a surfeit of slaves and that their further importation would in fact be injurious to the interests of slaveholders in the upper South.

It may be added that the liberal wave of the Revolution on this issue was short-lived. Other liberal movements of the era continued to grow toward a later fruition. But the Revolution left slavery undisturbed wherever it was important; and with the increasing profitability of slavery following the rise of cotton culture and the westward spread of the plantation system in the next century, attitudes hardened, slave codes were made harsher, the emancipation movement in the South —feeble as it was—was halted, and slavery came to be defended by Southerners as a positive good. Another and greater war was needed to renew even a limited progress toward freedom and equality.

11 ★★★★★★★★★

The Federal Solution

Thomas Hutchinson, an embodiment of empire set on the American borderlands, had said in 1773, "I know of no line that can be drawn between the supreme authority of Parliament and the total independence of the colonies." He was not alone in that inability. The political thought of the time simply did not include so fluid a conception of sovereignty as to permit it to be divided and geographically dispersed. Over one body of men there could be only one sovereign, only one ultimate power to declare the law. If there were to be both a central government and local governments, then one must be the creature and dependent of the other. A sovereign government like that of Britain could create counties or boroughs or other governmental corporations for its convenience, and from time to time could delegate such powers to them as it might choose; but such local governments were merely agents or extensions of the central authority, having of themselves no potency at all. Or a group of sovereign states could form a league and set up a central government, like the Continental Congress, as their servant to carry out for them such defined functions as they might choose to perform collectively; but such a league could not create law, or act upon the individual citizens of the associated states, or do anything else save as the agent of the powers that created it.

Neither of these conceptions was adequate to solve the problem of governing the dispersed American empire. The Americans were not prepared to accept the total subordination of their local governments to a distant Parliament. They would not have been prepared to accept it even had they been equally represented in that Parliament. The distinct and isolated interests of the individual colonies must, they believed, be expressed and protected by distinct and sovereign governments. They continued to believe this later, even when they were dealing with a central government of their own creation and geographically closer to their respective interests. In consequence the government set up by the Articles of Confederation was but the common agent of a group of sovereign states, powerless in itself.

But such localism was also inadequate to the times. For by the late eighteenth century the Americans had common interests extending the length of the great continent that required a sovereign government to express and protect them as fully as did the distinct interests of Virginians or Rhode Islanders. These continental, or national, interests were of two broad kinds. One was the set of interests related to the national security: the control and exploitation of the West, the subordination and ultimate removal of the Indians, the defense of the frontiers, the protection of American trade on the high seas and in foreign ports, security against aggression. The other was the set of interests involved in the rapidly emerging commercial economy, which demanded a uniform and stable monetary system throughout the country, the removal of internal trade barriers, and a uniform and dependable enforcement of contracts and collection of debts, as well as a vigorous representation of American commercial interests with foreign powers.

With respect to the national security, the Congress of the Confederation had a responsibility broadly enough defined, but it lacked the power for its effective discharge because of its total dependence upon the individual states for troops and money and because it had no real authority to enforce the discharge of obligations imposed by treaties it might negotiate. With respect to the national economy, the Congress did not have even the shadow of power. The bond between America and Britain had been destroyed because the statesmanship of the time could not devise a means of establishing at once both general authority and local autonomy in terms flexible enough to be responsive to the changing needs of the time. The problem had been no better solved by the Americans among themselves.

Almost from the adoption of the Articles of Confederation the great majority of voting Americans were convinced that the central government needed greater power and that in particular it needed an independent source of income and at least such minimal authority over trade as would allow the passage of navigation acts. But, as we have seen, no single formulation of the needed authority was ever able to gain the unqualified approval of all thirteen states and hence to become an amendment to the Articles of Confederation. By 1786 it had become apparent that efforts to amend the Articles in any important way by the unanimous consent of the states was futile.

In that year the Congress appointed a major committee to review the whole problem of enlarging its authority. The committee brought in a series of amendments that would have enabled Congress to enforce the payment of requisitions levied upon the states, granted it a limited authority over trade, and established the rudiments of a federal judiciary. But it was obvious they had no real chance of unanimous ratification, and the dispirited Congress did not even present them to the states.

Meanwhile, even as the Congress debated these proposals in the summer of 1786, the men who were most anxious for a stronger central authority had already turned their hopes to the possibility of creating a wholly new government by means of a direct approach to the states. Their determination was hardened by a continuing worsening of the financial and commercial situation.

Recent research has dispelled the old image of the years of the Confederation as a time of economic disaster. Once the disturbances of the war were over and labor could be applied steadily to the endless and fertile land, agricultural production rose swiftly. Most Americans were still farmers living upon their own products. They were well fed and well clothed, and a quiet prosperity touched most American homes.

It was not so in the cities and towns and among the planters who lived by export. Trade was still uncertainly adjusting to its new channels. A pall of uncertainty inhibited investment and economic growth. The value of securities, especially of obligations of the Confederation and the state governments, was uncertain and indeed undeterminable. Who could prudently invest in manufactures, when no national tariff protected him and when at any time state tariffs in adjoining states might bar him from his customers? What merchant could wisely expand his sales in other states when his efforts to collect his debts might be frustrated by "stay" laws to postpone their recovery or by the uncontrolled issuance of paper money? Who could safely invest in Western lands when there was no government able to force the British from their frontier posts or subdue the Indians or guarantee the peace along the frontier? Commerce and investment languished, trade fell sharply from its postwar peak, and the impatient expectation of a booming prosperity to match the new nation's hopes was frustrated.

Worst of the economic problems was simply that of money. America had always been short of gold and silver. It was shorter than ever now that every coin had to go to pay interest on the foreign debt and meet the increasingly unfavorable balance of trade. Yet every state had to levy much heavier taxes than before independence because of the unprecedented wartime debts that must be met and because the considerable British contribution to the cost of American defense and administration was no longer available. These taxes were sought in nearly nonexistent "hard money." At the same time, private creditors both at home and in Britain were pressing for the payment of their debts, some contracted in the immediate postwar boom, some carried over from before the war and inflated by years of interest. A severe deflation was a result. Men were idled, prices dropped sharply, and the burden of debt became heavier and heavier as it had to be paid in more and more valuable dollars.

A consequence was that in the mid-1780's there was a struggle in every state over the issue of paper money. During an eighteen-month period, from March, 1785 to August, 1786, seven states emitted paper currency in varying amounts to meet the crisis; and the question was hotly debated in the remaining six. Such currency was not viewed with the horror in which it was to be held by conservatives throughout the nineteenth century, when the increased supply of precious metals had made paper money less essential. Businessmen in eighteenth-century America knew that a carefully regulated paper currency could be a useful and even necessary lubricant of trade. But they had in vivid and recent memory the total collapse of the Continental currency and the chaos of unregulated wartime issues of the individual states. What they believed they urgently needed was a national government able to prevent monetary experiments by the states and yet to maintain an adequate, stable, uniform, national money supply.

While the movement toward a new constitution was under way, it was given a sharp impetus by an uprising in Massachusetts known as Shays' Rebellion. More than any of the other states, Massachusetts had been firmly devoted to the sanctity of hard money and of state obligations. It had taxed heavily to meet its debts, and the taxes fell most grievously on the subsistence farmers of its more isolated and rural counties. When the legislature firmly refused to issue paper money that the farmers could have borrowed on the security of their land in order to pay their taxes and debts, and when it also refused to enact "stay" laws halting or postponing the numerous foreclosure sales, many of these farmers took arms. Protest meetings and riots began in August, 1786, shortly after the legislature had adjourned. Two or three bands embracing over a thousand farmers marched about rather aimlessly during the autumn and broke up the sittings of a number of courts. The principal band was led by a Revolutionary War captain, Daniel Shays, from whom the uprising took its name. By February, 1787, the "rebellion" had been crushed by Massachusetts state militia commanded by General Benjamin Lincoln. Subsequently some ameliorative legislation was passed, and the participants, including even Shays himself, were pardoned.

While it lasted, however, this uprising had given a shock to conservative leaders throughout the country. Its spread to other states was feared, and the more alarmist businessmen saw it as the beginning of anarchy. Even the more level-headed saw another evidence of the turmoil through which they had lived for so many years and which had so disrupted the economic progress in which they were interested. Their apprehensions, together with concern for the federal arsenal at Springfield, led the Congress to authorize General Knox to raise a national force against the uprising. This army was in fact never used or needed, but it had not escaped the attention of the nationalist leaders that they had been able to justify such a force legally only by falsely stating that it was intended for use against the Indians. This whole experience gave a powerful stimulus to the nationalist movement that was already under way.

The concrete steps in this movement that led to the Constitution had begun in March, 1785, with a meeting at Alexandria, later adjourned to Mount Vernon, in which representatives of Maryland and Virginia met to discuss their common problems in connection with shipping and navigation on Chesapeake Bay and the Potomac River. They settled these easily enough and proceeded to make a more sweeping set of recommendations to their respective legislatures for setting up uniform trade regulations, currency, and commercial arrangements in general. A further conference, to which Pennsylvania would be added, was suggested to explore the possibility of a

Potomac River canal. James Madison of Virginia, a hitherto inconspicuous little man, but a wise and indeed a brilliant one, had been a delegate to the Mount Vernon meeting. He had become convinced of the necessity for a complete revision of the Articles of Confederation through a convention called for the purpose; and in a very real sense he became the leader of an informal national movement to achieve this objective. He saw his opportunity in the recommendation of the Virginia commissioners to the Mount Vernon conference, and he persuaded the Virginia legislature when it acted on the report in the following year to go beyond its terms and invite all the states to send delegates to a conference to meet at Annapolis in September, 1786, to discuss common problems of trade and navigation.

Most states accepted Virginia's invitation, but delegates from only five—Delaware, New Jersey, New York, Pennsylvania, and Virginia—actually appeared in Annapolis on the appointed date. The twelve delegates who were there, led by Alexander Hamilton, Madison's comrade in the effort to achieve a national government, abandoned the original purpose of their meeting and instead devoted themselves to calling on all the states to send delegates to still another convention. This was to meet in Philadelphia the following May in order "to take into consideration the situation of the United States, to devise such further provisions as shall appear to them necessary to render the constitution of the federal government adequate to the exigencies of the Union; and to report such an act for that purpose to the United States in Congress assembled, as when agreed to, by them, and afterward confirmed by the legislatures of every state, will effectually provide for the same." They recommended this enlargement of their original purposes to embrace not only commerce but also the whole political structure of the country because, as they said, "the power of regulating trade is of such comprehensive extent, and will enter so far into the general system of the federal government, that to give it efficacy, and to obviate questions and doubts concerning its precise nature and limits, may require a correspondent adjustment of other parts of the federal system."

This was not an isolated or spur-of-the-moment action of the handful of men at Annapolis. Those who most clearly perceived the need for an effective national government were men with national interests. They had business, political, or personal associations with the leaders in other states. They wrote each other frequent letters and met in the Congress or on business occasions. Many of them had close friendships founded on common service during the war. Though there was nothing approaching an organized political party, there was a loose but effective association of like-minded leaders. The twelve men at Annapolis were expressing the views of this much larger group, which had members in every state.

To this association is no doubt due the quick response to the Annapolis call. Though it came to the states not represented at that meeting only as an unofficial copy of the report of the delegates to their own five legislatures, it was heeded as though it had a formal, official status. Within relatively few weeks after the receipt of the invitation, the legislatures of Virginia, New Jersey, Pennsylvania, North Carolina, Delaware, and Georgia had chosen delegations. Faced with action on the part of so many states, the Congress, which had hesitated to approve this extralegal process of governmental change, was forced to add its blessing. On February 21, 1787, it too issued a call for delegates from the several states to meet at the same time and place; but Congress sought to limit the new convention to the "sole and express purpose" of proposing amendments to the Articles of Confederation, which should be reported to the Congress and the states for action in the manner prescribed in the Articles. The Congress intended, in other words, that the convention should serve only as a sort of citizens' committee to make suggestions that would in themselves have no legal effect and that before adoption would have to traverse the same impossible course of unanimous consent of the state legislatures that had defeated every earlier effort at improvement.

The members of the convention thought otherwise. Following Congress' invitation, all the other states except New Hampshire and Rhode Island chose delegates. (A New Hampshire delegation was later selected, and arrived when the convention was about half through its work; Rhode Island was never represented.) On the appointed date, May 14, 1787, only the Virginia delegation had reached Philadelphia to join their Pennsylvania colleagues, and eleven more days were to pass before the convention could organize with a bare quorum of seven states. By early June, however, eleven states were represented, and by mid-July the New Hampshire delegation had arrived. All told, fifty-five men served as members of the convention. They have been praised as an assemblage of near demigods who miraculously wrote out a perfect instrument of government, fabricating it whole from their own inspiration. Part of the legendry of the Constitutional Convention was due to its long-preserved secrecy. Not until the publication of James Madison's notes more than a half century later was anything publicly known of the bickering, the debates, the compromises that characterized its work. The Founding Fathers were very human beings who put together a constitution of compromises based almost entirely on existing patterns. But there were some pieces of new and creative genius. And the men themselves were the best America could produce.

John Adams and Thomas Jefferson were abroad on diplomatic missions and hence could not be present. A few men suspicious of the convention's purposes, like Samuel Adams and Patrick Henry, refused to seek positions on their states' delegations. John Jay was serving as secretary of foreign affairs. But otherwise almost every great political figure of the Revolutionary period was present. To mention the leaders only, there were Washington, who presided; Benjamin Franklin, too old for active debate but able usefully to conciliate differences; Elbridge Gerry and Rufus King, from Massachusetts; William Samuel Johnson and Roger Sherman, from Connecticut; Alexander Hamilton, from New York; William Paterson, from New Jersey; Thomas Mifflin, Robert and Gouverneur Morris, and James Wilson, from Pennsylvania; John Dickinson, from Delaware; James Madison, George Mason, Edmund Randolph, and George Wythe, from Virginia; William R. Davie, from North Carolina; John Rutledge and the two Pinckneys, from South Carolina.

The delegates to the Congress differed violently on a number of points, but on the truly fundamental decisions of the convention they were from the beginning generally agreed. This is not surprising, for with few exceptions the men who bore the thankless burdens of service through the long sweltering Philadelphia summer were men who cared deeply about the national union and who were convinced of the absolute necessity of strengthening it. Those definitely hostile to a strong union remained away deliberately; the indifferent simply did not seek election to the delegations; the mass of small farmers isolated from national and international commerce, among whom opposition to the Constitution was strongest, had only a limited interest and an even more limited role in public affairs of this complexity. Hence the near unanimity of basic purpose among the delegates.

This fact has tended to distort the significance of the various acts of the convention. Because its more fundamental decisions were quickly made with little debate, they have received less attention than questions of much more limited importance, like the apportionment of state representation, upon which the delegates were nearly evenly divided. The course of the convention's debates and acts has been described brilliantly and thoroughly in such works as Max Farrand's *The Framing of the Constitution of the United States* (1913) and Carl Van Doren's *The Great Rehearsal* (1948), and here it will be necessary only to summarize the proceedings very briefly.

The advocates of a true national government had not come to Philadelphia with a concerted plan already worked out, but they knew in general what they wanted. In the nearly two weeks between their arrival and the formal organization of the convention, the Virginia delegation devised such a plan, no doubt taking counsel with like-minded members of other delegations. James Madison seems to have been its principal draftsman, but Edmund Randolph, as governor of Virginia and head of the delegation, presented it to the convention as soon as it began its deliberations. It was a great tactical advantage to the advocates of a very strong central government to have the consideration of such a proposal become, in effect, the agenda of the convention.

The Virginia Plan proposed that there should be a national legislature with each state's representation based on its free population or its share of taxes. It should have two houses, the lower elected by the people, the upper by the lower house from among the nominees of the state legislature. There should be an executive—which might be one man or several—chosen by the legislature, and a national judiciary with a supreme and lower courts that should have jurisdiction over suits between citizens of different states as well as over cases involving national laws. The Congress should have all the powers granted under the Articles of Confederation, together with a very general power to legislate in any matter in which the individual states were not competent to act or ""in which the harmony of the United States may be interrupted by the exercise of individual legislation." The Congress should also have the power to veto laws of the individual states when in its opinion they were unconstitutional and to use force against any state failing to fulfill its duties. Officers of the states would be bound by an oath to support the national Constitution. This plan, though providing a national government and local governments each chosen by and acting directly on the people, clearly made the national government supreme over the states. The power to veto state laws, to use force on the states, and to extend its authority to any national object would have made the national government very nearly omnipotent in its relation to the states.

The convention immediately took up Randolph's resolutions, which were introduced on May 29, and considered them daily until June 13. During this period it sat technically as a committee of the whole, which enabled it to proceed informally in shaping proposals in a tentative fashion for final later review by the convention in formal session. On the very first day of this consideration it adopted as its first act, by a vote of six states to one, a resolution that fixed the course of the convention: "that a *national* government ought to be established consisting of a *supreme* legislative, executive and judiciary." In the course of the debate in the committee of the whole, the Virginia Plan was modified in a number of respects and made more specific in others. It was agreed that the upper house should be chosen by the state legislatures rather than by the lower house. The authority to use force against a state was dropped, but the power to veto state laws in contravention of treaties was added. A one-man executive was decided on. Terms were fixed for the President and members of both houses.

The principal contest in the review of the Virginia Plan had been over the question of the size of state representation. The smaller states were alarmed at the prospect of being overwhelmed by the votes of their larger neighbors, and united in support of an effort to return to the equal representation of states in one or both houses. On this issue they lost only six to five, having gained in strength from the appearance of new delegations since the first, six-to-one, vote for a centralized government. Unwilling to accept this defeat, the smaller states felt the need to propose some general alternative to the tentatively accepted Virginia Plan. Hence when the Virginia Plan was reported by the committee to the convention proper on June 14, a delay was asked to enable the smaller states to bring in a counterproposal. This was presented the following day by William Paterson, leader of the New Jersey delegation. It represented the views of that state and of a number of delegates from Connecticut, New York, Delaware, and Maryland as well. Had they been represented, it would probably have commanded New Hampshire's and Rhode Island's support as well.

The New Jersey Plan would have retained the basic characteristics of the Articles of Confederation but would have given the Congress the additional power to levy import duties and stamp taxes, to regulate foreign and interstate commerce, and to use force in the collection of requisitions on the states. A supreme court was proposed with the authority to hear cases involving federal laws and treaties, admiralty and maritime cases, and cases in which foreigners were interested. It was also proposed that there be an executive board of several persons elected by the Congress. Congress itself, however, would still be an assemblage of ambassadors from the several states, chosen, paid, and instructed by the state governments and voting by states.

The New Jersey Plan was referred in its turn to the committee of the whole, and the Virginia Plan was recommitted so that they could be considered together. For several days all basic issues were again reviewed, and on June 19 the committee of the whole voted seven to three, with Maryland divided, to reaffirm its support of the Virginia Plan. This left the Convention at an impasse, for the delegates of the smaller states were hardening in their opposition to a union in which there would be no recognition of the equality of the states as such. There were threats to withdraw from the convention and to refuse to ratify the Constitution. At this point the Connecticut delegation offered the fundamental compromise that made acceptance of the Constitution possible. This was to have the lower house constituted as proposed in the Virginia Plan, with representation based on population and members directly elected by the people, and to have the upper house as proposed in the New Jersey Plan, with equal representation for each state and members chosen by the state legislatures. This proposal, with some further details, was reported to the convention on July 5 by a committee that had been created to resolve the impasse.

For ten days this report was debated. The central compromise became involved with a number of subsidiary compromises relating to the size of the lower house, the power of the federal government to control the importation of slaves, the counting of slaves for representation, and the priority of the lower house in connection with money bills. It was finally agreed that there would initially be sixty-five members in the House of Representatives, as the lower house was to be called. The number for each state in the first Congress was fixed in the compromise. Thereafter representation was to be based on population, as determined by a decennial census, with only three fifths of slaves counted. The importation of slaves could not be limited for twenty years. Money bills must originate in the House, but could be amended in the upper house, or Senate. There should be an equal number of senators from each state, who would be chosen by the respective legislatures. Over the negative votes of Virginia and Pennsylvania, who opposed state equality in either house, and of South Carolina and Georgia, who wanted the importation of slaves to be permanently protected, the compromise was adopted on July 16.

The largest states, and the delegates most devoted to a strong national government, bridled at the compromise. A strong executive power was vested in one man rather than a board, but the convention could not at that stage reach any really satisfactory agreement on his term or method of election. The power of the judiciary was increased, and the authority of Congress to negative state laws was removed.

Once the basic principles of the new government were fixed, the convention adjourned from July 26 to August 6 while a new committee worked out their detailed statement. This was a small group consisting of Oliver Ellsworth of Connecticut, Nathaniel Gorham of Massachusetts, Edmund Randolph of Virginia, John Rutledge of South Carolina, and James Wilson of Pennsylvania. Little is known of its detailed proceedings, but Wilson was probably the most active member in preparing the draft that was reported back to the convention when it reconvened. That body now had an actual proposed constitution before it, not, as hitherto, only a set of resolutions defining the sort of government to be set up. For more than a month, until the tenth of September, it debated this document line by line. Nor was its consideration merely verbal. On a number of points it made significant changes in the substance of the Constitution.

The most debated of these were in relation to the term and mode of election of the President. Throughout the convention there had been a continuing trend toward strengthening this office. A single officer, later to be termed the President, had been substituted for a board. He rather than a council of revision had been given the power of veto. Appointments were concentrated in his hands, including the appointment of federal judges, which it had originally been proposed to vest in the Senate. Command of the armed forces and the conduct of foreign affairs, subject to the Senate's concurrence in treaties, were entrusted to him. Efforts to set up an executive council that might dilute the President's authority were defeated. With each increase in the power of the President, the manner of his election became more important.

The initial proposal in the Virginia Plan, which had survived all the debates and revisions to this point, had provided for an executive to be elected by Congress. This procedure offended those who believed in a complete separation of executive, legislative, and judicial powers. The President's veto of congressional legislation was viewed as a safeguard of minority rights, especially those of property owners against the "mere democracy" of Congress. For the President to be chosen by the Congress would, it was feared, make him its creature. To preserve his independence, a long term without reelection was proposed. Yet this in turn created apprehensions that a bad President might be for too long vested with irrecoverable power. An obvious answer was direct election by the people; but in the primitive state of communications that then existed, it was believed that the people simply would not know men from states other than their own or be able to judge their ability. Finally the convention adopted the idea of indirect election through electors chosen in each state for the specific purpose.

Once these decisions had been made, the amended document was referred to a committee on style charged with drafting its final wording. The dominant one of its five members was Gouverneur Morris, to whose elegant pen is primarily due to the terse clarity of the Constitution. The committee quickly produced its report, which was carefully reviewed, phrase by phrase by the whole convention and amended in minor detail. On September 15 the convention approved, by a unanimous vote of the states represented, the final draft. It was engrossed over the following day, and on September 17, 1787, it was signed by the delegates. After arranging for the submission of the Constitution to the Congress and to the thirteen states, they dissolved the convention and departed for their homes.

William E. Gladstone, British Prime Minister a century later, thought the document submitted by the convention was "the most wonderful work ever struck off at a given time by the brain and purpose of man." We are perhaps more skeptical than Gladstone's generation in our use of superlatives and less willing to accept the notion of the intervention of some sudden inspiration in the affairs of men; and we have become accustomed to see all social institutions as products of a long and continuous process of evolution rather than as wholly new creations.

And certainly the Constitution was the product of such an evolution. We have seen that it came at the end of more than a quarter century's effort to solve the problem of providing a central government adequate to meet those rapidly growing problems that transcended the boundaries and the competences of the individual American commonwealths. Efforts to create such a government within the British empire, such as the Albany Plan of Union and the Galloway Plan presented to the first Continental Congress, were rejected by British and colonials alike. The efforts of King and Parliament to make themselves such a government were defeated in the Revolutionary War itself. The American response, in the Articles of Confederation, had proved itself inadequate. Yet from all these unsuccessful experiments the members of the Constitutional Convention had learned a great deal. In particular, they knew by experience what sorts of powers it was essential to vest in a central government and what sorts could best be left to the individual states. It is interesting that on this tremendously important question, in a sense the fundamental question confronting the convention, there was so little real difference of opinion. It was clear to all that foreign affairs, the army and the navy, the West, Indian relations, the regulation of interstate and foreign commerce, and an independent if limited power to tax must be vested in the central government. These were precisely the powers that had been claimed by Parliament, and they had been either granted to or found by experience to be essential to the Confederation. Even the language in which this division of powers between the national government and the states was recorded was largely borrowed from the Articles of Confederation.

The Americans had also had a generation of experience in the organization of new governments through written constitutions in the individual states. Save for Rhode Island and Connecticut, which for a time continued to live under their free colonial charters, every American state had had at least one, and sometimes two, written constitutions within the preceding dozen years. Many of the members of the Constitutional Convention had had experience in drafting such a constitution for their own respective states, and all of them had had experience in living and governing under a written constitution. It is hence not surprising that they drew heavily on that experience in formulating the internal organization of the new government, and particularly in defining the role of the President. The language of the New York and Massachusetts state constitutions appears to have been especially useful to the drafters.

The members of the convention of course drew heavily on the long traditions of limited and partly popular government that were the heritage of their English descent and that had been more sharply defined by the Revolutionary controversy. To base the entire government upon the people by either direct or indirect election, to place primary responsibility for taxes and appropriations in the popularly elected lower house, to make the executive subject to the restraints of legislative and judicial action, and in general to provide a government of laws rather than of men were nearly instinctive actions, taken for granted almost without debate by the members of the convention. They drew similarly on the ideas of Locke, which underlay all political thinking of the period; of Montesquieu, the French political theorist; and of the liberal economic school whose ideas had been best stated by Adam Smith in his *Wealth of Nations* a decade before. All these bodies of ideas had emphasized the necessity of limiting the powers of government and of dividing them among legislative, executive, and judicial authorities in such a way as to minimize arbitrary action and to require a broad consensus of interests and people before the power of government could be exercised. They sought in government the firm maintenance of an orderly arena for the exercise of a lawful individual freedom. It is hence not surprising that the Constitutional Convention carefully separated executive, legislature, and judiciary, preserving their independence from one another and providing checks by each on the action of the other. Similarly, the states were balanced against the federal government and the powers of each further limited by restrictions in the Constitution itself.

But if the convention predictably embodied in its work the experience of the American colonies and states and of the Continental Congress and the Confederation, and if it drew on Locke, Montesquieu, and all the great strains of thought of its century, it nevertheless created from this experience and from these ideas something new. There were set forth in the Constitution some fundamentally important and genuinely new political creations. These were not, interestingly enough, the most debated sections of the Constitution; on the contrary, the most important actions of the convention were taken with little or no debate, sometimes indeed almost as if by chance. One has the feeling that the convention itself did not fully understand the implications of its most brilliant decisions.

Of these, the most brilliant was without question to provide that the national government and the state governments should derive their powers independently from the people, and not one from the other; and that hence their relation to each other would not be that of agent and principal, or subordinate and superior, but rather that of wholly independent governmental organs created for different purposes. We have seen how novel this conception was, and it was not quickly devised by the convention. Until nearly the end of its debates it was assumed that the national legislature or executive would be able to negative state laws, as the British government had been able to do with colonial statutes. It was seriously proposed by some that the President should be able to appoint state governors. In contrast to these proposals, obviously based on the patterns of the old empire, were the provisions of the so-called New Jersey Plan, which would have continued the Congress merely as a somewhat stronger collective agent of the states. And indeed, traces of the concepts underlying the New Jersey Plan survived in the Constitution itself in the equal representation of the states in the Senate, the election of senators by the state legislatures, and the election of the President by state-chosen electors.

The final form of the Constitution, however, presented an almost wholly new idea, under which the people organized themselves into one government for national affairs and into others for local affairs, with almost no connection between the two except in the election of senators. It was as though the same body of men organized themselves as a religious congregation for purposes of worship and as a series of corporations for the transaction of their business affairs. It was a brilliant creation, preserving the autonomy and local sovereignty of the states at the same time that the national government was endowed with sovereignty for national purposes. The members of the convention answered the argument of the indivisibility of sovereignty simply by dividing it.

Yet this did not fully answer the problem. Necessarily many cases would arise in which the boundary between national jurisdiction and state jurisdiction was vaguely or inadequately defined or was defined differently by the states and the federal government. Who then could decide these differences? And if the federal government were the arbiter, would it not then really be the sovereign over all, since it could itself determine the limits of its own powers? Even if the federal government did not have a clear-cut final power of this sort, would not disputes over the boundaries of power bring the states into a repeated direct and bruising conflict with each other and with the central government that would endanger the harmonious working of the whole system?

Here again the solution was a brilliant innovation. The Constitution itself and treaties entered into and laws enacted pursuant thereto were made the supreme law of the land, of the states as well as of the federal government. In the British legal tradition it was the specific and basic duty of judges to declare what the law was in cases that came before them. Hence the Constitution provided a means by which questions of the proper sphere of the federal government and of the states would not be resolved as political problems by legislative or executive actions, but as legal problems that a court must decide in hearing a case between private parties.

There was some precedent for this. Most of the basic declarations of the common law had been made in England, not as statements of abstract principle but as specific actions of courts in deciding the cases of individual human beings. Even more relevant was the provision of the Articles of Confederation that among the types of cases that could be brought before the rudimentary courts of the Confederation were those between claimants to a tract of land who based their conflicting claims on grants from different states. Thus the validity of the conflicting territorial claims of the various states could be decided not by legislation or by negotiation or by adjudication directly between the states—which would have raised the question of the validity of judicial processes served on a sovereign state—but rather as a part of the adjudication of the rights of private individuals who were clearly subject to the court. It was essentially this procedure that was taken over and enlarged by the Constitutional Convention.

The federal government and the states hence need never come into direct conflict with each other. The double insulation is provided by removing their controversies from a political to a legal arena and by deciding those controversies in terms of the concrete rights of individuals in real circumstances rather than in terms of the abstract powers of sovereign bodies confronting each other. The fundamental school segregation questions of our own day, for example, in which the real issue was the extent to which federal policies guaranteeing equal rights to all citizens could override policies of certain states insisting upon the segregation in the schools of children of different races, were not decided as political controversies by the Congress. Indeed, the inflamed state of emotions on the issue would have made any political or legislative solution quite impossible. Instead a decision was reached in a judicial determination of the rights of a small group of individual Negro parents to send their children to a particular school. The federal and state governments came into direct conflict only on occasions in which certain state officials briefly ignored the Constitution and refused to accept the judicial decisions as binding.

These two fundamental innovations were probably not explicitly formulated in the minds of the delegates to the Constitutional Convention. They realized that they were making the federal and the state governments independently responsible to the people, rather than making one dependent on the other; but there is little evidence that the delegates during the convention or the advocates of ratification afterward clearly understood what a radical departure from earlier schemes of federation this represented. The provision that the Constitution and statutes enacted pursuant to it should be the supreme law of the land was inserted with almost no discussion on the motion of Luther Martin, a Maryland delegate who opposed the majority of the convention, refused to sign the completed Constitution, and vigorously fought its ratification. Certainly he did not want to strengthen the central government, and probably he thought of his measure as a device to make the central government rely on the state courts rather than on its own legislative or executive for the local enforcement of its laws.

It was clear, however, that the federal courts would have the power to declare state laws unconstitutional and hence void whenever the validity of such statutes was at issue in cases that might come before them, and that this was a better way of preserving the boundary between federal and state authority than the vesting of a veto power over state legislation in the hands of the federal President or Congress. But there is little evidence indeed that the delegates foresaw a similar use of the judicial power against federal legislation; and indeed it was to be so used only very rarely before the Civil War.

But the delay in working out fully the implications of the

"supreme-law-of-the-land" provisions of the Constitution was due primarily to the fact that until after the Civil War there were relatively few problems involved in defining the respective areas of jurisdiction of the federal and the state governments. For all the cry over "states' rights," the issues leading to the Civil War were not so much over the question of the boundary between federal and state authority as over the question of whether powers undoubtedly vested in the federal government—for example, the authority to levy tariffs and to administer Western territories and determine the conditions for the admission of new states—were being used in ways damaging to the interests of the Southern states. The really complex issues of the boundaries of federal power arose in the late nineteenth and twentieth centuries, when interstate commerce, over which the federal government had unquestioned authority, came to dominate the economy and when the federal government began to use its authority for regulatory purposes. Meanwhile the Fourteenth Amendment had been enacted, which forbade the states to deprive any person of life, liberty, or property without due process of law; and this imposed on the federal courts a further responsibility of defining the limits of state authority, not only as against the federal government but as against the individual citizen. When these difficult questions arose, which could have found a political solution only after rancorous controversy, if indeed at all, there was ready at hand the admirably flexible use of the judiciary written into the Constitution, with however incomplete an understanding of its implications, by its legally minded drafters.

Another major innovation, new at least as an aspect of national government, was the creation of a powerful executive popularly elected but independent of the legislative power. In previous European governments either an autocratic ruler had himself exercised the legislative power, as in eighteenth-century France, or else an autocratic executive power was pitted against an elected legislative body, as in Britain. In the latter case the legislative body became the only direct spokesman of the people, and the contest for popular sovereignty became a contest between the legislative and executive powers. Hence the triumph of popular sovereignty in the late eighteenth and nineteenth centuries in Europe meant a victory of legislative authority, and executive power came to be vested in a committee of the legislature. This process was already happening in Britain, where executive authority was coming to be vested in a body of ministers drawn from and increasingly responsible to Parliament.

Only in America was the executive to stand as an independent expression of the popular will. The existence of this strong executive office, both liberated and hampered by its independence of the legislature, has been a unique and continuously important feature of American government. The office was, of course, rooted in the experience of the states' governorships, and particularly of those of Connecticut and Rhode Island, which had been elective from the beginning. But the convention throughout its preliminary debates had proposed an executive chosen by the legislature, rather than independently, if indirectly, by the people; it had entertained the idea of an executive board or committee rather than a single President; and some of its members at least had no doubt surreptitiously sighed for a monarchy. To abandon all these familiar patterns and to adopt for a whole nation a kind of executive that had earlier been tried only in administering the local concerns of individual colonies and states was a bold and creative act.

The Northwest Ordinance of 1787 was passed by the Congress of the Confederation while the Constitutional Convention was sitting. One of the most important acts of the convention, helping to shape the whole history of the United States, was to embody in the Constitution the basic concept of that ordinance: that new states were to be formed from the territories of the United States and admitted to the Union as equal states entitled to their equal representation in the Senate and their proper proportionate representation in the House of Representatives. The Constitution thus avoided the vesting of special privilege in the older states, such as the British at home had attempted to maintain over the British who settled in America, and as the colonists along the coast had maintained over the colonists in the back country. The United States was able in this way to avoid in its development the kind of rebellion of newly settled areas against the entrenched privileges of the old that had been expressed in such uprisings as the Regulator Movement in North Carolina or Shays' Rebellion in Massachusetts, and, indeed, in the American Revolution itself.

The final fundamentally important aspect of the Constitution was its guarantee of a uniform and stable legal environment for the growth of a national economy. We have noted that once uniform British navigation laws, trade regulations, and limitations on paper currency were removed, the legal structure of American economic life dissolved into a kaleidoscope of state patterns. Paper currencies of varying and unpredictable value circulated, state tariffs lay athwart the interstate flow of goods, "stay" laws delayed the enforcement of contracts, and easy and inconsistent bankruptcy statutes made the transaction of business across state lines hazardous. The Constitution made sweeping changes on all these points. Commerce among the states as well as with foreign countries was put under the jurisdiction of the national government. That government was also given the exclusive power to coin money and to regulate weights and measures. The states in turn were forbidden to impose tariffs, or to issue paper money, or to pass legal tender laws or stay laws, or indeed any law impairing the obligation of a contract. Nor could the federal government itself issue paper currency as such (though it could borrow money and issue securities that could circulate, like the later Civil War greenbacks). Uniform bankruptcy laws were to be devised by the Congress. The federal courts were opened to a citizen of any state who might have reason to sue a citizen of another.

At the same time that these measures assured the opportunity of the national economy to develop as a unit, without regard to state boundaries and without fear of state interference, the national government was given power to encourage American industry, through navigation laws in favor of American shipping, through tariffs to protect American enterprises, and through a system of patents to stimulate invention. This was to provide the constitutional basis for Hamilton's bold economic program during Washington's first administration as President.

The Constitution was signed on September 17, 1787, on behalf of all the states represented. On that day, too, the convention adopted a resolution of revolutionary importance. It provided that though the completed document should be submitted initially to the Congress sitting at New York, it should also be sent to every state, without any requirement for prior approval by the Congress. Moreover, it would be acted on in the states not by the legislatures but by conventions elected by the people for that specific purpose. Finally, ratification by nine of the thirteen states would be sufficient to bring the Constitution into force among those states that had accepted it. By this resolution the delegates freed their handiwork from a dependence on the possible hostile action of the Congress and of the state legislatures, which would be abolished or curtailed in power by its adoption. Moreover, they escaped the requirement of unanimity that had defeated all prior efforts to strengthen the Articles of Confederation.

Congress acted on the Constitution without delay. Many, perhaps most, of its members had some reservations about the document; there were serious questions about the propriety of Congress acting on a proposal to change the government by a procedure contrary to the existing Articles of Confederation; a number opposed the Constitution outright. Yet none was willing to oppose its submission to the states, and on September 28 the Congress voted unanimously to transmit the document to the states with the recommendation that it be submitted to ratifying conventions, but without any recommendation of approval.

Then began the great struggle over ratification. No doubt only a minority, probably only a small minority, of Americans understood the issues involved and actively supported the proposals of the convention. The majority of the population, to the extent that it considered the issues at all, was doubtless well enough content with the government it knew—locally based, agrarian-oriented. Apathy, indifference, dislike, and fear of the unfamiliar had to be overcome if the Constitution were to be ratified.

On the other hand, the Federalists, as the supporters of the Constitution came to be called, had certain advantages. They were, as a group, the men whose personal, business, and political connections were national and not merely local; and hence they were able to act together as a national party. Though there were exceptions, like Patrick Henry and George Mason, almost all the major leaders of the Revolution were among the supporters. Washington's support alone was of decisive value. Madison, Jay, Franklin, Hamilton, Knox, and Dickinson; from a distance, John Adams and Jefferson; and, belatedly, Hancock and Samuel Adams were also for ratification. Moreover, the actively organized support of those who were determined to achieve ratification was far more effective than the negativistic and even apathetic hostility of the anti-Federalists, few of whom were prepared to wage a planned and energetic campaign. The Federalists were largely concentrated in the cities, and they had a predominant influence in the newspapers and other means of influencing public opinion.

As soon as the Constitution was published, a propaganda campaign was begun in pamphlets and newspaper columns. In this contest the Federalists had a clear advantage, quantitatively and, especially, qualitatively. By far the ablest and most influential contribution to this national debate was *The Federalist,* a series of eighty-five contributions to New York newspapers that appeared regularly from October, 1787, to April, 1788, collected in the spring of 1788 into a two-volume compilation. The essays were written primarily by James Madison and Alexander Hamilton, with some contributions by John Jay. Lucid, dispassionate, persuasive, the essays clarified the understanding of the convention's proposals, alleviated many of the public's fears, and raised the debate to a high level. Though written primarily to influence the contest over ratification in New York, essays from *The Federalist* were widely reprinted and had a considerable influence in other states as well.

The anti-Federalists could present no such reasoned and consistent statement of their position. Many of the arguments in opposition to the Constitution were simple bizarre, based on wild notions of an armed and walled Federal City from which mercenary troops could descend on the populace, or on dark fears of a monarchy. Almost all the more articulate and thoughtful anti-Federalists in fact agreed with the Federalists that the Articles of Confederation were inadequate and that a substantial strengthening of the national government was needed. They thus conceded the validity of the principal argument for the Constitution and differed from the Federalists, as they differed among themselves, only as to the particular form the stronger government should take. The greatest weakness of the anti-Federalist position was precisely that they could not unite on any alternative proposal for remedying weaknesses that they conceded had become intolerable.

The nearest the anti-Federalists could come to a definite proposal was that the Constitution should be remanded to a second convention with instructions to revise it by the incorporation of greater safeguards for state sovereignty and individual liberty. The impracticality of so long a delay, the uncertainty of any new convention's being able to improve upon the work of the old, and the difficulty of arranging such a solution all combined to make this proposal unfeasible. However, the pressures of the anti-Federalists for reassurances on this point forced the Federalists into an informal but clear understanding that amendments to cover the points of their major concern would be submitted to the first Congress to meet under the Constitution. It was in fact this sequence of events that led to the adoption of the Bill of Rights, set forth in the first ten amendments to the Constitution.

The anti-Federalist apprehensions were of two kinds. Southerners feared that the comprehensive powers over the national economy granted the federal government could be and would be used to the detriment of the special interests of their region. They foresaw the termination of the slave trade as soon as the twenty-year period of its constitutional protection was ended. They anticipated that this would be the forerunner of other measures hostile to slavery. (It should be added that not all Southerners took this view. Virginians, though slaveholders, usually deplored the institution; and its temporary protection of the slave trade was one of the reasons given by George Mason for his opposition.) The Southern economy was based on the export to Europe of agricultural products in exchange for manufactured goods. Southerners feared that federal tariffs to encourage Northern manufactures and federal navigation acts to encourage Northern shipping would substantially increase the cost of their imports and indirectly limit their markets broad.

The other set of apprehensions related to protection of individual rights. The written guarantee of such rights was a long Anglo-American tradition. Magna Charta was still cherished. The English Bill of Rights of 1689 was a more recent model, and almost every state constitution adopted in the Revolutionary epoch contained such a statement of rights. The absence of any such instrument in the new Constitution was viewed as ominous. There was no guarantee of freedom of press or speech, or of trial by jury in civil cases, or of freedom of religion, or against the establishment of a state religion. Nor was there guarantee against unreasonable searches and seizures, or other similar procedural protections. Advocates of the Constitution pointed out that since the federal government had only those powers specifically granted to it, no bill of rights was necessary to limit its exercise of powers it had never possessed. They went farther and suggested that it might even be dangerous to list certain rights of this sort in a constitution because the omission of any right from the list might then be taken to mean that the right did not exist or was not protected. This argument was weakened, however, by the fact that certain elements of a bill of rights were already present in the Constitution, including guarantees of the writ of habeas corpus and of jury trials in criminal cases before the federal courts.

After the first few states had ratified, it became increasingly clear that it would be most difficult to obtain the consent of the necessary nine, not to speak of the entire thirteen, without some clear assurances on this subject. The struggle was particularly close in Massachusetts, where in fact opponents of the Constitution at first controlled the ratifying convention. To win the support of enough of those initially hostile to gain even the barest of majorities, it was necessary for the Federalists themselves to draw up a set of amendments guaranteeing individual rights, to propose their submission along with the instrument of ratification, and to pledge their most vigorous efforts to obtain the earliest possible ratification of the amendments under the new government. This same tactic was followed in other states, notably New Hampshire, the crucial ninth to ratify, and Virginia, the tenth and most important to assent. In neither case could ratification have been won without the promise of such amendments. This precedent was followed also in New York, and the Federalists as a national group considered themselves pledged to the adoption of a bill of rights as a set of amendments to the new Constitution. This pledge, it may be added, was promptly redeemed in the first Congress under the Constitution by the passage of twelve proposed amendments, ten of which were finally adopted by the states and make up our Bill of Rights today.

Both sets of apprehensions about the new Constitution proved to be well founded. Though there can be no doubt that the Constitution has proved a blessing to the citizens of the Southern states as to others, the forebodings of the more radical Southerners that it would threaten certain Southern "'interests" that they were anxious to protect—including especially the preservation of human slavery and the economic status of slave-based agriculture—were fulfilled. As they feared, the slave states were to become an increasingly small minority, with increasingly imperiled interests, until at last they were to feel impelled to renounce the Constitution and leave the Union, with tragic consequences for all. Even more farseeing was the opposition based on the absence of specific guarantees of personal freedom. Had that opposition not forced the adoption of a bill of rights, it is quite true that the cornerstone of liberty in our system of government would have been lacking.

These were the principal nationwide issues in the ratification struggle. In the individual states these basic issues were complicated by a maze of local issues and personalities, which it would be profitless to review here state by state. It was the strategy of the Federalists to obtain a very quick ratification by a major state in order to start a procession of adoptions. For this purpose they chose Pennsylvania, where the convention had just been sitting and where the Federalists were clearly the dominant party. Steps were taken to rush through the legislature a call for a ratifying convention and to ram the Constitution through the convention with a minimum of delay and debate. Though the Federalists were successful in obtaining almost immediate action in summoning a convention to meet on November 21, and though they had a two-thirds majority in that body, opposition to their high-handed tactics prolonged the debate for three weeks. Pennsylvania, ratifying on December 12, lost the honor of being the first state to do so to Delaware, which had ratified on December 7, Further quick ratifications came from New Jersey on December 18, 1787, and Georgia on January 2, 1788. In both the action was unanimous, as it had been in Delaware. The smaller states had become convinced that approval of the Constitution would be very much in their interest. Connecticut followed with a three-to-one vote on January 9. Massachusetts was the first state whose convention had a strong anti-Federalist representation—indeed an initial majority. Only by the compromise on amendments was ratification achieved on February 6, and then only by a vote of 187 to 168. The seventh and eighth states were Maryland and South Carolina, on April 28 and May 23, both by large majorities. Only one more state was necessary to complete the formal adoption, but the adherence at least of New York and Virginia would be essential to a successfully functioning union. In both of those states opposition to the Constitution was strong and ably led. Rhode Island had already rejected the Constitution and the New Hampshire convention had adjourned without approving it. North Carolina seemed certain to disapprove. The struggle was far from over.

It was at this stage that the informal agreement to adopt a bill of rights made success possible. On this basis the New Hampshire convention reconvened and acted favorably on June 21, making the ninth state. Four days later, without having learned of New Hampshire's priority, Virginia also ratified by a close vote and after a long debate, and again in reliance on commitments to seek a bill of rights. New York's convention was clearly anti-Federalist and would no doubt have rejected the Constitution or ratified it only conditionally had not Alexander Hamilton been able to win a postponement until news of New Hampshire's and Virginia's adherence was received. Once it was clear the new government was to be a reality, New York could hardly remain apart. Reluctantly, and by a vote of only thirty to twenty-seven, its convention ratified on July 26. Within ten months after the Constitutional Convention's adjournment, there had been a clear-cut acceptance by the states. In contrast, it had taken four years to win approval of the far less radical Articles of Confederation, even under the immediate pressure of war. The strategy of the Federalists in bypassing Congress, in assuring that the Constitution would be referred to specially elected conventions and not to the state legislatures, and in requiring ratification by only nine states had made success possible. It had been finally realized by their tireless and brilliant campaign tactics, state by state. The Congress of the Confederation acted promptly to bring the new government into being, providing that the election of Presidential electors and members of the House of Representatives should be held on January 7, 1789, that the electors should meet to vote for President on February 4, and that the first Congress should convene on March 4.

These events took place on their specified dates. The members of Congress, opening the sealed ballots of the Presidential electors, discovered—to no one's surprise—that they had unanimously chosen George Washington. Messengers were sped to Mount Vernon to inform the waiting general. Once more summoned from his beloved estate to assume public responsibility, he set out within a few days for New York, the temporary capital. There on a balcony of Federal Hall, overlooking Broad and Wall streets, he took the oath of office as the first President of the United States of America. The new government had begun and the era of the Revolution was over. Within a few months the remaining states, North Carolina and Rhode Island, finding isolation impractical, submitted their actions of ratification, and the Union was complete.

For the past fifty years historians have hotly debated the motives of the Federalist leaders and the relation of the Constitution to the democratic forces of the Revolution. The traditional view, as advanced by such popular nineteenth-century historians as George Bancroft and John Fiske, was that the achievements of the Revolution were falling into chaos during the Confederation, that the Federalists were a group of brilliant and selfless men whose leadership in drafting and ratifying the Constitution itself completed and perfected the Revolution. This view was explosively challenged in 1913 by a young historian later to become famous—Charles A. Beard. Beard's book *An Economic Interpretation of the Constitution* was based in part on a painstaking examination of the property holdings of the individual members of the Constitutional Convention. He discovered that the delegates who favored a strong Constitution were in general men of substantial property whose holdings were largely in Continental and state bonds and other evidences of debt, public and private. From this and other evidence Beard concluded that the Constitution had been drawn and "put over" by a small minority of men whose property was primarily of this sort, in opposition to the interests of the vast majority whose property, if any, was primarily in land. As the instrument of a small wealthy class, the Constitution, in Beard's view, marked a counterrevolution aimed at halting the democratic trends of the Revolution itself. Beard's youth had been spent in the Midwest in a period of severe agricultural depression, when desperate, debt-ridden farmers formed the Populist Party to seek cheaper money and laws to prevent foreclosures and delay debt collection. To some extent, and with considerable justification, this work reads back into the period of the Constitution the emotions and the points of view of the Populists, who saw bankers and financiers as the scheming enemies of farmers and the Constitution as a barrier to their regulation by the farmer-controlled state legislatures. In the era of Franklin D. Roosevelt, when many of the same issues presented themselves, there was an interest in the period leading from the Revolution to the Constitution. The historians whose work took shape in those years, like Merrill Jensen, did much to create an improved understanding and a better opinion of the Articles of Confederation and the anti-Federalists.

More recent work, by such men as Robert Brown and Forrest McDonald, has called Beard's views into serious question. A more searching analysis has been made of the economic interests, not only of the few dozen men who made up the Constitutional Convention, but of hundreds of both Federalist and anti-Federalist leaders, including the members of all the state conventions. This has destroyed Beard's clear-cut picture. Among the consistent supporters of the Constitution were frontier farmers and urban artisans. Among its opponents were wealthy property owners such as George Mason, Patrick Henry, and Richard Henry Lee. Among the hundreds of state delegates studied, it is impossible to establish a division of rich and poor or even of personal-property holders versus real-property holders that corresponds with any consistency to the division between Federalist and anti-Federalist. The possibility of personal profit from the increase in the value of Continental and state bonds that Beard saw as a principal and somewhat venal motive for supporting the Constitution becomes on examination an obviously superficial and relatively unimportant factor.

There do, however, emerge certain broad interest groupings. By and large the principal support for the Constitution came from two groups. One was made up of those who were dependent on a strong national government for frontier defense. This included the residents of a state like Georgia, weak itself and confronted with hostile Spaniards and Indians, as well as settlers in what are now Tennessee, Kentucky, and West Virginia and the western frontiers of the original states. The dependence of these frontier dwellers on a vigorous and well-armed national government overrode all the economic and occupational considerations that might otherwise have disposed them to oppose the Constitution.

The other, and more important, Federalist group consisted of those whose economic interests were involved in interstate and foreign trade and in the emergence of a commercial money economy. This included not only the wealthy merchants, moneylenders, securities holders, and businessmen of Beard's account, but also a vast number of humbler men such as workers in shipyards, artisans and indeed all townsmen, farmers and planters growing crops for export, workmen in the incipient factories, newspaper publishers, seamen as well as shipowners—indeed all those whose stake was in the emerging national economy. In the state ratifying conventions, almost all representatives of the towns and cities voted for the new Constitution, and they appear to have had the substantially unanimous support of their constituents, of whatever social level or economic class. So too did the representatives of those rural counties near coastal cities or along navigable rivers, where the produce of farms was exported or extensively traded and where a commercial agriculture had developed.

The opposition to the Constitution came primarily from the more isolated rural counties, the concerns of whose subsistence-farming residents did not extend beyond the familiar boundaries of their states. They were the spokesmen of the traditional, local, agrarian interest that had persisted throughout the Revolutionary decades in its opposition to the integration of their separate commonwealths into any larger domain, whether a strengthened British empire or a powerful American union. These same more isolated rural areas were also those most remote from newspapers, from travelers, from all the eighteenth-century means of communication. Their residents had had little chance to become familiar with the issues in the constitutional controversy or to understand the new proposals. Much of their opposition was simply an uninformed clinging to the traditional in the face of the new and unfamiliar.

Certainly the Federalists were, on the average, wealthier men than their anti-Federalist opponents. And there is some truth in Beard's identification of the Federalists with the owners of mercantile property, stocks, bonds, other evidences of debt, and the anti-Federalists with the landed interests. But fundamentally what distinguished the two was not so much wealth or class as the degree of participation in and identification with the growing network of trade and communication that was forming the new national economy.

Was the Constitution, then, counterrevolutionary? In a sense it was, in that it undertook to create a central government empowered to perform precisely those functions of defense, taxation, and economic regulation that the Americans had just fought the Revolution in order to deny to the British government. Among those who most heartily welcomed the new government were men like John Dickinson who in the days before 1776, however much they might object to British domination, had still clung to the central British government as an ultimate necessity. But it is not realistic to equate the powers of a distant and half-hostile British government in whose choice the Americans had no part with those of a government at home of their own choosing. And otherwise the charge of counterrevolution is not easily supported. It is true that the Constitution favored creditors by protecting them against state action that might impede them in the collection of their debts or by inflation might depreciate the value of their holdings. And the holders of governmental bonds and notes benefited by the assurance of adequate income for their payment. But the states themselves were moving in the same direction, and the importance of the Constitution in this area is not so much that it favored creditors over debtors as that it provided for a single uniform statutory basis for the development of the national economy.

Otherwise the weight of the Constitution was on the side of democracy. It simply adopted the suffrage requirements of the states themselves. Unlike most of the state constitutions, it imposed no property or religious qualifications for office. A part of the agreement that led to its ratification was the adoption of a bill of rights more comprehensive than that of any state. Its provisions with respect to the admission of new states opened the way to a steady flow of democratizing influences for more than a century. There was no reason to suppose that the new national government would be any less democratic or any less responsive to the public will than the state governments; and in fact, it has been proved to be more democratic and more responsive.

Nor are the charges well founded that the Constitution was "put over" on a majority of the people by an organized minority through a sort of conspiracy or peaceful coup d'etat. It is true that the process by which it was ratified was not that prescribed by the Articles of Confederation and had no prior basis in law. But the departure from the requirement of congressional action and unanimous approval by the state legislatures was made not in order to frustrate the majority will but rather to permit it to prevail. Few other major issues in American history, if any, have been so fully, lucidly, and candidly debated; none has been more directly decided by the people themselves.

The Constitution was in no sense a suppression of the democratic forces of the Revolution; rather it incorporated them in a final and brilliant resolution of those issues of central versus local government over which the Revolution had been fought. We have reason to be proud of it.

12 ★★★★★★★★★

The Meaning of the American Revolution

We are perhaps now in a position to try to see the meaning of the series of events that began two hundred years ago. The American Revolution in fact embraced four distinct developments: the secession from the British empire, the formation of the Union under the Constitution, a further democratization of life within the United States, and the formulation of a body of political theory. The true meaning of the Revolution was not in any one of these alone. The new nation was one of many nations, and many dozens of others have come into existence since. The political theory of the Revolution was drawn from British and, in slight degree, French sources, and introduced little in the way of wholly new ideas. What was unique up to that time was not that there was a system of political ideas, but that the system could be embodied in an actual state; not that there was a new nation, but that there was a nation shaped by an idea—"conceived in liberty and dedicated to the proposition that all men are created equal."

We have seen that the swift growth of the colonies by 1763 had shattered the relative isolation in which the several American commonwealths had lived their nearly independent lives, and had confronted them with exigent problems that could be met only by a central government. The colonies individually could not defend themselves in the swirling imperial rivalries of the late eighteenth century, or maintain their positions in the fierce international commercial competition of the time, or assert their claims to the vast Trans-Appalachian wilderness into which their people were beginning to overflow, or deal with the restless Indians along the new frontier, or provide a large enough trading area of uniform and dependable currency and uniform commercial law within which the emerging mercantile and industrial economy could develop. Some central body must undertake these tasks and must have the power to raise a revenue to meet the necessary costs.

The British ministries in power after 1763, however vaguely and confusedly, saw these needs and moved erratically to meet them—but did so for British ends. The commercial regulations they imposed or strengthened were intended to make the colonies subservient to the British economy. The deployment of forces for American defense suited British strategy rather than the immediate needs of the unconsulted Americans. The Western policies, blocking Americans from the new lands across the mountains, were exclusively of British design. All of these British activities were to be financed in substantial part by taxes levied on the Americans by Parliament. The fundamental decisions affecting the whole future of the American colonies were, in fact, to be taken in London without American participation.

The American resistance from 1765 to 1774 was simply an effort to prevent such an exercise of what the colonists considered a novel and unconstitutional claim to power. They did not want to leave the empire; they wanted to remain in, but with conditions as they had been prior to 1763. They certainly wanted no central government, American or British, to exercise the powers being claimed by Parliament. Initially at least, in most of the colonies the controversy with Great Britain had little to do with the internal disputes over the distribution of power and wealth within the colonies. The men who resisted British authority were generally themselves those who exercised authority and possessed wealth within the colonies. They wished to protect their power and property from mobs at home as well as from the exactions of the British.

And the Americans had little interest in the construction of a systematic political theory for its own sake. Indeed no systematic political treatise was written during the whole of the Revolutionary epoch. The pamphlets, addresses, and declarations in which the revolutionists expressed their political views were lawyers' briefs or propaganda appeals designed to gain a point in debate or to win support for a program of action. Hence they were constructed out of the commonplace political ideas of the time in an effort to identify the American cause with political truisms already accepted by those to whom they appealed. The political theory of the American Revolution was the product rather than the blueprint of the program of Revolutionary action, though the theory ultimately began in turn to shape the realities out of which it grew.

The American rejection of the British efforts to set up an integrated imperial policy was, as we have seen, almost wholly negative. Prior to the Revolution the Americans were simply unwilling to admit the necessity of a central military establishment in peacetime, or of a vigorous and consistently enforced Western policy, or of new commercial policies, or most particularly of an imperial revenue derived from America. Almost the only recognition of the existence of such problems, coupled with constructive suggestions for their solution in ways that would not depend on unilateral British dominance, came in the Albany Plan of Union and in Galloway's much later proposals to the Continental Congress, and less formally in Benjamin Franklin's correspondence and conferences. British intransigence in attempting to enforce a unilateral solution confronted American stubbornness in refusing to limit the now somewhat anachronistic independence of the individual colonies. This conflict left, as we have seen, no way of maintaining the empire peacefully. When Americans refused any longer to obey a British authority that had in fact been exercised only by their consent, that authority simply disappeared in America, and the colonists were all but forced to declare an independence that was in fact already theirs.

So long as they were debating with the authorities in London the proper role of the colonies under the Crown, the American advocates were free to base their position on an interpretation of the constitution, laws, and traditions of Britain. But in order to justify their actions in denouncing the authority of the Crown and leaving the empire, they must of course rely on principles valid for all men and not solely for subjects of the Crown. This necessity led to the more abstract and universal statement of political theory expressed in the years after 1774, and most notably in the preamble of the Declaration of Independence itself.

We have seen too that none of the problems of central authority disappeared with British rule and that the Americans were confronted in their independence with the necessity of constructing a national government that could exercise the authority over national defense, international relations, the West, the Indians, and interstate and foreign commerce formerly claimed by Parliament; that could play Parliament's former role in maintaining a uniform currency and a uniform respect for contracts and obligations throughout the American commonwealths; and that could go far beyond Parliament's earlier pretensions in acting upon individuals and in assessing and collecting an independent revenue. In the course of setting up this central government—that is, of drafting and ratifying the Constitution—it was necessary to formulate a new body of thought with respect to federalism, which was expressed in the Constitution itself and in such commentaries as *The Federalist.*

The fundamental political philosophy upon which the Americans drew to justify their secession from the British empire and which they later used as the basis for designing their new governments came to them primarily through Locke, Harrington, and other seventeenth-century British writers; but some parts of its roots go far back, through Thomas Aquinas and other medieval philosophers, ultimately to the Roman Stoics. This philosophy rested on a series of basic assumptions.

One of these was that government is a human creation that can be designed and assembled like a machine to serve predetermined purposes. It is not, except ultimately and indirectly, of divine origin, beyond human right to alter. Nor is it a creation of history, having sanctions of tradition and developing by its own laws of growth. Government and the state have no ends of their own save to serve the purposes of the human beings who have created them and live under them.

Another of the fundamental assumptions is that all government is subject to natural law, antedating and superior to all human ordinances, and that under the natural law all men have certain natural and inalienable rights. Government is legitimate only to the degree that it is established and acts in accord with the natural law. The Americans of the Revolutionary period, like European writers of the time, thought of natural law in very much the same way that they thought of fundamental laws of physics and astronomy—as uniform and orderly rules rather readily ascertainable by contemplation and logical construction. Indeed the ready acceptance of both these two initial assumptions is due to their compatibility with the Newtonian ideas described in Chapter I.

Another assumption, going deep into Christian history, is that of the equality of all men when stripped of political status. The Christian belief in the equality before God of men's souls when divorced by death from earthly rank equated itself easily with the idea that in a state of nature, before any government has been created to differentiate them, men are also equal.

There were other assumptions about the nature of men besides that of their inherent equality. The Americans, like most thinkers of the Enlightenment, believed that men were generally good, rational, and socially inclined. They would be able readily to agree together for the common interest, almost all of them would voluntarily obey the rules of a just government, they would have the rational capacity to understand natural law and the fundamental principles of government. In other words, they could and would, if allowed to do so, join to create a sound government. And it would not need to be a leviathan state built on force and powerful enough to restrain the selfish and violent passions of its subjects. Government could rather be a mild and lenient mechanism using compulsion only against an occasional malefactor.

But their optimism about mankind was not a fatuous one. They believed that self-interest was the strongest human motive. This very self-interest, properly enlightened, could be trusted to lead society at large to act in its own general interest, so that it was safe to diffuse power among the people. But if a few men were singled out and given authority, it was very necessary to guard against their natural impulse to use that authority to gain or perpetuate special privileges for themselves.

These fundamental assumptions were woven together into a concept of the origin of government that was set forth by John Locke and other writers of the seventeenth and eighteenth centuries and became a basic element in American political thought. This concept pictured men as being originally in a "state of nature," having no government and no means of keeping order among themselves. In the absence of all political status, men retained their innate equality. As rational and social creatures, in order to protect their lives, their liberty, and their property from the dangers of anarchy, they would agree among themselves to establish a government. To that government they would consent to delegate certain powers over life, liberty, and property, but only to the degree necessary to protect those very rights, which were naturally and inalienably theirs. The only legitimate origin of government was in such a social contract, actual or implied, and in the consent of the people, which the contract expressed. Since government was created by the people solely for the purpose of protecting their lives, liberty, and property, if it seriously failed to do so, and especially if it acted arbitrarily to deprive citizens of those very rights, it forfeited any claim to loyalty and obedience; and its subjects were free to dissolve it and erect in its stead a government better calculated to serve their ends. Moreover, since all men had been equals in the state of nature and had equally joined in the hypothetical creation of government, they retained their equality before the law under the governments they had jointly established.

Except that Jefferson substituted the term "pursuit of happiness" for the term "property" in the phrase elsewhere always stated as "life, liberty, and property," this fundamental philosophy was most succinctly and most nobly set forth in the preamble to the Declaration of Independence.

As the intellectual descendants of Darwin and Freud as well as of Newton, it is easy for us to see this basic political philosophy not only as almost entirely and uncreatively derivative from English and French thinkers but also as itself shallow and inconsistent. We know (no doubt many eighteenth-century thinkers did too) that the vision of men in a state of nature entering into a social contract to establish government is at best an illuminating myth and certainly not a historical description of the origin of government. We know that governments evolve rather than are created by the fiat of a body of citizens. We are sadly aware of the passion and unreason of man and of the black currents of hatred and hysteria that blind his judgment. We are skeptical of the existence of any objective body of "natural law," believing that men, instead of discovering natural law in the universe, project upon the universe as "natural law" their own subjective beliefs, uncritically accepted because of long familiarity.

Yet if the fundamental political philosophy of the Enlightenment, which the Americans shared and used, is superficial as psychology, ignorant as history, and inconsistent as logic, it still has nobility as an ideal. Men may not in fact have been created equal, they may derive from nature no rights that are in fact inalienable, there may never have been a state of nature or a social contract, there may be in the blind universe no self-evident truths of government. But to say that we propose to regard men as equal, that we propose to guard certain rights as though they were inalienable, that we recognize no basis of government except in the general consent of those governed, and that we concede no proper purpose to government except to serve its citizens is to set forth goals that do indeed have a kind of timeless and universal validity.

The political philosophy of the Enlightenment—based on natural law, natural rights, the equality of men, social contract, and a grounding of legitimate government in the consent of the governed—supported the Americans' claim of the right to abandon their allegiance to the Crown and create new governments. But it did not in itself define the specific characteristics of the governments they should create. In particular it did not answer the question of the arrangements that were best calculated to protect the people's life, liberty, and property from the very government that was set up to safeguard them. The political philosophy said that every man had an inalienable right to his life, liberty, and property; yet it was of the very essence of government that it must have an ultimate power to take all three. How could this power be made legitimate and consistent with the natural-rights philosophy?

The Revolutionary generation developed an extensive and consistent body of ideas on this subject as well, derived less from political theorists and more directly from British and colonial political experience.

In the first place, they were convinced that government should be based on a written constitution emanating directly from the people, superior to any statute, and binding upon executive, legislative, and judicial authorities alike. Though their esteem for written constitutions undoubtedly was based largely on the protection afforded the rights of the colonists by the colonial charters, it also accorded with the basic beliefs in natural law and social contract. The state constitutions and later the federal Constitution were veritable social contracts and played the role of a tangible and written natural law above all other acts of government and forms of law.

This concept of the special status of the Constitution was only vaguely defined at the beginning of the Revolutionary movement, and some of the early state constitutions were simply adopted by the legislatures or provincial congresses, just as statutes of constitutional significance were adopted in England by Parliament. But its particular character as the direct expression of the fundamental will of the people came to be more clearly conceived, and from the time of the Massachusetts constitution of 1780 it was accepted that a constitution should be drafted by a convention directly elected by the people for that specific purpose and no other and should be ratified by a vote of the people at large.

In the second place, the Americans believed that there was no place for inherited status in the political order. Here they advanced far beyond their British and European mentors like Locke and Montesquieu, who not only tolerated a hereditary monarchy and nobility but indeed saw in them a valuable equipoise to the popular element in the government. But in the American view, as expressed in Virginia's bill of rights, ". . . no man or set of men are entitled to exclusive or separate emoluments or privileges from the community, but in consideration of publick services; which, not being descendible, neither ought the offices of magistrate, legislator or judge to be hereditary."

The Americans gave enthusiastic lip service to the doctrine of separation of executive, legislative, and judicial powers advanced by Locke and especially by Montesquieu. But in fact the principal concern of the Americans was to protect the independence of the legislature and judiciary from the executive authority, which they still associated with the Crown and with Britain. There was initially little recognition of the reciprocal importance of a strong and independent executive. In the early state constitutions the governor was usually elected by, and hence in a sense responsible to, the legislature; his appointive and veto powers were severely curtailed; and his term was short. It was made clear that his function was only to execute the decrees of the legislature. The development of the concept of an independent executive truly coordinate with the legislature came only late in the Revolutionary period, reaching its full expression in the federal Constitution. But the fact that the executive was directly or indirectly elected by the people in America gave the separation of powers a different meaning from that it held for British and European writers. They thought of the separation of popular legislative authority from inherited executive authority as a means of holding in check both royal tyranny and popular excess. The Americans thought of that separation not as limiting the popular will but as protecting it against distortion by either the legislative or the executive agents of the people.

The primacy of the legislature was one of the articles of Revolutionary faith. Here was where the people spoke and determined the policy of the state. Here was where the law was made, which it was the function of the executive and the judiciary only to execute and to apply. Hence special importance attached to the proper constitution of the legislature. It should be annually and freely elected, with reasonably equitable geographical representation. The members should be rotated frequently and should be subject to instruction by the constituents. Generally there was high regard for the idea of a two-house legislature, derived in fact from the centuries-old colonial and British experience with bicameral legislatures, but rationalized as a device to provide a representation of property in the upper house countervailing the popular representation in the lower house.

In the minds of the Revolutionary generation, as in the whole Anglo-American tradition, there was a heavy reliance upon the courts to protect citizens against arbitrary acts of government. The courts occupied an even greater role than today because in the almost total absence of a bureaucracy to carry out the laws, most acts of the state applying to an individual citizen were carried out through the courts. Hence the emphasis upon independent judges chosen to serve during good behavior—that is, normally until death or voluntary retirement. Hence also the fundamental importance assigned to the writ of habeas corpus, by which the courts could prevent the detention of any person without due process of law. Indeed the concept of due process of law was central to the whole ideology of the time, and it had a rather precise content derived from long British legal tradition. Trials must be in open court, on charges explicitly set forth, and on the basis of general laws in effect at the time of the alleged act. In both civil and criminal cases trial must be before an impartial jury of the vicinity. The defendant must have an opportunity to confront and question the witnesses against him and to summons witnesses in his behalf.

Implicit in the thought of the men of the Revolution was the further strengthening of the courts and of the concept of the constitutions as the embodiment of the fundamental law by investing in the courts the power to annul statutes that were contrary to the Constitution. This power had been exercised only half accidentally in sporadic cases before 1789 and was not to be explicitly claimed for the courts until 1803. It was, however, to become a central and distinguishing characteristic of American government, and one of the greatest importance.

The ideas of the Revolutionary generation were intended to provide a government directly responsive to the general public will and yet so limited as to prevent arbitrary action against any individual. But structural measures of this sort could not alone assure good government. Without the opportunity for a free flow of information and an open exchange of views among the people, the expression of the popular will in the legislature would become relatively meaningless. Hence the emphasis on freedom of speech and of the press, freedom of association and of assembly, freedom to petition for redress of grievances. Hence too the emphasis on the goal of universal education in order to equip men to take part in the process of communication that forms the popular will. The Revolutionary leaders were convinced that guarantees of these rights must appear in the basic constitutional documents side by side with the provisions establishing the structure of government.

When the Americans finally addressed themselves to the problem of a central government, they solved it, as we have seen, by a further extension of the concept of a separation of powers. Just as the supremacy of popular will was protected within a state by having the people designate separate sets of men to exercise their executive, legislative, and judicial authority, each separately responsible to the people, so that supremacy was protected within the federal framework by separate delegations of authority to deal with national and with local matters. Nowhere outside the people themselves did the Americans envision the existence of any general and all-embracing authority.

The political ideas of the Revolutionary thinkers cannot be fully understood apart from their economic ideas and from the nature of the American economy of the time. The political theory of seventeenth-century England, and especially of Locke, was developed by a class of men of property who had come to be the most vigorous economic force of the England of their day, but who had limited political power under the Stuarts. It was important to these men to establish limits on arbitrary political power so that their property could not be seized or taxed away from them and so that they could carry on their businesses in a free and stable political environment. The men of John Locke's generation who led the Glorious Revolution of 1688, rid the throne of the Stuarts, and enacted the Bill of Rights did not want to use the state to achieve a social revolution. Rather the reverse: they wanted to limit the power of the state to interfere with private property and its individual control, and to assure that any actions the state did take had the concurrence of men of some means, whatever their lack of feudal status.

This is why this philosophy was so congenial to the Americans of the Revolutionary era. To a far greater degree than even the commoner landowner or businessman of England, the American had been freed of the burdens of feudal privilege and arbitrary government. Only the tiniest portion of his income went to support royal grandeur or churchly estates or to pay feudal dues or even the costs of ordinary government. The regulations of guilds and magistrates did little to hamper or control his economic freedom, and his industry was more abundantly rewarded than anywhere else in the world. The Americans felt less need for a protective social order on the medieval pattern than men anywhere else. They wanted only to be free to exert themselves in achieving the good life for themselves and their families, and their view of the state was primarily as an institution that would provide a stable and uniform legal structure at minimum expense, within which men would be free to use and develop their property and pursue happiness with the least governmental burden or interference.

Because property was so much more widely diffused and so much easier to obtain in America than in Britain, these Whig political views, however identically expressed, had a far more democratic impact in America than in Britain. The view of government as an instrument to protect individual property owners against arbitrary exactions in England meant delivering the state to a rather small number of large landowners and merchants; in America the same doctrines meant a broadly democratic control of government on behalf of the populace—or at least the white populace—generally. The equality of all men, proclaimed by Locke and the Americans alike, really meant the equality of all active members of the political community—of those who were assumed to be parties to the social contract and who had a requisite stake in the polity formed by that contract. In England this meant that only small minorities were actually admitted to that equality; the democratic organization of the American economy meant that the same doctrine produced a nearly democratic political order in which almost all white men had, or could have, substantial equality.

This belief in a government of limited powers intended primarily to maintain an arena for the free and orderly exercise of individual liberty carried with it a belief in an economic policy of laissez-faire. It is by no means entirely a coincidence that the same year, 1776, witnessed the Declaration of Independence and the publication of Adam Smith's *Wealth of Nations*, arguing, as we have seen, the social advantages of a policy of individual liberty in the economic field. There had been a considerable amount of governmental control of economic life in the colonial period, imposed by British authority in order to fit the American economy into the British imperial economy in a generally subordinate relation. This pattern of bounties, prohibitions, customs duties, and navigation and staple acts all of course ceased to have effect with the coming of independence. Statutes regulating the economy and fixing prices that had been passed by the states during the war years to encourage the production of military supplies and to fight inflation were repealed or fell into disuse with the end of hostilities. A number of state tariffs were enacted, but they were necessarily low and of little general economic consequence because of their being confined to so small a territory. Meanwhile, from 1776 to 1789 there was no central government empowered to enact tariffs, navigation laws, or any other economic legislation, with the result, as we have seen, that there was necessarily a national economic policy of complete laissez-faire. A relatively small group of entrepeneurs did look to the new government under the Constitution to aid, if not to regulate, manufacturing and commerce through tariffs, navigation acts, and bounties. Under Hamilton's leadership a modest program of this sort was to be initiated in Washington's first administration, but the almost total laissez-faire tradition fixed during the Revolutionary period was too strong and would quickly return to dominance.

The Americans were aware, however, that a policy of economic laissez-faire was consonant with a democratic political and social order only if the economy itself remained open and relatively egalitarian. Hence the opposition to monopolies, preemptive land grants, and similar privileged economic institutions, and the suspicion of banks and other corporations as means of centralizing economic power. In view of the overwhelming importance of land ownership in the American economy of the time, however, clearly the most important contribution to economic democracy and individualism was the development of a pattern of land distribution in relatively small tracts at very low cost to individual settlers. The application of this liberal policy to the vast and fertile wilderness back of the mountains was to assure a steady force driving toward economic democracy and equality for a century to come—a force that was to persist in effect long after the last land grant was issued.

The meaning of the American Revolution for other countries and for subsequent generations is to be found not in the words uttered in 1776 but in the survival of its principles in the living institutions of other lands and later times. Perhaps the most fundamental of its legacies is the simplest and most obvious—the divided British empire and the independent United States of America. Had it been possible somehow to work out a pattern of federalism within the empire that could have averted the American secession and permitted those colonies, like Australia and Canada, to remain within a vaster commonwealth, the consequences would have been incalculable. On the one hand the preservation of the unity of the English-speaking world might have given it so overwhelming a predominance of power in the nineteenth and twentieth centuries as to have enforced an Anglo-American peace and avoided the great wars of our century. On the other hand, to have failed to gain its independence would undoubtedly have slowed the development and blurred the distinctive character of the United States, diminishing what it has been able uniquely to offer its own citizens and the world.

Within our own history the institutions of the Revolutionary period have proved to be surprisingly durable. The government of no other country in the world is so close in form or doctrine to its antecedents of the 1770's and 1780's as the American. There have been many totally unforeseen developments: political parties have had a role in our government, for example, that was never thought of by the Founding Fathers and that they would have deplored, but without which the system they established would never have worked. The fact that the governmental concerns that they recognized as national—defense, foreign relations, interstate and foreign commerce—have come to play a dominant role in our lives has meant that the national government has become more important and the states less important than they envisioned, even though the distribution of spheres of responsibility between the two levels of government remains much as they had planned it. The power of the President has grown, but again primarily because of the growth in importance of the responsibilities placed on him in the Constitution for foreign affairs and the command of the armed forces. Genuinely new and unforseen have been the creation of a large bureaucracy operating directly on the people without going through the courts (though ultimately under judicial control) and the variety of patterns of federal-state cooperation through grants and joint programs. The role of the judiciary has enormously increased, especially in its power to declare legislation unconstitutional, but this was implicit in the Constitution—indeed was its implicit keystone. But these developments have demonstrated rather the flexibility of the Revolutionary institutions in meeting unforeseen conditions than any inappropriateness in the institutions themselves. On the whole the enduring validity of the Revolutionary philosophy and the vitality of the machinery set up to put it into effect have been a remarkable and profound tribute to the realistic political wisdom of the Revolutionary generation.

There are three areas, however, in which our experience is still testing the meaning of the American Revolution. One of those is the conflict between the Revolutionary conviction of the sanctity of private property and the Revolutionary awareness that a democratic and equal political order must go hand in hand with a democratic and equal economic order. The devotion of the Founding Fathers to private property was due not so much to its own importance as to their belief that its wide diffusion among the people was essential to a free and democratic government and to the health of the state. In the economy of the eighteenth century, they feared monopoly—and indeed could conceive of it—only as it might be established by the state or as it might derive from churchly or feudal landholdings. These types of monopoly the Revolutionary generation undertook to destroy or prevent, and one of the ways of preventing such state-fostered monopolies was severely to limit the powers of the government over the economy. By the late nineteenth century unforeseen developments in transportation and manufacturing created enormous concentrations of economic power and extremes of wealth and poverty. Though these seriously endangered the democratic principles derived from the Revolution, the government for a long time was made helpless to deal with them by the limitations on its economic powers also derived from the Revolution.

This conflict was in large part resolved in legislation and Supreme Court decisions of the 1930's, so that it is now manifest that the Revolutionary tradition of the liberty and equality of men must be served by rather than itself serve the Revolutionary tradition of the sanctity of property. But the question of the boundaries of these rights and the wisest way of resolving conflicts between them will be with us always.

A second question, far less well resolved, arises from the Revolutionary doctrine of separation of powers, especially of the legislative and the executive authority in the federal government. In the major countries of Western Europe this doctrine atrophied in the nineteenth century because there the executive power that was pitted against the legislative was monarchical, whereas the legislative was popular. Hence the inevitable triumph of popular authority meant that executive power passed to a parliamentary committee acting as a cabinet and solely responsible to the legislative body. (Paradoxically, this acquisition of executive power by the legislative body meant that in the long run the latter lost its legislative autonomy and came to be almost totally subservient to the executive group chosen from its midst.) This reunion of separated powers has had a number of weaknesses, but it has meant that major legislative programs can be planned and carried through with assurance.

In America, because both the executive and the legislative derived their authority from the people, each was able to retain it; and hence an eighteenth-century political concept has survived here as it has almost nowhere else in the world. The tension in authority between the two, as the forefathers intended, has been so great that it has been possible to enact major legislation altering fundamental domestic arrangements only when there is overwhelming public support to which both respond. In the nearly half a century following our entry into World War I, such a nearly unanimous consensus for major domestic reforms has existed only in the early years of the New Deal; and only during those years, 1933–1937, was there domestic legislation that actually changed the structure of the economic and social order. The desirable stability envisioned by the Founding Fathers has approached a dangerous rigidity, indeed a paradoxical heritage from a Revolutionary past.

The most serious problem inherited from the Revolution was its failure to carry out its declaration of the equality of all men. We have pointed out that half consciously the leaders of the Revolutionary period confined the application of equality to those men whom they recognized as parties to the social contract and members of the political community. Even among them equality was never rigorously asserted. Property qualifications for voting and unequal representation of sections in the state legislature gave distinct political advantages to the wealthier men and the wealthier areas. Literacy tests as the years passed were substituted for property tests as a more defensible means of disfranchising the poor, but with almost the same effect. Those inequities have persisted to the present day, operating now primarily to give white men an advantage over Negroes, and rural areas an advantage over urban areas at the ballot. They have proved to be exceptionally difficult flaws to remove, in part because of the resistance to change imbedded in the separation of central and local governments and of executive and legislative authorities, and in part because the very inequalities have given those who benefited from them enough power to prevent their change. For example, dominant white officials, even in counties in which there is a Negro majority, can prevent all or most Negroes from registering to vote; and rural legislators, though representing a minority of a state's voters, may be a majority of the legislature and hence able to defeat bills aimed at redistricting.

The most grievous flaw in the Revolutionary settlement was, of course, the total exclusion of Negroes from the political community and the accompanying perpetuation of Negro slavery. This failure to carry through the ideals of the Revolution has lain like a curse over the United States ever since. It almost destroyed the Union in 1861. Even after the abolition of slavery, the denial of political and economic equality has persisted through all the following decades as an unjust, impoverishing, and embittering stain on American life. Again this very inequality has been protected by the separation of power between federal and state governments and between executive and legislative authorities and in general by the Revolutionary system of checks and balances that has made major legislation almost impossible in the face of opposition from a determined minority.

But if part of the Revolutionary settlement has tended to paralyze us in the face of needed reform, another part has opened a way to solution. Generations of thinkers before the period of the Revolution had asserted the primacy of natural law in the affairs of men, but none before that time had dealt successfully with the problem of how to make that natural law actually operative. The political thinkers of the Revolution achieved this by embodying what they conceived to be the principles of the natural law in supragovernmental constitutions that were declared to be the supreme law of the land, enforceable in the courts. Though, as we have pointed out, the constitution-writers of the 1780's by no means saw to the end of the path they opened, in fact they had made it possible for the original principles of the Revolution, as written then or later into the Constitution, to cut through legislative and administrative deadlocks, override statute law, and be applied directly to human situations. This has happened in our time in the Supreme Court decisions on racial segregation and legislative districting. The Revolution has been reasserting itself directly.

The American Revolution was followed almost immediately by the French Revolution, which in turn initiated a process of political change that ultimately created parliamentary democracies in almost all the countries of Western Europe. It was followed as well, at an interval of a generation, by wars of independence in Latin America that freed that vast area from Spanish and, later, Portuguese control and established governments in republican form. New governments are being formed in our generation for previously dependent countries throughout Asia and Africa. This sequence of events has made it easy for Americans to see the American Revolution as a new, almost divinely inspired, political dispensation that opened a new era for Europe and Latin America as well as for ourselves and that now provides a ready-made pattern for countries newly acquiring their independence.

But this ready assumption of primacy and universality for the American Revolution overlooks some of the unique characteristics that distinguish it sharply from the revolutionary movements elsewhere, and in particular from those movements in the patterns of the French or the Russian revolution. These unique characteristics—like those of the related Glorious Revolution in Britain a century earlier—were largely due to the fact that the economic and social order was more, not less, democratic than the government. As we have pointed out, the Revolutionary leaders were men who wanted to take over the government in order to restrict its powers and to subject it to more democratic control. Their object was not to change the social and economic order, but to protect that order from arbitrary political action. They wanted a government that would be consistent with a society and an economy with which they were already pleased.

In contrast, the French Revolution, the Continental revolutions of the nineteenth century, and the Communist revolutions of the twentieth century took place in societies in which the economic and social order was highly unequal and burdened with arbitrary privilege, and in which the economic lot of the majority of the people was bitter and hopeless. The revolutionists in these situations sought to take over the state in order to use its powers to destroy the economic and social order and thereafter rebuild it on a juster and more equal basis. To do this it was necessary to strengthen and centralize rather than to limit and diffuse the authority of the state; to unite rather than to separate the power to legislate and the power to act; to break down rather than to guarantee the sacredness of life, liberty, and property insofar as they were imbedded in the old order. What emerged from the French Revolution and the Communist and Fascist revolutions was the totalitarian state, bound by no higher law, exercising unrestrained the whole power of the community, and crushing rather than protecting the legal and economic resources by which men could individually assert their dignity.

It is not surprising, therefore, that the American ideology has played a relatively minor role among those European reformers of the nineteenth and twentieth centuries who saw in the society and economy around them not a rich and free environment in which men could develop easily and individually if only protected from political tyranny, but an infamous and strangling set of institutions that must be forcefully eradicated. Except occasionally, as in the confiscation of the vast holdings of Tory landlords in New York and elsewhere, the Americans were not confronted with the necessity of seizing property and curtailing liberty in order to eradicate deeply rooted special privilege. Later generations in older countries were not so happy in the choices before them.

Nor was the American pattern really followed in Latin America, although in the countries of that region its forms were faithfully adopted. None of the roots of a democratic social order had been implanted there. The power of an established church had not been broken. Landholding was vast and feudal. The economy was based on exploited labor. Education, like wealth, was in the hands of a small elite. There had been no generations of training in the responsibilities of democratic self-government in local matters. It is not surprising that only the form and not the substance of the American Revolutionary patterns survived and that the petty dictatorships that rose within the forms of democracy in Latin America in the nineteenth and early twentieth centuries had neither the will nor the strength to reform the social order.

The events of the nineteenth and especially of the twentieth century have discouraged our easy optimism about the spread of democracy in the American pattern throughout the world.

They have shown only too painfully that a limited and democratic government of divided and restricted powers pledged to the sanctity of individual life, liberty, and property can take root and survive only in a just society in which property, education, and habits of responsible freedom are widely diffused among the people. Indeed, when the safeguards of liberty and property, intended in our society for the individual protection of the people at large, are applied to unjust societies in which feudal property holdings, or worse, survive along with harsh exploitation, they may well appear to be the bulwarks of oppression. Indeed they have appeared so to the suffering masses of many countries of Latin America, Asia, and Africa.

But the promise of the totalitarian state has been even more bitterly fulfilled. The mobilization of the state's unrestrained authority in disregard of individual status or rights has been justified by revolutionary necessity. Men have been promised that once the injustices of the old order have been eradicated, a free political society can be allowed to grow on the basis of the new and healthy social and economic order. But it has proved to be as impossible to foster a free social and economic life within a totalitarian government as it has been to create a stable free government within an unfree society. Freedoms of economic choice, of speech, and of assembly are turned immediately against the totalitarian government, which must curtail them to protect its own survival. None of the totalitarian governments of the nineteenth and twentieth centuries has in fact yet permitted the growth of free social and economic institutions or has itself been transformed toward free and limited government except following military defeat. This is not to say that such a transformation is forever impossible, but it is certainly most difficult.

No doubt a critical need of the twentieth century is to develop the political techniques by which economic and social orders based on privilege and exploitation can be modernized and made free without the use of political techniques of compulsion that in the long run destroy freedom in the political and in the economic realm alike. The liquidation of privilege by parliamentary methods in Britain and Western Europe over the last century affords a hopeful example, and experiments in such countries as India and Nigeria and the liberal governments of Latin America may answer the question of how to obtain equality without sacrificing freedom.

But if it is true that the American Revolutionary experience did not provide the ideology or the pattern for the liberating revolutions and movements of the two following centuries, it is also true that it did provide the stimulus and the ideal goal for many of those events. The mere existence across the waters of a land of dreamed-of freedom and plenty—a land conceived in liberty and dedicated to the proposition that all men are created equal—not only drew millions of emigrants from Europe to the New World, but exercised a constant and relentless pressure to reform the governments of the Old.

And as the earliest, the most nearly complete, and the most realistic embodiment of the optimistic and humane political ideas of the Enlightment, the Revolution gave those ideas a vitality, a force, and a permanence in the life of the world that could never have been achieved by their mere exposition in treatises. Just as the Russian Revolution of 1917 transformed Communism from a turgid body of economic theory into an awesome force that has laid its hands on the lives of hundreds of millions of men, so the American Revolution transformed the very different body of political theory of Locke and his colleagues into a living power. Men like Washington and Jefferson did not conceive the ideas that all men are created equal, that they are endowed by nature with rights beyond the authority of any government to reach, that governments exist only to protect and foster those rights of individual men, and that they can be properly based only on the consent of the governed. But it was their deeds and the deeds of their Revolutionary comrades that first made those ideas, however imperfectly, incarnate in a free government and a living society.

The force of those fundamental ideas has grown from generation to generation. However any government may try to evade their application, no one today can afford publicly to deny their validity, and they constitute the core of the world's and our own unsilenceable political conscience. As such, they and the Revolution that embodied them are constantly finding new meanings. Twist and turn as we have down the generations in our own national dealings with Negroes, we have never been able to escape altogether from our inheritance of the declaration that all men are created equal. Finally we must redeem it. And so it is throughout the world where these ideas continue to exert their implacable revolutionary force, leaving, for example, no metropolitan power any longer able to hold a colony in subordination against its will, asserting in the work of young Soviet writers the faith that there are yet individual rights beyond the state or party, forcing a rich Western world to act to make more nearly equal the chance of all men, including those in the poorest and least developed lands, to be free from want and to pursue happiness.

So long as this ferment of its fundamental ideas continues, the meaning of the American Revolution, of those long-dead events and men, will continue to grow and to find new expression.

Chronology

1763	February 10. Treaty of Paris ends Seven Years' War, giving Britain Canada and all of the present territory of the United States east of the Mississippi except New Orleans.
	July. Rockingham succeeds Grenville as Prime Minister.
	October 7. Proclamation of 1763 bars settlement west of the Alleghenies.
	May–November. Pontiac's Rebellion.
1764	April 5. Passage of Sugar Act.
1765	March 22. Stamp Act approved.
	March 24. Quartering Act passed.
	May 30. Stamp Act Resolutions in Virginia.
	August 15. Mob forces resignation of stamp-tax collection in Massachusetts.
	October 7–25. Stamp Act Congress meets.
1766	March 18. Stamp Act repealed. Declaratory Act passed.
1766	July. Chatham succeeds Rockingham as Prime Minister.
1767	June 29. Townshend Acts passed.
1768	February 11. Massachusetts Circular Letter on Townshend Acts.
	Summer. Nonimportation agreements made.
	September 29. Arrival of British troops at Boston.
1769	May 16. Virginia Resolutions attacking Townshend Acts.
1770	February. Lord North becomes Prime Minister.
	March 5. Boston Massacre.
	April 12. Townshend duties, except tea duty, repealed.
1773	May 10. Tea Act.
	December 16. Boston Tea Party.
1774	March 31. Boston Port Act.
	May 20. Massachusetts Government Act and Administration of Justice Act.
	June 2. Quartering Act.
	June 22. Quebec Act.
	September 5. First Continental Congress meets.
	October 14. Congress adopts Declaration and Resolves.
	October 18. Congress adopts Continental Association.
	October 26. First Continental Congress adjourns.
1775	March 30. New England Restraining Act.
	April 19. Battles of Lexington and Concord.
	May 10. Second Continental Congress convenes.

	June 17. Battle of Bunker Hill.
	July 3. Washington takes command of army.
	July 8. Olive Branch Petition.
	November 13. Montreal captured by Montgomery.
	December 30. Attack on Quebec fails.
1776	February 27. Battle of Moore's Creek Bridge.
	March 17. British evacuate Boston.
	May 10. Congress recommends new state governments.
	June 28. British attack on Charleston fails.
	July 2. Resolution declaring independence voted.
	July 4. Declaration of Independence adopted.
	August 26–27. Battle of Long Island.
	October 28. Battle of White Plains.
	November 16. Surrender of Fort Washington.
	December 26. Battle of Trenton.
1777	January 3. Battle of Princeton.
	September 11. Battle of Brandywine Creek.
	September 26. Philadelphia falls to Howe.
	October 4. Battle of Germantown.
	October 17. Burgoyne surrenders at Saratoga.
	November 17. Articles of Confederation adopted by Continental Congress.
	December 18. Occupation of winter quarters at Valley Forge.
1778	February 6. Treaty of Alliance with France.
	June 17. France opens hostilities against Britain.
	June 28. Battle of Monmouth.
	July 4. Clark captures Kaskaskia.
	December 29. British capture Savannah.
1779	February 23. Clark captures Vincennes.
	May 21. Spain declares war against Britain.
1780	May 12. Charleston captured by Britain.
	August 16. Battle of Camden.
	September 25. Benedict Arnold revealed as traitor.
	October 7. Battle of Kings Mountain.
1781	January 2. Virginia agrees to turn western lands over to Confederation.
	January 17. Battle of Cowpens.
	February 20. Robert Morris becomes superintendent of finances.
	March 1. Articles of Confederation ratified.
	March 15. Battle of Guilford Courthouse.
	October 19. British surrender at Yorktown.
1782	March 20. Lord North resigns as Prime Minister.
	November 30. Preliminary peace treaty.
1783	September 3. Treaty of Paris with Great Britain.
	November 25. British turn New York over to Washington.
1784	April 23. Congress adopts ordinance for government of the Western territories.
1785	May 20. Congress adopts ordinance for sale of Western lands.
1786	January 16. Adoption of Virginia Statute for Religious Liberty.
	August. Outbreak of Shays' Rebellion.
	September 11–14. Annapolis Convention.
1787	May 25. Constitutional Convention meets.
	July 13. Northwest Ordinance adopted.
	September 27. Constitutional Convention adjourns.
	December 7. Delaware ratifies Constitution.
	December 12. Pennsylvania ratifies Constitution.
	December 18. New Jersey ratifies Constitution.

1788	January 2. Georgia ratifies Constitution.
	January 9. Connecticut ratifies Constitution.
	February 6. Massachusetts ratifies Constitution.
	April 28. Maryland ratifies Constitution.
	May 23. South Carolina ratifies Constitution.
	June 21. New Hampshire ratifies Constitution.
	June 26. Virginia ratifies Constitution.
	July 26. New York ratifies Constitution.
1789	March 4. First Congress meets under the Constitution.
	April 30. Washington inaugurated as first President.
1789	November 21. North Carolina ratifies Constitution.
1790	May 29. Rhode Island ratifies Constitution.

Bibliographical Note

The records of the period of our national birth are copious. The Founding Fathers themselves were very conscious that they were engaged in acts of great importance, and they took pains to record them. Generations of scholars have used these sources to produce an enormous number of works, and the history of the Revolution and the Constitution has been almost continuously written and rewritten since the events themselves. From this outpouring, the bibliography that follows attempts to call attention only to a limited number of works that may interest the amateur student of the period. The reader who wants to make an exhaustive study will find an invaluable tool in the *Harvard Guide to American History* (1954), which provides a detailed guide to the bibliography of American history up to the date of its publication. More recent publications may be followed through the reviews and bibliographical notes in the *American Historical Review* and the *William and Mary Quarterly.*

Sources. The official records are contained in Worthington C. Ford, ed., *Journals of the Continental Congress, 1774–1789,* 34 vols. (1904–1937); Max Farrand, ed., *Records of the Federal Convention of 1787,* 3 vols. (1911–1937); Jonathan Elliot, ed., *Debates in the Several State Conventions on the Adoption of the Federal Constitution,* 5 vols. (1861); and Francis Wharton, ed., *Revolutionary Diplomatic Correspondence,* 6 vols. (1889). Many documents, mostly official, are brought together in Peter Force, ed., *American Archives,* 9 vols., covering the period March 7, 1774, to December 31, 1776 (1837–1853). Edmund C. Burnett, ed., *Letters of Members of the Continental Congress,* 8 vols. (1921–1938), is a valuable supplement to the *Journals.* The *Harvard Guide* lists British, French, and Spanish official sources.

The Founding Fathers were voluminous letter-writers, and most of them were careful record-keepers. Various editions of their writings edited in the late nineteenth and early twentieth centuries are now being superseded by thorough, complete, and scholarly editions being done by a number of university presses under the general sponsorship of the National Historical Publications Commission. Jefferson's writings are being issued by the Princeton University Press, John Adams' by Harvard, Franklin's by Yale, Madison's by Chicago, Hamilton's by Columbia. The Bicentennial Edition of Washington's writings, authorized by Congress and edited by John C. Fitzpatrick (39 vols., 1931–1944), remains the definitive one.

Various brief compilations of selected sources are very convenient for the general reader. The best of these, consisting primarily of official documents, is Samuel E. Morison, ed., *Sources and Documents Illustrating the American Revolution, 1764–1788* (2nd ed., 1929). Limited in period is John Braeman, *The Road to Independence: A Documentary History of the Causes of the American Revolution: 1763–1776* (1963); a companion volume is Hugh F. Rankin, *The American Revolution* (1964). Henry Steele Commager and Richard B. Morris, eds., *The Spirit of 'Seventy-Six*, 2 vols. (1958), is a large compilation of personal letters and other less formal documents. George F. Scheer and Hugh F. Rankin, *Rebels and Redcoats* (1956), is a popular narrative history of the war incorporating the texts of many original sources. Saul K. Padover, ed., *The World of the Founding Fathers: Their Basic Ideas on Freedom and Self-Government* (1959), brings together brief excerpts from the writings of the Revolutionary leaders that give the flavor of Revolutionary thought. A convenient collection of documents is Charles C. Tansill, ed., *Documents Illustrative of the Formation of the Union of the American States* (1927). *The Federalist* has appeared in many editions, as has Thomas Paines' *Common Sense*.

Background. Among the hundreds of works on eighteenth-century Britain may be mentioned Lawrence H. Gipson, *The British Empire Before the American Revolution*, 9 vols. (1936–1956); G. L. Beer, *British Colonial Policy, 1754–1765* (1907); J. Steven Watson, *The Reign of George III, 1760–1815* (1960); J. Holland Rose, A. P. Newton, and E. A. Benians, eds., *The Cambridge History of the British Empire*, Vol. I: *The Old Empire, from the Beginnings to 1783* (1929). More specialized are Robert L. Schuyler, *Parliament and the British Empire* (1929); Richard Pares, *King George III and the Politicians* (1953); and the many works of Lewis Namier and his followers, including *The Structure of Politics at the Accession of George III* (1929), *England in the Age of the American Revolution* (1930), and Bernhard Donoughue, *British Politics and the American Revolution: The Path to War 1773–75* (1964).

Within these limits it is impractical to list general studies of Western civilization in the eighteenth century, but attention should be called to Walter Dorn, *Competition for Empire, 1740–1763* (1940); Leo Gershoy, *From Despotism to Revolution, 1763–1789* (1944); Carl Becker, *Heavenly City of the Eighteenth-Century Philosophers* (1932); R. R. Palmer, *The Age of the Democratic Revolution: A Political History of Europe and America, 1760–1800*, Vol. I (1959) and Vol. II (1965); and Hannah Arendt, *On Revolution* (1963).

General works on the causes of the Revolution include Charles M. Andrews, *Colonial Background of the American Revolution* (1924); John C. Miller, *Origins of the American Revolution* (1943); Lawrence H. Gipson, *The Coming of the Revolution* (1954); Curtis P. Nettels, *Roots of American Civilization* (1938), an excellent history covering the entire colonial period; Claude H. Van Tyne, *Causes of the War of Independence* (1922).

Specialized studies of various aspects of the pre-Revolutionary decade include Oliver M. Dickerson, *The Navigation Acts and the American Revolution* (1951); Michael Kraus, *Intercolonial Aspects of American Culture on the Eve of the Revolution* (1928); Leonard Labaree, *Royal Government in America* (1930); Bernhard Knollenberg, *Origin of the American Revolution, 1759–1766* (1960), which attaches special importance to developments at the close of the French and Indian Wars and during the Grenville administration; Arthur M. Schlesinger, *Prelude to Independence* (1958), which covers the Whig newspaper campaign in the colonies; Carl Ubbelohde, *The Vice-Admiralty Courts and the American Revolution* (1960); Edmund S. and Helen M. Morgan, *The Stamp Act Crisis: Prologue to Revolution* (1953).

General Histories of the Revolution. The older general histories of the United States, such as those by George Bancroft and Edward Channing, have largely been replaced, so far as the Revolution is concerned, by recent studies. Among the best of many are: Claude H. Van Tyne, *The War of Independence* (1929); John C. Miller, *Triumph of Freedom* (1948); John R. Alden, *The American Revolution, 1775–1783* (1954); Evarts B. Greene, *The Revolutionary Generation, 1763–1790* (1943), primarily social history. Edmund S. Morgan, *The Birth of the Republic, 1763–1789* (1956), is an excellent and readable brief account of the whole period. Richard B. Morris, *The American Revolution: A Short History* (1955), is an even briefer account to which are appended a number of the basic documents. Readable popularizations are Bruce Lancaster, *From Lexington to Liberty* (1955), and *The American Heritage Book of the Revolution* (1958). From the British point of view, an excellent recent study is Piers Mackesy, *The War for America, 1775–1783* (1964).

Military History. An excellent brief account is Howard H. Peckham, *The War for Independence: A Military History* (1958). Christopher Ward, *War of the Revolution*, 2 vols. (1952), a posthumous work edited and completed by John R. Alden, is perhaps the best general military history. Gardner W. Allen, *A Naval History of the American Revolution*, 2 vols. (1913), remains the standard work on its subject. Almost every major battle of the Revolution has been the subject of a book. A few of these are: Joseph B. Mitchell, *Decisive Battles of the American Revolution* (1962); Alfred Hoyt Bill, *Campaign of Princeton, 1776–1777* (1948), and *Valley Forge: The Making of an Army* (1952); William S. Stryker and William S. Myers, *The Battle of Monmouth* (1927); and Donald B. Chidsey, *Victory at Yorktown* (1962); John W. Shy, *Toward Lexington: The Role of the British Army in the Coming of the American Revolution* (1965).

Economic History. Curtis P. Nettels, *The Emergence of a National Economy, 1775–1815* (1962), is the best recent economic history of the period as a whole. Useful specialized studies include Percy W. Bidwell and J. I. Falconer, *History of Agriculture in the Northern United States, 1620–1860*, 2 vols. (1933); L. C. Gray, *A History of Agriculture in the Southern United States to 1860*, 2 vols. (1933); E. R. Johnson and others, *History of the Domestic and Foreign Commerce of the United States* (1915); Victor S. Clark, *History of Manufactures in the United States, 1607–1860*, 3 vols. (1929); R. M. Robbins, *Our Landed Heritage: The Public Domain, 1776–1936* (1942); Thomas P. Abernethy, *Western Lands and the American Revolution* (1937); Arthur M. Schlesinger, *The Colonial Merchants and the American Revolution* (1918); Robert A. East, *Business Enterprise in the American Revolutionary Era* (1938); James B. Hedges, *The Browns of Providence Plantations* (1952); E. James Ferguson, *The Power of the Purse: A History of American Public Finance, 1776–1790* (1961); Jackson Turner Main, *The Social Structure of Revolutionary America* (1965).

Political Theory. The ideas of the Revolution are treated in Vernon L. Parrington, *Main Currents in American Thought*, 3 vols. (1927–1930); C. H. McIlwain, *The American Revolution: A Constitutional Interpretation* (1923); C. F. Mullett, *Fundamental Law and the American Revolution* (1933); Moses C. Tyler, *Literary History of the American Revolution, 1763–1783*, 2 vols. (1897); Philip Davidson, *Propaganda and the American Revolution, 1763–1783* (1941); Randolph G. Adams, *Political Ideas of the American Revolution* (1922); Max

Savelle, *Seeds of Liberty* (1948); Clinton Rossiter, *Seedtime of the Republic* (1953); J. Franklin Jameson, *The American Revolution Considered as a Social Movement* (1926); Carl L. Becker, *The Declaration of Independence: A Study in the History of Political Ideas* (1922); Seymour Martin Lipset, *The First New Nation* (1963).

Specialized Studies. Among almost innumerable specialized works may be mentioned: Alice M. Baldwin, *The New England Clergy and the American Revolution* (1928); Weldon A. Brown, *Empire or Independence: A Study in the Failure of Reconciliation, 1774–1783* (1941); Edmund C. Burnett, *The Continental Congress* (1941); A. E. McKinley, *The Suffrage Franchise in the Thirteen English Colonies in America* (1905); Clarence Alvord, *The Mississippi Valley in British Politics,* 2 vols. (1916); Elisha Douglass, *Rebels and Democrats* (1955); Carl Bridenbaugh, *Cities in Revolt* (1955); John Bakeless, *Turncoats, Traitors, and Heroes* (1959); Dale Van Every, *A Company of Heroes: The American Frontier, 1775–1783* (1962); Samuel F. Bemis, *Diplomacy of the American Revolution* (1935); Richard B. Morris, *The Peacemakers: The Great Powers and American Independence* (1965); Paul H. Smith, *Loyalists and Redcoats,* (1965); Claude H. Van Tyne, *Loyalists in the American Revolution* (1929).

Confederation and Constitution. Merrill Jensen, The *Articles of Confederation* (1948) and *The New Nation: A History of the United States During the Confederation, 1781–1789* (1950); Max Farrand, *The Framing of the Constitution of the United States* (1913); Carl Van Doren, *The Great Rehearsal* (1948); Charles A. Beard, *An Economic Interpretation of the Constitution of the United States* (1913); Robert Brown, *Charles Beard and the Constitution* (1956), and *Reinterpretation of the Formation of the American Constitution* (1963); Edward S. Corwin, *The Constitution and What It Means Today* (1920); Jackson T. Main, *The Antifederalists: Critics of the Constitution, 1781–1788* (1961); Forrest McDonald, *E Pluribus Unum, The Formation of the American Republic* (1965).

Biographies. Among the more important biographies are: Page Smith, *John Adams,* 2 vols. (1962); John C. Miller, *Sam Adams* (1936); William B. Willcox, *Portrait of a General: Sir Henry Clinton in the War for Independence* (1964); C. J. Stillé, *The Life and Times of John Dickinson* (1891); Carl Van Doren, *Benjamin Franklin* (1938); S. W. Patterson, *Horatio Gates* (1941); Theodore Thayer, *Nathanael Greene, Strategist of the American Revolution* (1960); John C. Miller, *Alexander Hamilton* (1959); Broadus Mitchell, *Alexander Hamilton,* 2 vols. (1957); H. S. Allan, *John Hancock* (1948); Robert D. Meade, *Patrick Henry, Patriot in the Making* (1957); Frank Monaghan, *John Jay* (1935); Dumas Malone, *Jefferson the Virginian* (1951), *Jefferson and the Rights of Man* (1959), and *Jefferson and the Ordeal of Liberty* (1962)—three volumes of a biography still in progress, but carrying Jefferson through the Revolutionary period; North Callahan, *Henry Knox, General Washington's General* (1958); Louis Gottschalk, *Lafayette Comes to America* (1935); *Lafayette Joins the American Army* (1937); and *Lafayette and the Close of the American Revolution* (1942); John R. Alden, *General Charles Lee* (1951); Irving Brant, *James Madison,* 6 vols. (1941–1961); Ellis P. Oberholtzer, *Robert Morris, Patriot and Financier* (1903); Esther Forbes, *Paul Revere and the World He Lived In* (1942); Arnold Whitridge, *Rochambeau* (1965); Charles P. Whittemore. *A General of the Revolution: John Sullivan of New Hampshire* (1961); Douglas S. Freeman, *George Washington,* 7 vols. (1948–1957); Bernhard Knollenberg, *Washington and the Revolution* (1940).

Regional and State Histories. Among the profusion of studies may be mentioned: Allan Nevins, *The American States During and After the Revolution, 1775–1789* (1924), an exhaustive study, now being revised, of the developments within the individual states; James Truslow Adams, *Revolutionary New England, 1691–1776* (1923), and *New England in the Republic, 1776–1850* (1926); Richard F. Upton, *Revolutionary New Hampshire* (1936); Robert E. Brown, *Middle-Class Democracy and the Revolution in Massachusetts, 1691–1780* (1955); Oscar Zeichner, *Connecticut's Years of Controversy, 1750–1776* (1949); W. C. Abbott, *New York in the American Revolution* (1929); E. Wilder Spaulding, *New York in the Critical Period, 1783–1789* (1932); Richard McCormick, *Experiment in Independence: New Jersey in the Critical Period, 1781–1789* (1950); Theodore Thayer, *Pennsylvania Politics and the Growth of Democracy, 1740–1776* (1954); R. L. Brunhouse, *The Counter-Revolution in Pennsylvania, 1776–1790* (1942); Carl and Jessica Bridenbaugh, *Rebels and Gentlemen* (1942); Charles A. Barker, *The Background of the Revolution in Maryland* (1940); Philip A. Crowl, *Maryland During and After the Revolution* (1943); John R. Alden, *The South in the Revolution, 1763–1789* (1957); Hamilton J. Eckenrode, *The Revolution in Virginia* (1916); Carl Bridenbaugh, *Seat of Empire* (1950); Charles S. Sydnor, *Gentlemen Freeholders: Political Practices in Washington's Virginia* (1952).

Index